BOETHIUS'S

In Ciceronis Topica

Also by Eleonore Stump

Boethius's *De topicis differentiis* (trans.)

BOETHIUS'S
In Ciceronis Topica

TRANSLATED, WITH NOTES

AND AN INTRODUCTION BY

ELEONORE STUMP

Cornell University Press

ITHACA AND LONDON

First published 1988 by Cornell University Press.
First Printing, Cornell Paperbacks, 2004

International Standard Book Number 0-8014-8934-2

Printed in the United States of America
Librarians: Library of Congress cataloging information appears on the last page of the book.

The paper in this book is acid-free and meets the guidelines for permanence and durability of the Committee on Production Guidelines for Book Longevity of the Council on Library Resources.

Paperback Printing 10 9 8 7 6 5 4 3 2 1

For Donald

Namque tu solebas
Meas esse aliquid putare nugas.

Catullus, *Carmina* i

CONTENTS

Notes to the Translation

ACKNOWLEDGMENTS

In the course of producing this book I have accumulated many debts of gratitude. A grant from the National Endowment for the Humanities, supplemented by Virginia Polytechnic Institute and State University, freed me from teaching duties and enabled me to work full time on this project. I am particularly grateful for the support and encouragement of Susan Mango at NEH. I am also deeply indebted to my outstanding dean, Henry Bauer. His willingness to further the research of his faculty and his enlightened and creative ways of doing so made a great difference to my work. Without his support I could not have finished this book. I count myself very lucky too in having as the head of my department Richard Burian, who has been willing to find ways (often unconventional and personally inconvenient for him) in which I could participate fully in the life of my department and still meet my children at the school bus every day. Without his support I would not have finished this book. The Society for the Humanities at Cornell University under the directorship of Jonathan Culler generously provided me with office space during the summers I was working on this book. Vanessa C. Alexander and Christine H. Duncan, secretaries of my department, were unfailingly helpful and efficient in the messy business of producing neat computer copy for the press. Norman Kretzmann generously supported the research of this book in many ways. I am grateful to him for innumerable helpful suggestions and unflagging encouragement. Finally, I am indebted to my husband, Donald Stump, to whom this book is dedicated. His patience, good humor, and willingness to participate in the madcap life entailed by having two careers and three children in one family have been the foundation of all my work.

ELEONORE STUMP

Blacksburg, Virginia

ABBREVIATIONS

(For complete bibliographical information, see the bibliography.)

An. Pos.	Aristotle, *Posterior Analytics*
An. Pr.	Aristotle, *Prior Analytics*
CAG	*Commentaria in Aristotelem graeca*
Cat.	Aristotle, *Categories*
De hyp. syll.	Boethius, *De hypotheticis syllogismis*
De int.	Aristotle, *On Interpretation*
De inv.	Cicero, *De inventione*
De top. diff.	Boethius, *De topicis differentiis*
ICT	Boethius, *In Ciceronis Topica*
In Isag.	Boethius, *In Isagogen*
Metaph.	Aristotle, *Metaphysics*
Nic. Eth.	Aristotle, *Nicomachean Ethics*
PL	*Patrologia latina*
Soph. el.	Aristotle, *Sophistical Refutations*
Top.	Aristotle, *Topics*

BOETHIUS'S
In Ciceronis Topica

INTRODUCTION

Boethius

Anicius Manlius Severinus Boethius, "the last of the Romans" and the tutor of the MiddleAges, was born into a patrician family in Rome in 480.[1] Orphaned at an early age, he was brought up by the illustrious and aristocratic Quintus Aurelius Memmius Symmachus, whose daughter he eventually married. He gained a reputation as a man of learning, and his brilliant public career was marked by honors. For many years he occupied a position of trust under the Arian king Theodoric the Ostrogoth; in the year 510 he became consul, and his two sons were made joint consuls in 522. Eventually, however, he fell out of favor with Theodoric and was accused of treason. The official charges against him include the implausible accusation of practicing magic and astrology, but the principal reason for his imprisonment seems to have been Theodoric's suspicion that Boethius was corresponding with the orthodox Byzantine emperor Justin in a conspiracy to overthrow Theodoric. In 524 (or 526), after a term of imprisonment at Pavia, Boethius was put to death. Though there is still controversy, it is widely accepted now that Boethius was unjustly accused.

Scholars disagree over where Boethius was educated and what his sources were. An old theory, still considered arguable, is that Boethius studied in Athens and learned his philosophy in Neoplatonist schools there.[2] Pierre-Paul Courcelle, on the other hand, maintains that Boethius studied not at Athens but at Alexandria in the school of the Greek commentators on Aristotle and that the head of that school,

1. Except for the last paragraph, this section on Boethius is taken from my book *Boethius's De topicis differentiis* (Ithaca: Cornell University Press, 1978).
2. See, for example, R. Bonnaud, "L'education scientifique de Boèce," *Speculum*, 4 (1929), 198–206; and C. J. de Vogel, "Boethiana" I and II, *Vivarium*, 9 (1971), 49–66, and 10 (1972), 1–40.

Ammonius Hermiae, was one of the main influences on Boethius.[3] More recently a theory has been gaining currency that Boethius studied neither in Athens nor in Alexandria but got the material for his logical works from the marginalia in a copy of Aristotle's *Organon* which he owned.[4] Whatever the final outcome of the controversy, it is clear that Boethius was heavily influenced by both Neoplatonism and Aristotelianism.

Boethius's works include the *Consolation of Philosophy*, one of the masterpieces of Western literature; five theological treatises, important in the development of medieval theology; and three books on the quadrivium: two treatises on mathematics and a textbook on music. He intended to translate all the works of Plato and of Aristotle into Latin and to reconcile the two, but he accomplished only a small portion of that enormous task, namely, translations of and commentaries on most of Aristotle's logical works. In addition, he wrote several independent works on logic, including treatises on categorical and hypothetical syllogisms, a book on ways of analyzing things (*Liber de divisione*), and a treatise on Topics, the *De topicis differentiis* (*De top. diff.*).[5] Finally, he translated Porphyry's *Isagoge* and wrote commentaries on it and on Cicero's *Topica*; the commentary on Cicero, *In Ciceronis Topica (ICT)*, is the text presented in this book.

Boethius's influence on medieval philosophy was considerable. The early scholastics knew as much of Aristotle as they did know largely through Boethius's translations; his commentaries and treatises were used very widely and served to establish, among other things, a basic Latin philosophical vocabulary. In some cases—for example, in certain developments in medieval logic—his work is the principal source, and his discussion of the ontological status of predicables seems to have sparked the long medieval controversy over universals. In short, he

3. See *Late Latin Writers and Their Greek Sources*, tr. H. Wedeck (Cambridge, Mass: Harvard University Press 1969; 1st ed., Paris, 1948), pp. 275ff.; also, idem, "Boèce et l'école d'Alexandrie," *Mélanges d'Archéologie et d'Historie*, 52 (1935), 185–223; and idem, "*La Consolation de philosophie*" *dans la tradition littéraire, antécédents et postérité de Boèce* (Paris: Etudes Augustiniennes, 1967). See also Philip Merlan, "Ammonius Hermiae, Zacharias Scholasticus, and Boethius," *Greek, Roman, and Byzantine Studies*, 9 (1968), 193–203.

4. James Shiel, "Boethius' Commentaries on Aristotle," *Mediaeval and Renaissance Studies*, 4 (1958), 217–244. See also Lorenzo Minio-Paluello, "Les traductions et les commentaires aristotéliciens de Boèce," *Studia Patristica II*, 5th ser., 9 (1957), 358–365; and L. M. de Rijk, "On the Chronology of Boethius' Works on Logic" I and II, *Vivarium*, 2 (1964), 1–49, 125–162. See also my article "Boethius's Works on the Topics," *Vivarium*, 12 (1974), 77–93.

5. The name of this treatise is traditionally given as *De differentiis topicis*. For evidence that its proper name is *De topicis differentiis*, see Samuel Brandt, "Entstehungszeit und zeitliche Folge der Werke von Boethius," *Philologus*, 62 (1903), 263 n.16.

was one of the main influences on the early scholastics and was an authority for them second perhaps only to Augustine among Christian philosophers.

L. M. de Rijk has made a detailed study of the chronology of Boethius's logical works and believes that he can establish with reasonable reliability the following list:

In Porphyrii Isagogen, editio prima	ca. 504–505
De syllogismis categoricis	ca. 505–506
In Porphyrii Isagogen, editio secunda	ca. 507–509
In Aristotelis Categorias	ca. 509–511
In Aristotelis Perihermeneias, editio prima	not before 513
In Aristotelis Perihermeneias, editio secunda	ca. 515–516
De syllogismis hypotheticis	between 516 and 522
In Ciceronia Topica	before 522
De topicis differentiis	before 523

Of the Boethian works on logic not included on this list, two are pertinent to the study of Topics: *Liber de divisione* and Boethius's lost commentary on Aristotle's *Topics*. De Rijk estimates that the former was written between 505 and 509 and the latter sometime before 523, before *De top. diff.*[6]

In recent years, partly because of the fifteen-hundredth anniversary in 1980 of Boethius's birth, there has been a spate of publications on Boethius's life and work. Among the most noteworthy recent books and anthologies are *Boethius and the Liberal Arts*, edited by Michael Masi[7] (more than half of which is devoted to Boethius's views on mathematics and music); *Atti congresso internazionale di studi Boeziani*, edited by Luca Obertello[8] (which includes several articles on Boethius's place in his historical, cultural, and political context); *Boethius: His Life, Thought and Influence*, edited by Margaret Gibson[9] (which among many excellent articles includes two very helpful ones on Boethius's logic); and *Boethius: The Consolations of Music, Logic, Theology, and Philosophy*, by Henry Chadwick[10] (an outstanding book that includes a detailed discussion of Boethius's logic and a lengthy bibliography). For detailed scholarly analysis of Boethius's life and role in society, the reader is directed to the relevant portions of these books.

6. de Rijk 1964: 159–161.
7. Berne: Peter Lang, 1981.
8. Rome: Editrice Herder, 1981.
9. Oxford: Basil Blackwell, 1981.
10. Oxford: Clarendon Press, 1981.

The Tradition of Dialectic

Boethius's *In Ciceronis Topica* is one of two treatises Boethius wrote on the subject of the Topics or *loci*. The other treatise is *De top. diff.*,[11] one of the last philosophical works he composed.[12] Together these two treatises present Boethius's theory of the art of discovering arguments, a theory that was enormously influential in the history of medieval logic.[13] *De top. diff.* is a fairly short treatise, but it is Boethius's advanced book on the subject; it is written in a concise, even crabbed style, and it clearly presupposes acquaintance with the subject matter. In contrast, *ICT* is Boethius's elementary treatise on the Topics. It was written shortly before *De top. diff.*[14] and is a commentary on Cicero's *Topica*, though it is a much larger and more comprehensive work than the *Topica*; it is more than twice as long as the more tightly knit *De top. diff.*

The tradition of dialectic in which these Boethian treatises stand and to which they contribute has its roots in the work of Aristotle, especially in Aristotle's *Topics*.[15] In that book, Aristotle's purpose is to present an art of arguing, more precisely the art of dialectical disputation or Socratic arguing, and most of the book is devoted to a method for the discovery of arguments. The main instrument of this method is a Topic, by which Aristotle understands primarily a strategy of argumentation (such as, "If the species is a relative, [one must] examine whether the genus is also a relative") and secondarily a principle confirming the line of argument produced by the strategy (for example, "If the species is a relative, the genus is also").[16] Six of the eight books of the *Topics* consist largely in a loosely ordered compilation of such strategies and principles. Aristotle considers these Topics part of dialectic and distinguishes them from two different but analogous sorts of Top-

11. An edition of this text can be found in J. -P. Migne, *Patrologia Latina* (*PL*), vol. LXIV (Turnholt: Brepols, n.d.), 1174–1216. For a translation and notes, see Stump 1978.

12. de Rijk 1964: 159–160.

13. See Stump 1978, and idem, "Topics: Their Development and Absorption into Consequences," in Norman Kretzmann et al., eds., *The Cambridge History of Later Medieval Philosophy* (Cambridge: Cambridge University Press, 1982), pp. 273–299. See also Niels J. Green-Pedersen, *The Tradition of the Topics in the Middle Ages* (Munich: Philosophia Verlag, 1984).

14. de Rijk 1964: 159–161.

15. For discussion of Aristotle's *Topics*, see Stump 1978: 159–178. See also Walter de Pater, *Les Topiques d'Aristote et la dialectique platonicienne: La méthodologie de la définition*, Etudes thomistiques, 10 (Fribourg: Editions St. Paul, 1965); and idem, "La fonction du lieu et de l'instrument dans les *Topiques*," in G. E. L. Owen, ed., *Aristotle on Dialectic: Proceedings of the Third Symposium Aristotelicum* (Oxford: Clarendon Press, 1968), pp. 164–188.

16. Aristotle, *Top.* 124b15–16.

ics, rhetorical Topics (which aid in the construction of rhetorical arguments)[17] and mnemonic Topics (which aid in recalling things committed to memory).[18]

Topics received considerable attention in later antiquity from the Greek commentators on Aristotle[19] and from Latin rhetoricians,[20] including Cicero, whose treatise *Topica* is a presentation of Topics considered primarily as useful for arguments in law courts.[21] In the course of their work, the discipline of the Topics changed until by Boethius's time it had become very different from Aristotle's art of Topics, particularly in its understanding of the nature of a Topic.

According to Boethius, who is dependent on both the Greek and Latin traditions,[22] two different sorts of things are Topics: a Topic is both a maximal proposition and the Differentia[23] of a maximal proposition. On Boethius's view, a maximal proposition is a self-evidently true, universal generalization, such as 'Things whose definitions are different are themselves also different.' Boethian Topics of this sort probably have as their ancestors the Aristotelian Topics that are principles. Their official function, on Boethius's account, is to aid in the discovery of arguments, but in practice Boethius tends to use them to confirm arguments.[24] Differentiae are theoretically the differentiae dividing the genus *maximal proposition* into its subaltern genera and species, and in that capacity they serve to classify maximal propositions into groups. Some maximal propositions have to do with definition, for example, and other with genus; so *from definition* and *from genus* are

17. See Stump 1978: 170–172.
18. For mnemonic Topics in the Latin rhetorical tradition, see, e.g., *Rhetorica ad Herennium*, tr. Harry Caplan (Cambridge, Mass: Harvard University Press, 1954), III.xvii–xxiv, pp. 208–224. See also Frances Yates, *The Art of Memory* (London: Routledge and Kegan Paul, 1966); and Richard Sorabji, *Aristotle on Memory* (London: Duckworth, 1972).
19. See esp. Alexander of Aphrodisias, *In Aristotelis Topicorum libros octo commentaria*, in Maximilian Wallies, ed., *Commentaria in Aristotelem graeca*, sup. vol. II, pt. 2 (Berlin: G. Reimer, 1891).
20. See, e.g., Tacitus, *Dialogus de oratoribus*, ed. M. L. de Gubernatis, Corpus scriptorum latinorum Paravianum (Turin: G. B. Paravia, 1949), p. 31; Quintilian, *The Institutio oratoria of Quintilian*, tr. H. E. Butler (London: Heinemann, 1920–1922), V.x.20ff., V.x.100ff., V.xii.15ff.; Cassiodorus, *Institutiones*, ed. R. A. B. Mynors (Oxford: Clarendon Press, 1937), pp. 125ff.; and the following in Charles Halm, ed., *Rhetores latini minores* (Leipzig: Teubner, 1863): Victorinus, *Explanationum in Ciceronis rhetoricam libri II*, pp. 213ff.; Martianus Capella, *Liber de arte rhetorica*, pp. 465ff.: Fortunatianus, *Artis rhetoricae libri III*, pp. 105ff.
21. For a brief historical survey of Cicero's *Topica* and the literature on it, see Stump 1978: 20–23.
22. For a summary of the controversy over Boethius's sources, see Stump 1974.
23. I am capitalizing 'Differentia' here to distinguish this technical use of the word from its more ordinary use designating one of the predicables.
24. For a detailed analysis of Boethius's use and understanding of Topics, see Stump 1978, especially pp. 179–204.

Differentiae. Much more important, however, is the role Differentiae
play in Boethius's method for the discovery of dialectical arguments.
For the most part, Boethius thinks of dialectical arguments as having
categorical rather than conditional conclusions, and he conceives of the
discovery of an argument as the discovery of a middle term capable of
linking the two terms of the desired conclusion. Boethian Differentiae
are, for the most part, the genera of such middle terms. (In those cases
where the arguments are hypothetical rather than categorical, Boethius
generally but not invariably thinks of Topics as validating the conditional proposition in the argument.) To find an argument using
Boethius's method, one first chooses an appropriate Differentia (criteria for appropriateness are left to the arguer's intuition). The genus of
middle terms, determined by the Differentia chosen, and the two
terms of the desired conclusion then indicate the specific middle term
of the argument and so indicate a dialectical argument supporting the
conclusion.

Boethius's understanding of dialectic and Topics was highly influential in the Middle Ages.[25] In the early medieval period, there is considerable evidence that Boethius's work on the Topics was known and
used. There are some scattered allusions, in examples and maximal
propositions, to De top. diff. and ICT in Alcuin's Dialectica.[26] One of a
series of anonymous treatises stemming from Saint Gall in the ninth
century includes a discussion of the distinction between whole and
parts and genus and species which is based on ICT. The work on
syllogisms composed by Notker Labeo (d. 1022) is influenced by ICT.
And Gerbert's teaching at Reims in the tenth century was dependent
on both De top. diff. and ICT. Until the mid-twelfth century, in fact, ICT
was one of the works that formed the basis of the study of logic.[27] In
the work of Garlandus Compotista[28] and in many of the early twelfth-
century logic texts, there is a great deal of interest in Boethian sorts of
Topics but understood as warrants for the validity of arguments, especially hypothetical arguments, rather than as instruments for the
discovery of arguments. Abelard's Dialectica has extensive discussion

25. See Stump 1982: 273–299 and Green-Pedersen 1984. See also Jan Pinborg, "Topik
und Syllogistik im Mittelalter," in F. Hoffman et al., eds., Sapienter Ordinare (Leipzig: St.
Benno Verlag, 1969), pp. 157–178.
26. Alcuin, Dialectica, PL 101 968A–972C, esp. 968D, 970B–D, 971A–C.
27. See John Marenbon, Early Medieval Philosophy (480–1150): An Introduction (London:
Routledge and Kegan Paul, 1983), pp. 76–77, 81–82, and 130.
28. Garlandus Compotista, Dialectica, ed. L. M. de Rijk (Assen: Van Gorcum, 1959).
For a study of Garlandus's work on the Topics, see Eleonore Stump, "Garlandus Com-
postista and Dialectic in the Eleventh and Twelfth Centuries," History and Philosophy of
Logic, 1 (1980), 1–18.

of the Boethian Topics;[29] although it is dependent more on *De top. diff.*, it also shows some influence of *ICT*.[30]

By the early thirteenth century in the work of the terminist logicians, interest in the Boethian Topics is relegated to a rather routine chapter in logic texts, and the Topics are understood primarily as the guarantors of the validity of enthymemes. But in the remainder of that century and the first decades of the next, philosophical analysis of dialectic revives as philosophers begin to reconsider previously accepted Aristotelian views on demonstration and its relationship to dialectic. With the decline of Aristotelianism in logic goes a rising interest in consequences, or conditional inferences. Many streams of thought come together in the flood of fourteenth-century work on consequences, including, for example, earlier study of syncategorematic words, analysis of the fallacy of the consequent, and examination of Aristotle's views on the conversion of inferences. But one of these contributory streams is also the complex tradition of scholastic work on the Boethian Topics. In the works of Ockham,[31] Buridan,[32] Albert of Saxony,[33] and the Pseudo-Scotus,[34] for instance, many of the rules of consequences bear a strong resemblance to or are simply identical with certain Boethian Topics.

Thus Boethius's work on dialectic, expressed primarily in *De top. diff.* and *ICT*, stands in the center of a long, rich tradition of thought stretching from Aristotle through the fourteenth century, in which the name, nature, and logical role of what Boethius took to be a Topic slowly evolved until what had been the chief instrument for discovering dialectical arguments (in Aristotle's sense of 'dialectical') became just one more means for validating certain sorts of conditional inferences. Boethius's influence, direct and indirect, on this tradition is

29. Abelard, *Dialectica*, ed. L. M. de Rijk, 2d ed. (Assen: Van Gorcum, 1970). For a study of Abelard's work on the Topics, see Eleonore Stump, "Boethius's Theory of Topics and Its Place in Early Scholastic Logic," in Obertello 1981: 249–62. See also Otto Bird, "The Logical Interest of the Topics as Seen in Abelard," *Modern Schoolman*, 37 (1959), 53–57; and Niels J. Green-Pedersen, "The Doctrine of 'maxima propositio' and 'locus differentia' in Commentaries from the Twelfth Century on Boethius' 'Topics,'" *Studia Mediewistyczne*, 18 (1977), 125–163.

30. See, e.g., Abelard, 1970, pp. 561 and 582.

31. See esp. *Summa logicae*, ed. Philotheus Boehner, Gedeon Gál, and Stephen Brown (St. Bonaventure, N.Y.: Franciscan Institute, 1974), tr. III, chaps. 2–9.

32. See, e.g., Niels J. Green-Pedersen, "The Summulae of John Buridan, Tractatus VI De locis," in Jan Pinborg, ed., *The Logic of John Buridan* (Copenhagen: Museum Tusculanum, 1976), pp. 125–126 and 136–137.

33. *Perutilis logica* (Venice, 1522), ff. 36vb–37ra and 37rb.

34. *Super librum I Priorum*, in John Duns Scotus, *Opera omnia*, editio nova juxta editionem Waddingi xii tomos continentem a patribus Franciscanis de observantia accurate recognita (Vives, 1891), II: 105.

enormous and readily evident in logic treatises from the time of Garlandus Compotista to that of Ockham. A survey of this tradition can be found in my forthcoming volume of collected essays, *Dialectic and Its Place in the Medieval Development of Logic.* It can also be traced in the many scholastic commentaries on Boethius's dialectical work, as Niels J. Green-Pedersen has recently done.[35] (I regret that I was unable to take account of his book here because the work for my book was completed before his book appeared.)

In Ciceronis Topica

Cicero's treatise *Topica*, on Cicero's own account,[36] is his attempt to explain to his friend Trebatius what he himself takes to be Aristotle's sytem for discovering arguments. There is some mystery about this claim of Cicero's because, as has been recognized not only by modern scholars[37] but even by Boethius,[38] there is a vast difference between what Aristotle presents in his *Topics* as an art for the discovery of arguments and what we read in Cicero's *Topica.* Aristotle's sytem of discovery was transmitted and developed both by rhetoricians and by commentators on Aristotle, including, for example, Theophrastus, Eudemus, and Strato.[39] What we find in Cicero's *Topica* is an art of discovery which reflects the alterations and adaptations of Aristotle made by generations of both rhetoricians and philosophical commentators in the three intervening centuries.

Unlike Aristotle's treatment of the Topics, Cicero's is neither highly philosophical nor tied to the nature of the predicables (genus, property, definition, and accident). And the tools for aiding the discovery of arguments—the so-called Topics—are not a host of general principles, as they are in Aristotle, but rather a small set of classifications or differentiae for such general principles. In his *Topica* Cicero is attempting to teach Trebatius, in a brief and summary fashion, how to use these Topics, these differentiae of general principles, to generate a

---

35. Green-Pedersen 1984.

36. Cicero, *Top.* I.1–5, and *The Letters to His Friends,* tr. W. G. Williams, Loeb Classical Library (Cambridge, Mass: Harvard University Press, 1928), II: vii.xix.

37. For bibliography on this long-standing scholarly discussion, see H. M. Hubbell, tr., *Cicero's Topics,* Loeb Classical Library (London: Heinemann, 1960), p. 380; and Stump 1978: 20–21.

38. *De top. diff.* 1195C and 1200Cff.; and *ICT,* pp. 280–283 [*PL* 1051–1054]. In all references to *ICT,* the page reference is to the Orelli edition; the subsequent reference is to the *Patrologia (PL)* edition.

39. Stump 1978: 208ff.

great variety of arguments that will be useful to him in arguing cases in courts of law. Because his *Topica* is an abbreviated treatment of the subject, Cicero does not spell out the way in which he expects the Topics to aid in the discovery of arguments, but Boethius in his leisurely and extensive commentary does. Consider, for example, the following passage.

Marriage by purchase was carried out by established ceremonies. The parties being married by purchase asked one another question; the man asked whether the woman wanted to be a materfamilias, and she answered that she did. In the same way, the woman asked whether the man wanted to be a paterfamilias, and the man answered that he did. In this way, a woman came under the authority of her husband, and the marriage was called marriage by purchase. The woman was a materfamilias to her husband and had the status of a daughter of his. Ulpian describes this ceremony in his *Institutes*. Now a certain man in his last will bequeathed to his wife Fabia all his silver on the condition that Fabia would be not only his wife but in fact a definite species of wife, namely, a *materfamilias*. The question is whether the silver was bequeathed to the wife Fabia. *The wife Fabia* is the subject; *bequeathed silver* is the predicate. So I ask myself what argument I can take from the things presented in the question, and I see that there are two kinds inhering in *wife*: one is only a wife and the other is a *materfamilias*, a status brought about by coming under the authority of the husband. If Fabia did not come under the authority of her husband, she was not a wife, that is, she was not that species of wife to whom all the silver was bequeathed. Consequently, since what is said of one species is not appropriately said of another, and since Fabia is not included in that species of wife which has come under the authority of the husband (that is, the species which is a *materfamilias*) but her husband bequeathed the silver to a materfamilias, it appears that the silver was not bequeathed to Fabia. So the question, as was said, is whether all the silver was bequeathed to the wife Fabia. The subject is *the wife Fabia*; the predicate is *bequeathed silver* The argument is taken from something that is in the thing asked about, that is, from something that is in *wife*, which is being asked about; for a species of wife is in *wife*, which is being asked about, namely, the species that has not come under the authority of the husband. And this is related to *wife*, for every species (that is, every kind) is related to its genus. The argument is therefore made from something that is in the thing at issue, namely, from related things—from a kind of belonging to a genus. The maximal proposition is 'what is said of a single species is not appropriate for another.'[40]

The argument in this case apparently has the following structure.

40. *ICT*, p. 299 [*PL* 1071]. All quotations from *ICT* are taken from *Ciceronis Opera*, ed. J. C. Orelli (Zurich: Fuesslini, 1833), vol. V, pt. 1.

(1) The silver was bequeathed to a woman who was materfamilias.
(2) The wife Fabia is not materfamilias.
(3) *Materfamilias* is a species of wife.
(4) What is said of a single species is not appropriate for another. (the maximal proposition)
(5) Therefore, the silver was not bequeathed to the wife Fabia.

The Topic for this argument is *kind*, or *species*; it has a double role in the argument. First, it serves to suggest a class of middle terms which can unite or disjoin the subject and predicate terms of the question (*the wife Fabia* and *bequeathed silver*) and which thus provides the argument needed to prove the conclusion. In this case, the Topic gives rise to premise (3) and the general strategy of the argument. And second, it is a differentia for a genus of general principles, picking out those generalizations or maximal propositions that concern species. In this way the Topic helps discover the general principle, premise (4), which in some sense warrants the argument. A great deal more could and should be said about Boethius's theory of discovery in general and about this argument in particular, but this is enough to show briefly how Boethius intended his art of discovery to work and what sort of example he used to illustrate it.

Although the scholastics made extensive use of Boethius's works on the Topics, they relied on *De top. diff.* much more than on *ICT*. That relative neglect is also characteristic of contemporary historians of medieval philosophy, who have in general concentrated on *De top. diff.* more than *ICT*. As far as we know, there are thirty manuscripts of *ICT* extant from the tenth to the fifteenth century.[41] But there are 170 manuscripts of *De top. diff.* from the same period,[42] and that greater number is indicative of the greater use made of *De top. diff.* Part of the reason that more attention has not been paid to *ICT* by contemporary historians of philosophy (and perhaps this is true also of scholastic philosophers) is that by the standards of scholastic philosophical Latin, the Latin of *ICT* is difficult, certainly more difficult than that of Boethius's other philosophical treatises. But even more of an obstacle is the nature of the many examples Boethius discusses in great detail. Because Cicero is writing for a lawyer, he deliberately tries to make the bulk of his examples legal issues; because Boethius is writing a commentary on Cicero, he takes over the legal examples he finds in Cicero's text and labors to explicate them as well as the more theoretical portions of the *Topica*. It is unlikely that the technical termi-

41. de Rijk 1964: 151 n.2.
42. Ibid., p. 153 n.1.

nology of these examples would have been very familiar to scholastic philosophers. The laws involved in Cicero's examples were designed to regulate institutions, some of which had ceased to exist even by Boethius's time, as seems evident from the effort Boethius expends in explaining them; in some instances Boethius himself had to have recourse to textbooks of Roman law in order to clarify Cicero's example. For instance, in discussing Cicero's example about marriage quoted above, Boethius refers to a passage of Ulpian's manual, which is now no longer extant, to describe the rituals of a certain archaic form of marriage. In fact, Boethius's description of this ceremony, apparently taken from Ulpian's text, is still one of our main sources for this part of Roman law and culture.⁴³

This fact indicates one of the characteristics of *ICT* which should make it especially interesting to contemporary scholars: it is a marvelous source of information both about Roman rhetoric and philosophy as well as about Boethius himself. There has been a tendency in recent years to portray Boethius as a hack, as someone who relied very heavily on just a few sources and whose writings are essentially just reproductions of someone else's thought. There has even been the suggestion that virtually all of Boethius's philosophical writings (except, of course, the *Consolation*) are nothing more than his verbatim translations of the marginalia he found in his particular copy of Aristotle's *Organon*.⁴⁴ What we see in *ICT*, however, is a Boethius conversant with a wide variety of thinkers, doctrines, and works. Besides the various Roman jurists he cites, such as Ulpian,⁴⁵ Gaius,⁴⁶ and Julius Paulus,⁴⁷ and his general knowledge of Roman law demonstrated throughout *ICT*, the text shows that Boethius is acquainted with a broad range of texts and thought. He cites four different works of Cicero's: *Pro Caelio*, *Brutus*, *De inventione*, and *Tusculan Disputations*.⁴⁸ He gives extensive paraphrases of Marius Victorinus's book on definitions,⁴⁹ and he is thoroughly conversant with Victorinus's commentary on Cicero's *Topica*, which is now lost.⁵⁰ He quotes from Virgil's *Geor-*

43. H. F. Jolowicz and Barry Nicholas, *Historical Introduction to the Study of Roman Law* (Cambridge: Cambridge University Press, 1972), pp. 115–116 n.1.

44. James Shiel, "Boethius' Commentaries on Aristotle," *Medieval and Renaissance Studies*, 4 (1958), 217–244. For critical discussion of Shiel's thesis, see Eleonore Stump, "Boethius's Works on the Topics," *Vivarium*, 12 (1974), 77–93.

45. *ICT*, p. 299 [*PL* 1071].

46. *ICT*, p. 322 [*PL* 1095].

47. *ICT*, p. 303 [*PL* 1075–1076].

48. *ICT*, p. 341 [*PL* 1117]; p. 292 [*PL* 1063]; p. 355 [*PL* 1132]; p. 372 [*PL* 1152].

49. *ICT*, pp. 324ff. [*PL* 1098ff.]. For discussion of Victorinus's book on definitions, see Pierre Hadot, *Marius Victorinus* (Paris: Etudes Augustiniennes, 1971), pp. 163ff.

50. See, e.g., *ICT*, pp. 270ff. [*PL* 1041ff.]; p. 273 [*PL* 1044]; p. 284 [*PL* 1055]; p. 377 [*PL* 1156]. For a discussion of Victorinus's commentary, see Hadot 1971: 115–141.

gics;[51] he twice cites the fifth-century Latin rhetorician Merobaudes;[52] and he also seems familiar with Greek rhetorical terms and theory.[53] Finally, besides exhibiting familiarity with Aristotle's logic and the later commentators on it, he discussed Aristotle's *Physics* at some length;[54] he devotes considerable attention to Stoicism, mostly Stoic logic but also Stoic physics.[55] In short, *ICT* gives us strong evidence for supposing that Boethius had a good library, as he says in the *Consolation*,[56] that it had much more in it than a copy of Aristotle's *Organon* with marginalia, and that he made excellent use of what he had in that library.

Besides what *ICT* shows us about Boethius, it is also a valuable source as a witness to the thought and culture of his period. For example, in its testimony to the contents of works no longer extant, such as Victorinus's commentary on the *Topica* or Ulpian's legal text, *ICT* provides an important source for scholarship; even when Boethius is not giving us evidence concerning books no longer extant but is instead just presenting philosophical doctrines, *ICT* sheds light on some important issues. For instance, in *ICT* Boethius explains his views on the nature of universals and on the relations between metaphysics and logic,[57] he gives a lengthy exposition of Aristotelian and Ciceronian theories of causation,[58] and, in an interesting digression, he discusses Stoic views of Fate in a way that helps explain why the Stoics should have thought that the governance of all things by Fate is compatible with genuine freedom in human actions.[59] Perhaps the most interesting unexplored section in *ICT* is Boethius's presentation of Stoic logic. In *ICT* Boethius gives a detailed exposition of the seven Stoic undemonstrated argument forms. His exposition of Stoic logic is at variance with some influential interpretations of it by contemporary scholars, who in their reconstructions of Stoic logic have generally neglected *ICT*. But Boethius's account is consistent and philosophically sophisticated, and it contains intriguing suggestions for a solution to interpretative problems perplexing scholars of Stoic logic.[60]

51. *ICT*, p. 356 [*PL* 1134].
52. *ICT*, p. 335 [*PL* 1109], and p. 368 [*PL* 1147].
53. See, e.g., *ICT*, p.297 [*PL* 1068]; pp. 325ff. [*PL* 1099ff.]; and pp. 384ff. [*PL* 1165ff.].
54. *ICT*, pp. 367ff. [*PL* 1145ff.], esp. p. 373 [*PL* 1152].
55. Stoic logic is discussed throughout Book V of *ICT*. For some discussion of Stoic physics, see *ICT*, pp. 367ff. [*PL* 1146ff.].
56. See *The Consolation of Philosophy*, Bk. I, prose 4 and 5.
57. See, e.g., *ICT*, pp. 312ff. [*PL* 1084ff.]; pp. 283ff. [*PL* 1054ff.]; and pp. 293–297 [*PL* 1064–1068].
58. *ICT*, pp..367ff. [*PL* 1145ff.].
59. *ICT*, p. 367 [*PL* 1146].
60. See my notes to Book. V of this treatise for detailed discussion of Boethius's interpretation of Stoic logic.

The Translation and Notes

This book is a presentation and philosophical study of Boethius's text, designed to make the work available to scholars of medieval philosophy and also to those in other fields interested in *ICT*'s peculiar blend of philosophy, rhetoric, and law. As such, this book is intended to complement my earlier book *Boethius's De topicis differentiis*.[61] I have tried to limit the ways in which this book depends on that one, but I have not attempted to replicate here the studies on Boethius' theory of Topics and its historical context which were the main subject of the essays in the first book; I have also limited the number of notes referring to the text or notes in the earlier book. The selected bibliography accompanying this book is a list of those books and articles I found most helpful in annotating this treatise. Because of the technical nature of *ICT*, with its examples drawn from Roman law, a good part of the bibliography and the notes in this book is devoted to ancient law. The reader interested in more general bibliography on ancient dialectic or Boethius should consult the bibliographies in my earlier book and in Chadwick's *Boethius*.[62] Finally, because my purpose in the notes to *ICT* is to make a difficult technical treatise intelligible to scholars in a variety of fields, I have restricted purely philosophical notes to cases in which a philosophical perplexity about Boethius's view might hinder understanding of the text; I have entirely omitted notes considering whether Boethius has understood his sources correctly—not just Cicero, but also Aristotle, the Stoics, and various Roman jurists. Notes on Roman law predominate because Boethius's text abounds in legal examples that will be obscure to most readers without some help from notes.

This book differs in format in various ways from the earlier one. In every case I have altered the format to keep down expense in production of the book, but in such a way as not to inconvenience the reader. I have also had to modify my policy of translation. In the first book I took great pains to keep the translation literal, on the grounds that Boethius's philosophical language is precise and its precision ought to be preserved in the translation. It is, of course, difficult for a translation to be both a very literal rendering of the original and an example of flowing idiomatic English prose; in general it seems to me arguable that for medieval philosophical treatises precision should win out over readability in any struggle between the two. But *ICT* has proved to be an exception to the rule. In this treatise Boethius employs a legal vocabulary that often has no precise English equivalents because the social

61. Stump 1978.
62. Chadwick 1981.

institutions underlying the language no longer exist. Then, too, no doubt because he is commenting on Cicero and is influenced by his style, Boethius's language in this treatise is rich in a way that is often misleading or silly if preserved in translation. For example, he not only 'divides' a genus into its species, he also splits, sections, cuts, severs, and cleaves it. In the case of this treatise, then, precision would have destroyed, not undermined, readability. So although I have tried to preserve the precision of Boethius's vocabulary in this book as much as possible, this translation is not as literal as the first one.

Finally, *In Ciceronis Topica* exists in two modern editions, that in the *Patrologia latina* and that in the *opera omnia* of Cicero's works edited by Orelli and Baiterus in 1833. Neither of these is a critical edition; but, for a number of reasons, it seems unlikely that there will be a critical edition of *In Ciceronis Topica* for a long time. The edition in the Orelli and Baiterus series is quite good, so there is no urgent need for a critical edition; and it would be a big project to produce a critical edition of the treatise because of the very large number of extant manuscripts containing it.

So I have relied on the Orelli edition of *ICT* as the best available edition of the text, but for the convenience of the reader I have given parallel citations in the text and notes to the *Patrologia* edition. In all bracketed references to *ICT*, the first citation is the page and sometimes also line number of the Orelli text; the second citation is to the column number and paragraph letter of the *Patrologia* (PL) edition. I have checked worrisome textual passages in *Vat. lat.* 567ff. 1r–53r and *Reg. lat.* 1649ff. 1r–76v. I have indicated in the notes a very few places in which I think the Orelli edition should be questioned, but on the whole that edition seems to me sound. Numbers appearing between paragraphs in the text are standard reference numbers used in modern editions of Cicero and used to mark sections in the Orelli edition of Boethius's commentary.

Organization of *In Ciceronis Topica*

Because *ICT* is an extensive treatise, I include here a brief summary of its contents as an aid to the reader.

Book I

Introduction
Discussion of Victorinus's commentary on Cicero's *Topica*. The purpose of the Topics.

The nature of logic
What logic is according to the Stoics, Cicero, Plato, and Aristotle. Two partitions of logic; the nature of dialectic.
The nature of Topics
What Topics, arguments, and questions are. The purpose of an argument as regards questions; the nature of a proposition and its terms. Argument and argumentation; syllogism and enthymeme. The nature of maximal propositions and their role in arguments; Aristotle's understanding of maximal propositions. The nature of dialectical differentiae and their relationship to maximal propositions. The meanings of 'argument' and 'argumentation', and the role of maximal propositions in either. The difference between Aristotle's and Cicero's understanding of Topics.
The division of Topics
What the thing at issue is, and why the terms of a question cannot furnish arguments; the way in which the thing at issue gives rise to an argument. The major subdivisions of the Topics inhering in the thing at issue: *from the whole, from the parts, from a sign, from related things*. A problem: how these Topics differ from the thing at issue. Another problem: are there Topics for Topics? The Topics *from the whole, from parts,* and *from designation*, with examples and explanations of how these Topics function in arguments. An objection to one of Cicero's arguments.

Book II

Introduction
The nature of related things and their kinds: conjugates, genus, species, similars, differentiae, contraries, associated things, antecedents, consequents, and incompatibles, cause and effect, comparison of greater, lesser, and equal things. Why these are all related things. How related things are said to inhere in the thing at issue.
The Topic from related things
What the nature of each of the kinds of related things is. An example and an explanation for each of how it functions in arguments.
An extrinsic Topic
Its nature and role in arguments; an example.

Book III

Introduction
The Topics: their distinction from and relationship to the thing at issue; their function in arguments as a consequence of their rela-

tionship to the thing at issue. The logic of the order of the Topics,
based on their relationship to the thing at issue. A problem: whether
whole, parts, and designation should not also be considered related
things. The nature of a Topic: nothing is a Topic unless it can give rise
to an argument.

Definition

The nature of definition. The division of definitions into their species. Definition as either division or partition; how definition differs
from enumeration of parts. The kinds of definition. Victorinus's division of definition. The method for making definitions; Cicero's examples of definition. The difference between division and partition, between species and parts. The nature of genus and species. The
difference between Plato's view of forms and Aristotle's. The relation
of genus and species to partition and division. Definition by metaphor.

Book IV

Partition

The nature of partition. Why it is sometimes acceptable to omit parts
in partitioning; why it is not acceptable to omit species in a division. An
objection to Cicero's partition of guardianship. A perplexity about
Cicero's understanding of figures of speech.

Designation

The nature of designation. An example and an explanation of the
role of the Topic *from designation* in arguments.

Related things

The nature of the related things: conjugates, genus, species, en-
numeration of parts, similarity, and differentia. An explanation of how
each corresponding Topic functions in arguments, and an example for
each. Aristotle's account of opposites and its relation to Cicero's account of contraries. How the Topic *from* (Ciceronian) *contraries* functions in arguments; an example. The nature of associated things; the
role of the corresponding Topic in arguments, and an example. Antecedents, consequents, and incompatibles: why they form one conditional Topic. A perplexity: why are the Topics *from similarity* and *from a
contrary* not also one Topic? The nature of a conditional; the relationship of incompatibles to a conditional. How this conditional Topic
differs from the Topics *from associated things, from genus, from species,*
and *from contraries*. The relationship of categorical and conditional
arguments.

Book V

Introduction
Review of the nature of argument, question, proposition, and terms. The nature and sorts of conditional propositions; the nature of incompatibles.
The seven Stoic modes of hypothetical syllogisms
Presentation of the seven modes and review of them. The way in which arguments arise from antecedents, consequents, and incompatibles. An objection to Cicero's example of an argument drawn from consequents. A perplexity: how is this conditional Topic different from the Topic *from genus?* A commentary on and criticism of Cicero's presentation of the seven modes.
Causes
Aristotle's four causes and their relationship to Cicero's division of causes. Cicero's first division of causes into their kinds. Stoic views on Fate. A perplexity about this Ciceronian division. The role of causes in arguments. Three more Ciceronian divisions of causes. Cicero's definition of chance and its relationship to Aristotle's definition of chance; Boethius's own views of chance. The relationships among Cicero's several divisions of causes.

Book VI

Introduction
Review of the purpose of the art of Topics; the nature of Topics, arguments, questions, propositions, and terms.
Causes
The usefulness of the Topic *from causes;* its role in the arguments of jurists.
Effects and comparison
The nature of effects; how the Topic *from effects* functions in arguments. Comparisons: which things are preferable to which.
The division of Topics
Review of the logical division of Topics and reasons for thinking it complete.
The extrinsic Topic
The nature of the Topic *from authority* and its role in argument. What conditions and circumstances give rise to authority.

In Ciceronis Topica

BOOK I

[270/1039] I have deemed nothing more important, Patricius,[1] most skillful of rhetoricians, than your exhortation, which is based on both the worth of the present undertaking and its usefulness for future times. I have acquiesced very willingly in this task, not because I thought I might work at commentaries on Cicero's *Topica* in order to instruct you (indeed I would be ridiculous if, as they say, I wanted to teach letters to Minerva), but rather in order that a token of our friendship, taken from the store of the liberal arts, might always remain with you. For what task is more agreeable to those who love with the mind than that which shapes and instructs the parts of the mind itself? For other things are nearly always utterly destined to die, frail, fragile, and alien to us,[2] if you consider the vicissitudes of fortune. The present age does not weaken the power of the written word; even time itself, which wears all things out, only increases and strengthens its authority. Receive, therefore, this work undertaken not out of confidence in my workmanship but in reliance on our friendship, within which (by a sort of mutual pact) even chattering nonsense is not unbecoming. Furthermore, because I have presented you with this gift, you will be the more unjust if you refuse when I ask you for some of your work.

Since a rhetorician of great renown in the art of discourse, Marius Victorinus,[3] has written a commentary on Cicero's *Topica*, it would not have been right for me to touch on matters attempted by those who are perhaps my betters, unless there were something that my workmanship also could exercise itself on and provide. Victorinus wrote four books on the *Topica*. In the first of them he occupies himself only with explaining the principles of the book and considering introductory remarks that need to be discussed. The exposition in Victorinus's first book is then bounded by the exordium of the *Topica*, which is "Maiores nos res scribere ingressos, C. Trebati" and the passage "Sed iam tempus est ad id, quod instituimus, accedere."[4] In the second book he handles the parts of the dialectic (judgment and discovery)

21

and the definitions of Topics and of an argument. The explanation of his comments in the second book thus covers from this passage of the *Topica*, "Quum omnis ratio diligens disserendi duas habeat partes, unam inveniendi, alteram iudicandi," to this passage, "Itaque licet definire locum esse argumenti [271/1041] sedem: argumentum autem rationem, quae rei dubiae faciat fidem."[5] The third and the fourth books set forth in various ways the distinctions among the Topics and their examples. The third book lays out Ciceronian examples having to do with the law, and the fourth book shows the same Topics again by means of yet other examples drawn from the poets Virgil and Terence and from the orators Cicero and Cato. What is shown by rules is thus illuminated fully in various ways by examples. Advancing from this passage in the *Topica*, "Sed ex iis locis, in quibus argumenta inclusa sunt," the exposition does not go beyond this passage, "Valeat aequitas, quae paribus in causis paria iura desiderat."[6] The magnitude of the *Topica* itself, however, shows the size of the remaining part, which Victorinus did not concern himself with and could not have concerned himself with, caught up as he was in details, unless he had stretched out his work into a great multitude of volumes.

Let us carefully undertake, then, as best we can, even the small part Victorinus did concern himself with; we should, however, carry the exposition further, and not stop until the end of the *Topica*. So let us make a beginning suitable for setting forth the entire work. But before I deal with the theory of the Topical discipline, let me explain in a few words the proemium in which Cicero addresses Trebatius.[7] He says: [the reference here is to the lengthy proemium of Cicero's *Topica*]

[1.1–1.5]

As one learns in rhetoric texts, every proemium that aims at winning over its hearer seeks to obtain goodwill, prepares attentiveness, or produces aptness for learning.[8] In accordance with these three elements of a proemium Cicero makes Trebatius well disposed. Because he turned away from beginning greater subjects and devoted himself instead to the request of his friend, he earns the goodwill of Trebatius in these three ways, making him as it were a well-disposed judge. The greater subject, from the writing of which he turned away to this study for his friend, is the treatment of moral philosophy, for the theory of ethics is greater than skill at discourse. This, we conjecture, was at the time when he gave himself to leisure and to the philosophical disciplines because of the troubled times of the state.[9]

Because a belief in a writer's truthfulness, provided at the outset, inclines the minds of the readers to the author, Cicero here also uses these ways of preparing goodwill; by relating truly things Trebatius knows to be true, he inclines Trebatius to believe in those things that come later and about which Trebatius could be ignorant. The things Trebatius knows are these: In Cicero's Tusculan villa both Cicero and Trebatius opened books, each according to his fancy. Trebatius by chance happened on Aristotle's *Topics*. He wondered at the title of the work and asked Cicero for an explanation of it. Cicero relates that he explained to him that these books contain the science of discovering arguments, so that by a path and a straight way and a system one may come to the discovery of arguments without any error. Cicero's brief statement of these things shows the purpose of his book and makes his reader apt to learn. For the purpose of the *Topics* seems to be [272/1043] contained in this passage where Cicero says that it is a discipline of arguments—not that arguments are found, for this is fully supplied by nature, but rather that the mind might arrive at arguments without any toil or any disorder, by a path and by reason rather than by chance.

After he has obtained Trebatius's goodwill, Cicero adds praise of Trebatius, because he relates Trebatius's modesty in making his request, which, if Cicero had fulfilled, he would have been rewarded with honor and esteem. But Cicero maintains, he did not yield to his friend's entreaty to propound the *Topics* to him, not in order to avoid labor on his own part but rather for the sake of Trebatius. In this way too, then, Cicero hoped to avoid alienating Trebatius, who was then perhaps angry because he had been refused. It was of importance for Trebatius either that he read these books by himself and so become more practiced or that a learned rhetorician explain them to him more fully if he had any doubts. But, Cicero relates, Trebatius had told him about both alternatives, for Trebatius had tried to read these books by himself but was driven back by their obscurity, and the rhetorician from whom he had sought an explanation of the *Topics* confessed that he was not acquainted with these Aristotelian books. This point, the difficulty of the work, must render the hearer attentive; those things which we suspect are not easy to understand, we examine carefully.

In this connection, Cicero says that he was not at all surprised that the rhetorician was not acquainted with Aristotle, who seems to be unknown even to many philosophers. And he also rightly censures the sloth of such philosophers whom neither the usefulness of what is discovered nor the splendor of the language has attracted to the discipline of Aristotelian philosophy. In this way, too, he increases our attentiveness and makes it more acute, because censure of the sluggishness of others turns minds readily to study, and when we are attentive, we cannot help but be apt to learn. In this passage also he subtly introduces a certain praise of Trebatius. For it is impressive that when the philosophers have given up at what is their own task, Trebatius, hindered by going outside his area of expertise, nonetheless ferrets out the secrets of a science strange to him.

The very next passages even more clearly seek goodwill—for example, this, which is said very elegantly: Cicero was afraid that if he had denied Trebatius's modest and respectful request completely, Trebatius the interpreter of the law would have been somehow unlawfully treated. And also this: mindful of the favors he has received, Cicero relates Trebatius's previous service to him, namely, that Trebatius had written many things either for Cicero himself or for those whom Cicero defended. So, as Cicero says, he was afraid that he might appear to be either ungrateful or arrogant if he were unwilling to return the favor—ungrateful if he seemed to think little of Trebatius's great services, from which he himself had benefited (since he would then appear to think that there was no favor that needed to be repaid to Trebatius), but proud if he disdained him.

The other passages harp on the same point. Cicero relies on Trebatius himself as a witness that when he was in the city he was constrained by the necessity of business from repaying the favor due. As he came to Velia, he was reminded by meeting Trebatius's friends and had not wanted to neglect even Trebatius's silent demand. Furthermore, although he had no supply of books, nevertheless [273/1044] during his voyage he composed this book, relying on the storehouse of his memory, and sent it to Trebatius while still on his journey, so that he might add swiftness of compliance to the heap of his benefits for Trebatius. (Although all these things apparently seek Trebatius's benignant approbation, the brevity of the *Topica* drawn from memory must have to do with alerting the attention; the fact that it is drawn from memory shows that what he has put together is a summary.) And he wanted the book to be a token and memorial to rouse memory of himself. To this he adds, "although you need no admonition" lest he give offense by the obtrusiveness of his admonition, in case he might seem to accuse Trebatius of forgetfulness in virtue of thinking that he needs to be reminded.

All these passages, as I said, are replete with the ways of obtaining goodwill. But we have said enough about the proemium; now let us turn to the following passages. And if someone has found these passages discussed in more detail by Victorinus, we feel no twinge of envy for the missing fullness, for we do not want to hang on the individual words as he does, and we are hastening on to more of this book.

[2.6–2.7]

Philosophy expends its work and study on great subjects. It employs investigation into and contemplation of things in nature as well as actions in matters of morals, and it desires to shape morals in such a way that reason persuades a man of those things that make a life right. Therefore, philosophy must establish our judgment concerning the governing of life and exercise our faculties in accordance with what reason has determined we should adhere to or reject, do or leave undone. So both in contemplation of nature and in deliberation about moral actions, sure reason will necessarily discover the correct contemplation of things and will plan how life should be led. But unless reason proceeds along a certain path, it must often fall into many errors. To prevent reason from being exercised haphazardly and to ensure that it be practiced according to certain rules, the foremost of ancient philosophers thought it good first to discuss thoroughly the nature of reasoning itself, by means of which anything must be investigated, in order that we might use such reasoning purified and well ordered for the contemplation of truth or the exercise of virtues.

This discipline, then, which the ancient Peripatetics called logic,[10] is "mistress" of discourse. Cicero defined it as a careful system of discourse. It has been treated in a variety of ways by many authors and has been called by a variety of names. For, as we said, the careful system of discourse which provides expertise for both discovery and judgment[11] is called logic by the Peripatetics. The Stoics, however, treated the system of discourse somewhat more narrowly, for they did not work at discovery at all but dwelt only on judgment; they called this subject dialectic[12] and gave many rules about it. Plato, however calls dialectic the skill that can divide what is one into many parts (as, for example, we customarily divide a genus by the appropriate differentiae until we come to the lowest [274/1045] species) and that can collect by reason things that are many into some one genus.[13] Plato, then, calls this discipline dialectic; Aristotle calls it logic;[14] and, as we said, Cicero defined it as the careful system of discourse.

In one way, there is a threefold partition of logic, for the whole force of the logical discipline defines something, divides something, or deduces something.[15] Moreover, the skill of deducing itself consists in three different parts, for disputation progresses by means of true and necessary argumentations (this is called a discipline and demonstration), by means of readily believable argumentations only (this is said to be dialectic), or by means of argumentations that are very clearly false (this is taken to be sophistry or trickery).[16] So logic, which is expertise in discourse, deals with definition, partition, or deduction—

that is, with true and necessary argumentations, with readily believable (that is, verisimilar) argumentations, or with sophistical (that is, tricking) argumentations, for (as we said before) these are the parts of deduction. And this is one partition of logic, in accordance with which Aristotle calls dialectic the skill of deduction which uses what is readily believable.[17]

A different division of logic is that in accordance with which the whole careful system of discourse is separated into two parts, one of discovery and the other of judgment. The very definition of logic seems also to make this manifest. Because logic is a system of discourse, it cannot be separated from discovery; for since no one can engage in discourse without discovery, the system of discourse is the system of discovery. On the other hand, since logic is the careful system of discourse, judgment cannot be absent from it; for the carefulness of the system of discourse is judgment, and no one can discourse carefully unless he has judged the quality of the material he uses in arguing. And if the carefulness of the system is applied to the thread of the discourse, then judgment is undoubtedly suited to a variety of discoveries.

Now that we have explained these things in this way, we must consider how these divisions of logic are related to one another. Discovery is the basis for all the others, holding the place, as it were, of their matter[18] in the following way. For without discovery, there cannot be definition or partition, since we divide or even define a thing by the discovery of genera or differentiae.[19] Moreover, without discovery there cannot be deduction,[20] and so there will not be the necessary, the verisimilar, or the sophistical, for these three are added to discovery so that an argument becomes necessary, readily believable, or sophistical. Necessity, ready believability, and sophistry are forms of a sort; when they come to discoveries, they make arguments necessary, readily believable, or sophistical.[21] The same point applies to partitions and definitions, for the undifferentiated power of discovery can be called definitive or divisive when it is used to define or to partition things. In this way, composed of the discovery as matter and of the superimposed differentiae as forms, they become in turn matter for judgment. For the previous division of logic into three parts sets forth the parts in such a way that discovery is the matter for each of them, but the whole division itself furnishes the matter for judgment. When someone defines or [275/1046] makes a division of a thing, he discovers differentiae suitable for making a division and a definition, but judgment considers whether he has defined or divided rightly. In this way, these first parts of logic are conjoined to the members of the second division: they have discovery as their matter but are themselves the matter for judgment.[22]

This is the case also with the remaining part of logic, namely, deduction. The part of deduction which deals with readily believable things is based on discovery as its matter because it finds verisimilar arguments; judgment considers arguments of this sort, for there is a judgment that consists in discerning that what is discovered is not necessary but has verisimilitude. The part of deduction suited to necessary argumentations is based on the discovery of what is necessary as its matter; the judgment of it consists in the fact that because the things discovered are necessary, judgment considers them to be necessary. The part of deduction which is sophistical also contains within itself both discovery and judgment since false things can be discovered and can also be determined to be false by judgment.

So the first division of logic seems to contain the second division; for definition, partition, and deduction contain discovery and judgment, because without discovery they cannot exist and without judgment they cannot be recognized. But because all discovery is the basis for judgment and because the parts of the first division of logic cannot exist without both discovery and judgment, the first division conjoins both discovery and judgment. The second division, however (in accordance with which Cicero partitions logic), isolates these skills and severs the matter that is discovery from the part that is judgment.

Furthermore, judgment too has parts appropriate to it with regard to the nature of deduction. For every argumentation and every syllogism are constructed of propositions,[23] but everything that is a composite has two things of some sort in it, and these things, it seems, ought to be examined. One thing to examine is the nature of those things of which the composite is understood to be made up, and another is the conjunction of the parts by means of which the whole is composed. For example, in the case of a wall, if you examine the stones themselves by which the wall is constructed, you are looking at the "matter" of the wall. On the other hand, if you observe the arrangement and composition of the junctures of the stones, you are considering the nature of "the form." Similarly with regard to argumentations, which (as we related above) are conjoined and bound together by propositions, examination and judgment take place in two ways. One way determines and judges the nature of the propositions themselves—whether they are true and necessary, whether they are verisimilar, or whether they are used in sophistries. This is a contemplation of "the matter" of argumentations. The other way, however, considers the junctures and composition of the propositions among themselves, and it is a part of judgment. This way judges "the form" of arguments.

Hence, in this way a division comes to be made in what is continuous. The careful system of discourse has two parts, one of discovery and the other of judgment—sometimes judgment of the discovery itself, sometimes judgment of the deduction of the discovery, which is the form of an argumentation. The part that teaches about discovery supplies in abundance certain tools for discoveries and is called 'Topics'. (Why it is called by this name, I will say later on.) The part [276/1047] that has to do with judgment proffers certain rules making determinations and is called 'Analytics'. If it makes observations about the junctures of propositions, it is named 'Prior Analytics'. But if it deals with the discoveries themselves, then the part that discusses the determining of necessary arguments is named 'Posterior Analytics', and the part that discusses false and tricky (that is, sophistical) arguments is named 'Refutations'. The judgment of verisimilar argumentations is apparently not dealt with[24] because the nature of judgment concerning the middle is clear and uncomplicated when one is acquainted with the extremes. For if one knows how to judge discerningly what is necessary and is also able to judge false arguments, it is no trouble for him to determine verisimilar arguments, which are in the middle.[25]

I think, then, that I have explicated what Cicero means when he says that the careful system of discourse has two parts, one of discovery and the other of judgment. I have also set forth more carefully what this system is. The Stoics call it dialectic, and for them it consists in expertise in judging. Plato called it by the same name and understood it as skill at partitioning by differentiae and reducing to a genus. Aristotle used the same name, only he applied it not to the whole art of discourse as the Stoics do but only to the part that deduces verisimilar arguments for a question put forward. Aristotle, therefore, dealt with logic more completely since he discussed the two parts of logic (besides which there is no third), namely, discovery and judgment, whereas the Stoics neglected discovery and transmitted only tools for judgment.

Cicero, therefore, rightly upbraids the Stoics since they left entirely untouched a subject that is both prior in nature and more powerful in practice. It is prior in nature because one cannot judge a discovery unless the discovery itself first exists. And it is more powerful in practice because it is often far more advantageous to defend a case one has undertaken with discovery that is unadorned, artless, and naturally expressed than to exercise silently and unarmed a mute judgment while someone else does the discovering.[26] Cicero, however, gives his opinion concerning both judgment and discovery. He says that they are both equally of the greatest advantage and that if he had leisure, he would like to discuss them both. But he thinks he ought to begin with that which is prior, namely, discovery; as we said, this is called 'Topics'.

[2.7–2.8]

After the division of the discipline of logic, which Cicero defines as the careful system of discourse, he directs his attention toward explicating Topics, which as we previously said is the art of discovery. First he encompasses the Topics with a definition, and he indicates the purpose of the art called Topics with the special clarity of an example. The purpose of the Topics is the easy discovery of arguments. The Topics do not teach discovery, which belongs to our natural abilities, but rather easier discovery. Every art imitates nature; taking its matter from nature, the art fashions principles and a path, so that what the art promises may occur not only more easily but also more elegantly. For example, we can construct a wall by our natural abilities, but we do it better by art.

An argument is a reason that produces belief regarding something that was in doubt.[27] Many things [277/1048] produce belief, but because they are not reasons, they cannot be arguments either. For example, sight produces belief in the things seen, but because sight is not a reason, it cannot be an argument either. In addition, Cicero provided one differentia, namely, *which produces belief*, for every argument produces belief. If we then join this genus and differentia and say that an argument is equivalent to a reason that produces belief, would we have shown the whole nature of an argument? Not at all. Why not? Suppose someone wants to produce belief by means of a reason but regarding something about which no one is in doubt, will the reason that produces belief therefore be called an argument? In no way. For an argument is something that argues for (that is, proves) a thing, but nothing can be proved unless it was in doubt.[28] Therefore, unless something is uncertain and a reason producing belief in it is adduced, there cannot be an argument. Once another differentia has been added, namely, *regarding something that was in doubt*, the whole definition of argument, consisting of the genus and two differentiae, has been produced. The genus is *a reason*; one differentia is *which produces belief*, and the other is *regarding something that was in doubt*. The whole definition, then, is this: an argument is a reason producing belief regarding something that was in doubt.

Now, where something is in doubt, there must be a question. Hence, if there cannot be an argument apart from something that was in doubt, there cannot be an argument apart from a question either. A question is a proposition that is in doubt.[29] A proposition is an expression signifying something true or false.[30] So every proposition. whether it is put forward firmly and declaratively (for example, when someone says, 'Every man is an animal') or is directed toward an inquiry (for example, if someone inquires, 'Every man is an animal, don't you think?'), keeps its proper name and is called a proposition. But if the same thing is put forward as being in doubt, it becomes a question (for example, when someone asks, 'Is every man an animal?'). This does not seem a suitable place to set forth the many ways in which a question is divided, but we will discuss it in those books on the differentiae of Topics which we are endeavoring to compose.[31]

The whole purpose of an argument is directed toward a question, that is, toward a proposition that is in doubt—not in order to prove the whole question but rather to corroborate by reason a part of it, for one does not maintain a whole question but rather supports some part of it by argumentation. For example, no one maintains that the heaven is and is not spherical. (If someone did maintain this, he would apparently prove the whole question.) But when one considers whether the heaven is or is not spherical, one maintains only one part of the question, either that which affirms or that which denies that the heaven is spherical, for every question consists in contradictories. If something is affirmed by one person and denied by another, this whole thing is called a contradiction. For example, if someone says, 'The heaven is spherical,' and someone else denies it, saying 'The heaven is not spherical,' that the heaven is and is not spherical is called a contradiction. A proposition that is in doubt (which we said previously is a question) contains within itself both an affirmation and a negation, for by the very fact that it is in doubt, it seems to include a contradiction. For example, when someone is in doubt [278/1049] whether the heaven is spherical, it does not matter whether he adds 'or is not spherical' or refrains from saying it; the very fact that he is in doubt whether the heaven is spherical implies the other part.[32] For if a proposition defends one part, it is not a proposition in doubt and therefore is not a question.

So since every question has two parts, an affirmation and a negation, what one maintains is necessarily always based on one or the other part. One person maintains the part that is an affirmation and another person the part that is a negation, and each person seeks whatever arguments he can find, the first for support of the affirmation and the second for its destruction. For it makes no difference whether someone asserts an affirmation or destroys a negation, whether he maintains a negation or opposes an affirmation. Suppose there is a question whether the heaven is spherical. If someone maintains that it is spherical and adopts this part of the question, he must prepare for himself all arguments for establishing this part of the question; in doing so, he asserts an affirmation but destroys a negation. On the other hand, if someone denies this and says that the heaven is not spherical, he has adopted the other, remaining part of the question, namely, a negation, and this is where he takes his stand. He uses the arguments that he sought to prove this part of the question, and so he asserts a negation and overturns an affirmation.

Hence, I think I have demonstrated that one maintains not the whole question but some part of it. But whatever anyone maintains he also seeks arguments for. So arguments are adopted for the support or destruction of a part of a question. If someone does not understand these things very well, let him not defend himself by saying that we have spoken obscurely about them. If he is ignorant of what we have said in Latin about dialectic[33] or of what has been written about it by the Greeks,[34] it is no wonder that he is unable to attend to some part of our discussion here, and we should by no means be surprised that he does not comprehend everything.

Since (as we said previously) a question is a proposition in doubt, a question apparently retains the same parts as a proposition. Now every simple proposition has two parts consisting of terms. A simple proposition is of this sort: 'Every man is an animal.' Terms are what I call the simple parts of speech which comprise the proposition, such as 'animal' and 'man'. These are the predicate and the subject. A predicate is classified as the greater term in a proposition, the subject as the lesser term. The greater term is said of the subject, but the lesser term is never in any way predicated of the greater term. For example, since *animal* is greater than *man*, it is predicated of *man*, for we say, 'Every man is an animal.' But *man* is not said of *animal*, for no one says truly 'Every animal is a man.' So by this criterion we can discern which term in a proposition is greater and which is lesser.[35]

Since every question (as we said) has parts that are in doubt and arguments are adopted to prove those parts, anything in questions that is proved must be supported by the reasoning of arguments. But an argument will not be able to produce belief for something in doubt unless it is expressed in speech and arranged with the interweaving of propositions. The expression and arrangement of an argument by means of propositions is called an argumentation, and this is said to be an enthymeme or a syllogism [279/1050]. (We will explain the definitions of these more fully in connection with the Differentiae of Topics.)[36] And every syllogism or enthymeme consists of propositions. So every argument is expressed by a syllogism or an enthymeme. But an enthymeme is an incomplete syllogism, some of whose parts are omitted either for the sake of brevity or because they are already known, and so argumentation of this sort also does not fall outside the genus of syllogism.

Since every syllogism consists of propositions, and propositions consist of terms, and the terms differ from one another in that one is greater and the other is lesser, a conclusion cannot arise from propositions unless the propositions, which proceed by means of terms, conjoin the extreme terms by the intermediary of a third term. This is easily demonstrated with an example. Suppose there is a question whether a man is a substance or not. I adopt one part of the question in need of proof, namely, 'Man is a substance.' In this part there are two terms, *substance* and *man*; of these, *substance* is the greater and *man* is the lesser. This can be shown also from the fact that *substance* is expressed later in the expression; for example, in 'A man is a substance,' we give the name 'man' first and the name 'substance' later.[37] So in order for us to join *man* and *substance*, we must find a middle term that might unite both terms. Let this be *animal* and let this be one premise: 'Every man is an animal.' In this proposition *animal* is the predicate, and *man* is the subject. Then I add 'But every animal is a substance.' In this proposition *animal* is now the subject and *substance* is the predicate. And in this way I conclude, 'Every man is a substance.'[38] Throughout this argument *man* is always the subject. *Animal*, however, is predicated of *man* but made the subject for *substance*; *substance* itself remains always a predicate. Hence *man* is the lesser term, *substance* is a term greater than *man*, and *animal* is the middle term. Thus the extreme terms are united by the insertion of a middle term, and in this way the members of the question are coupled with each other and the doubt is resolved by the proof employed. Hence an argument is nothing other than the discovery of an intermediate, for an intermediate will be able to conjoin the extremes, if an affirmation is being maintained, or to disjoin them, if a negation is being asserted.

Of the two propositions and the conclusion (which is the third), the one that contains the greater term, that is, the one in which the greater term is the predicate and the middle term is the subject, is called the greater or major proposition—for example, 'Every man is an animal.' Since lesser things must be derived from greater things, the first premise appears to be the specific "producer" of the conclusion 'Every man is a substance,' although the conclusion arises from two premises. Anyone who has read our *Prior* and *Posterior Analytics*, which we translated from Aristotle, is not in the least doubt about this.[39] But if someone who does not know what is written in those books has rushed ahead to read these things, then even if he finds incomprehensible the explanation of those things that he does not understand, he should nonetheless believe that it is as I have said, and he should think that he himself would discover this more fully in Aristotle's *Analytics* [280/1051] if he were to read them.

The nature of things requires that where there is something greater and lesser, there must also be something greatest or maximal. Hence, there are certain maximal propositions, in the way in which we have shown that there are greater and lesser propositions; we should take their nature from the following partition of simple propositions. Every simple proposition is either affirmative or negative.[40] Of these, some are universal (as, for example, 'Every man is just'; 'No man is just'); some are particular (as, for example, 'Some man is just'; 'Some man is not just'); some are indefinite (as, for example, 'Man is just'; 'Man is not just'); and some are singular, containing something singular and individual (as, for example, 'Cato is just'; 'Cato is not just'). Of all these, some are to be doubted, and others are undoubted. We call highest and maximal propositions those propositions that are universal and known and manifest to such an extent that they need no proof but rather themselves provide proof for things that are in doubt, for those propositions that are undoubted are generally the principles of demonstration for those propositions that are uncertain. Propositions of this sort are 'Every number is either even or odd' and 'If equals are subtracted from equals, equals remain,' and others whose truth is known and unquestioned.[41]

In Aristotle's *Topics*, as we have observed,[42] maximal propositions, that is, universal and most known propositions from which the conclusion of syllogisms is derived, are called Topics. Because they are maximal (that is, universal) propositions, they embrace other propositions within themselves as places embrace bodies; because, however, they are most known and manifest, they furnish belief for questions and in this way contain proofs for things that are uncertain.[43]

Sometimes, we observe, maximal propositions inhere in syllogisms and argumentations themselves; other times, however, they are not contained in the argumentations themselves but nonetheless supply force to them. For example, if we want to show that a kingdom is better than a consulate, we will say, 'When it is good, a kingdom is longer lasting than a consulate; but every good that is longer lasting is better than that which is of shorter duration; therefore a kingdom is better than a consulate.' Here the proposition that is maximal, universal, known per se, and in need of no proof is incorporated in the argumentation; this is 'All goods that are longer lasting are better than those which are restricted to a short time.' But if we want to show that someone who is wise is not envious, we say, 'An envious man is one who grieves at the happiness of another; but a man who is made sad by the happiness of another is not wise; therefore an envious man is not wise.' Here the maximal proposition does not appear included in the argumentation, but although it is located outside the argumentation, it still supplies force to the syllogism. The maximal proposition is 'Things that have different definitions have different substances.'[44]

Whoever reads through Aristotle's *Topics* in Greek or in our translation will find that those propositions which are maximal, universal, known, and either necessary per se or readily believable per se are there called by the name 'Topics'.[45] [281/1052] But since such propositions must be many—in fact nearly innumerable—we are still in need of something that will enable the reasoning of our investigation to advance further. By dealing carefully with the theory, we can consider the differentiae of all maximal, universal propositions and can collect the innumerable multitude of maximal propositions known per se into a few universal differentiae. So we say some maximal propositions consist in definition, some in genus, and others in something else (as I will demonstrate more fully a little later). So, for example, all maximal propositions that fall under the nature of definition will be contained by the one name of 'definition'. As maximal propositions were said to be places or Topics for other propositions because maximal propositions contain the others within their scope, so these differentiae, to which maximal propositions have been reduced by an appropriate criterion, appear to be places or Topics (if not literally, then figuratively anyway) of those maximal, universal propositions that, as we said previously, are places or Topics for lesser propositions.

The differentiae of Topics or maximal propositions are themselves also given the name 'Topics' and can also be called genera of the propositions subordinated under them; for constitutive differentiae can usually also be regarded as genera.[46] For example, although *irrational* is a divisive differentia distinct from *rational,* it is nonetheless also a specific differentia for *horse* and *dog* and holds the place of a genus with respect to them, for *irrational animal* is the genus of *horse.*[47] Things are the same in the case of maximal propositions. Since some maximal propositions are from the whole and others are from parts,[48] *from the whole* and *from parts* in relation to one another are divisive differentiae. But in relation to maximal propositions themselves, which are constituted from the differentiae, they have the place of "a genus." The genus of a proposition arising from the whole is just *from the whole.*[49] Similarly, the genus of a proposition drawn from parts (however known and manifest the proposition) is *from parts,* and other differentiae are also "genera" of some sort for propositions that are maximal and yet seem to be included in these differentiae. I will discuss what these differentiae are a [281/1052] little later.

Here Cicero begins to deal with the Topics that contain and include the maximal propositions discussed above (that is, propositions that are universal and known per se); these Topics are the differentiae of maximal propositions. So he discusses the differentiae of statements that are universal and known per se, and he says that a Topic is just the seat of an argument. Every argument is brought to its conclusion by means of propositions, and all other propositions are contained in a first and maximal proposition,[50] which sometimes is part of an argumentation or syllogism and sometimes supplies force to an argumentation from without (and so in either case it appears to be a certain part of the argumentation since it completes the argument). Therefore, those differentiae which contain maximal propositions undoubtedly also contain all argumentations, so that the differentiae of maximal propositions are rightly regarded as Topics or places [282/1053] and as a sort of ultimate seat of arguments.

The two names 'argumentation' and 'argument' must have one of the following four significations. Either the expression and interweaving of the propositions together with the maximal propositions (whether located outside the syllogism or included within it) is called the argumentation, while the argument is the thought and meaning of the syllogism. Or the expression of the reasoning together with the maximal propositions and the meaning of the syllogism will be said to be the argument, and so argument and argumentation will be the same. Or the whole interweaving of the syllogism together with the meaning will be called the argumentation, but the maximal proposition will be called the argument. Or the whole arrangement of the reasoning apart from the maximal propositions will be said to be the argumentation, but the meaning of the argumentation is the argument, and the maximal proposition that remains is the Topic.[51]

Given this, if someone wants to call an argumentation both the interweaving and series of propositions down to the conclusion and the maximal proposition (whether located outside or included within the propositions of the reasoning), but calls an argument the meaning and thought of the reasoning, we nonetheless understand Topics as the differentiae of maximal propositions. Or if someone calls an argument the entire force and meaning of the reasoning together with the maximal proposition (whether located within or without the argument), the Topic for the whole reasoning is still undoubtedly the differentia of a maximal proposition, for it contains a maximal proposition, in which other propositions are contained. Or if it seems good to call an argumentation the entire interweaving of the reasoning but to call an argument the maximal proposition, again the Topic will be rightly reckoned as the differentia of a maximal proposition, which encloses and con-

tains the argument. And if the argument is understood as the sense of
the whole reasoning while the argumentation is understood as the
entire expression of the reasoning, but something different and apart
from them both is considered the Topic, then in this way also the
differentiae of maximal propositions will be regarded as Topics.[52] For
since a differentia contains a maximal proposition and is a place or
Topic for it, while a maximal proposition supplies the force for an
argumentation or argument, the differentia seems undoubtedly to be a
Topic for the whole argument because it includes within itself the
whole scope of the maximal proposition.

So we have shown what the seat of an argument is (places in which
arguments are enclosed, and these are the differentiae of maximal
propositions, which are called Topics), also what an argument is (that
which produces belief for something in doubt), what a thing in doubt is
(one or another part of a question), what a question is (a proposition in
doubt), and what a simple proposition is (a statement comprised of a
predicate and subject term signifying something true or false). All
these things should be remembered. The differentiae of maximal propositions (which as we said before are Topics), are drawn from those
terms that are primarily in a proposition and are secondarily considered in a question, namely, the predicate and the subject.

From what I have said above, the difference between Aristotle's
Topics and Cicero's *Topica* should be clear. Aristotle [283/1054] discusses maximal propositions, for he asserted that these are the Topics
for arguments, as we also related above; Cicero, however, calls Topics
not maximal propositions but rather their constitutive differentiae,
which is what he directs his attention toward teaching.[53]

[2.8]

After the definition of a Topic and an argument, Cicero makes an
exhaustive division of Topics. To begin with, every division ought to
embrace everything and neither insert anything superfluous nor omit
anything necessary.[54] Cicero accomplished this in his division, saying
that some Topics in which arguments are enclosed inhere in the thing
at issue[55] and others are taken from without. Nothing, it seems, can be
added to or subtracted from this division since in a few words it em-
braces everything;[56] for no matter which Topics for arguments we take,
they will either inhere in the thing at issue or they will not. (The
expression 'they will not' signifies that these Topics are external to the
thing at issue.) Now there is no intermediate between the Topics for

arguments that inhere in the thing at issue and those that do not, for there is no intermediary between an affirmation and a negation. Hence, since a Topic for arguments which does not inhere in the thing at issue is a Topic taken from without, there is certainly no intermediate between the arguments whose Topics inhere in the thing at issue and those whose Topics are taken from without.[57]

But it is easier to explain what the thing at issue is if we remember what was said above. When we spoke about a question, we said that a question is a proposition in doubt; but since a proposition consists of a subject and a predicate, we said that a question is also formed by the conjunction of a subject and a predicate. So a predicate or a subject is the thing at issue, for when one or another part of a question is in doubt, the doubt concerns whether or not the predicate term appears to inhere in the subject term.[58]

Given that every question is divided into an affirmation and a negation, if the predicate inheres in the subject, this gives rise to a true affirmation; if it does not, this gives rise to a true negation. When questions are debated, one man defends the affirmation and another defends the negation—that is, one man maintains that the predicate inheres in the subject, and the other maintains that it does not; what is maintained on the basis of one or another part of the question is the thing at issue.[59] An example will make this clearer. Suppose there is question whether Verres committed a theft.[60] Here *Verres* is the subject; *to commit a theft* is the predicate. If *theft* is conjoined to *Verres*, and this is proved by argumentations, the affirmation related to the question is demonstrated. On the other hand, if *theft* is disjoined from *Verres*, the negation related to the question is proved. Thus the thing at issue is nothing but one or another of the terms, either the subject or the predicate, put forward in a question.

By themselves these terms can neither be nor furnish arguments; for if they as they are could be arguments or furnish the material for arguments, [284/1055] they would leave no doubt in the question. But since there is still doubt in the question with respect to these terms concerning whether or not their conjoining can be confirmed, the terms by themselves can neither be nor furnish arguments. But those things that are in the terms or external to them supply an abundance of arguments.

What Victorinus asks and develops at length seems to me not even worthy of mention. He asks whether the question at issue itself has a Topic, which is very inappropriate. For (as was said) the Topic that is at issue here is not a Topic of just anything but is rather the Topic of an argument, and an argument is a reason producing belief for something that was in doubt, and a thing in doubt is part of a question. Now if an argument cannot be a question or part of question, and if the Topic at issue here is the Topic of an argument, there certainly cannot be a Topic for a question. Furthermore, every question admits of doubt, but an argument clears up all the uncertainty of a question. So an argument is not the same as a question, but Topics are Topics for arguments, and thus they are not Topics for a question.

With this settled, we should understand the thing at issue as one of the terms in the question, either the predicate or the subject.[61] Since these in themselves are things, they cannot themselves be an argument, but they can have within them that in which arguments are gathered and which is understood to be the seat of arguments.[62] Although these apparently inhere in the terms at issue, they are nevertheless not yet arguments but are rather places or Topics embracing arguments and establishing them as it were on a natural foundation. The same must be said of the Topics taken from without. These Topics are exterior to and somewhat distant from the terms of the proposition; they are things of a sort, but they enclose an abundance of arguments.

To summarize briefly, the thing at issue is just one of the terms in the question. But these terms cannot be arguments, nor can any argument be drawn from them. Hence the terms located in the question are neither arguments nor Topics, but only things. Furthermore, anything inhering in what is at issue is obviously itself a thing but contains in itself an abundance of arguments, so that when it is appropriate to take an argument from it, it acts as a Topic. Thus if someone contemplates it in its own right, it is a thing, but if someone seeks to base an argument on it, it becomes a Topic.[63] These points apply in general to principal and maximal Topics, which either inhere in the things at issue or are taken from without.

In order to make a complete division of Topics, Cicero severs the maximal Topics he presented simply before into certain "species": "Some Topics that inhere in the thing at issue are from the whole, some from its parts, some from a sign, and some from things somehow related to that which we are asking about." There is, then, a fourfold-division of Topics that are in the thing at issue, for Topics inhering in the thing at issue are understood to arise from the whole term that is at issue, from the enumeration of its parts, from a sign, or from related things. [285/1056] That this is the case will be supported with a brief explanation. Terms in a question must have appropriate definitions, parts, and names and must be conjoined with and traced back to other things by means of some relationship. The Topic that is called *from the whole* occurs whenever an argument is drawn from the definition of a term (either the subject or the predicate) in the question. The Topic *from the enumeration of parts* occurs whenever an argument is derived from the parts of a term in a question. The Topic *from a sign* occurs whenever an argument arises from the name of such a term. And the Topic *from related things* occurs whenever an argumentation originates from things connected by a certain relationship to a term put forward. I will develop instances of all these later when I deal with the examples Cicero presented to illuminate these matters.

Now we must consider this point: Cicero says that some of the Topics in which arguments are enclosed inhere in the thing at issue, and others are taken from without. This is apparently said in such a way as to make it seem that Topics that inhere in the things at issue are different from the thing at issue. For nothing could inhere in itself, and therefore what inheres in something is different from that in which it inheres. So if there are some Topics that inhere in the things at issue, they are undoubtedly different from the things at issue. Furthermore, although he says, "some Topics that inhere in the thing at issue are from the whole and some from its parts," he is nevertheless not speaking of different things when he says that some Topics that are in the thing at issue are from parts and some from a whole, as if the thing itself were different from the whole, or different from all its parts taken together, for every individual thing is identical with a whole. Rome is identical with the whole city, and every individual thing is identical with its separate parts connected into one thing. For example, a man is identical with his head, chest, abdomen, feet, and other parts conjoined and united into one thing. Therefore, how is it that at first he speaks as if he were talking about different things, since he said that Topics inhere in the terms at issue, but afterward he speaks as if he were talking about the same things, since he declares that some Topics that inhere in the thing at issue are from the whole and some from parts? For saying 'some Topics that inhere in the thing at issue are from the whole, and some from the parts' is the same thing as saying 'a Topic inheres in the thing at issue and is from that thing'; but this is absurd, for how could a thing inhere in that very thing since nothing inheres in itself, as I explained above?

But since every individual thing has both a definition and parts (as I described shortly before), this whole tangle of uncertainty will be resolved if we examine carefully the nature of definition and of parts. A definition is the unfolding of a thing that is compressed and involuted, as, for example, when we say that a man is a mortal rational animal; for what the name 'man' designated briefly and concisely, the definition unfolded, expressed, and disclosed by means of substantial parts of a sort.[64] Therefore, necessarily, the understanding of an involuted thing considered as [286/1057] constrained into one and compressed is one thing; the understanding of that same thing unfolded and set forth, considered as explicated and extended, is another. For although a definition signifies the same as a name, the definition nonetheless sets forth and discloses more plainly what the name designates concisely and in an undifferentiated way. And so it is right that the thing itself is not the same as its definition, even though one and the same thing is the basis for them both;[65] for (as was said) the thing itself is an individual, but the definition is a division and enumeration by means of parts of that individual thing. (The parts I am calling substantial here, however, are not those that are joined together to make up the bulk of a thing but rather those that make up the nature and formula of a substance.)[66]

What is said in a definition with regard to parts that join together to make up a substance must be understood also with regard to parts that unite to make up the bulk of a thing, as for example, a house is constituted by the conjoining of a foundation, walls, and a roof. For although a house is just the union of its parts, it is nonetheless one thing and conjoined. A partition of it by means of its "members" is a division. And so although the thing itself and its parts taken together are one thing, nevertheless understanding of the thing considered as a whole is not necessarily the same as understanding of it divided into the parts that make it up.

The Topic *from a sign* is most plainly different from a term in a question. For who would say that the word for some thing is the same as the thing that the word designates?

Those things related to what is at issue may appear to be external, but they nonetheless hark directly back to a term in the question. They must be divided into many parts; for every thing, whatever it is, is one thing, but it has many things associated with it. We understand these associated things to differ from things that are altogether external to what is at issue, because associated things are relative (as both the subsequent presentation of related things and the nature of the examples will show), but external things are not in any relationship to what is at issue. So the latter are called external only, but the former are called related things; for what is related to something is tied in some way to the thing it is connected with.

Almost all the Topics that Cicero now presents as simple and undivided he divides in his later discussion of them, just as he here divides the Topics that are in the thing itself when he declares that some arise from the whole, some from the parts, some from a sign, some from related things—and the related things themselves he cleaves into their own parts. He asserts that an external Topic consists in testimony; the force of testimony he locates in authority, and authority he draws out into its appropriate parts—but these things belong to the later discussion. Now, however, he presents these Topics as simple and undivided, and he appends examples for them considered as simple.

What we have left here is a question that we should apparently consider, namely, whether the Topics that are divided into other Topics can be Topics for the Topics they contain within themselves, for example, whether what is in the thing at issue is a kind of Topic for the Topics *from the whole, from the parts, from a sign*, and *from related things*. Now in fact there is nothing that would directly prevent us from thinking that there are Topics of Topics, for it can happen that a broader Topic contains narrower Topics within its scope, as provinces [287/1058] contain cities. But this example is not appropriate here. For a Topic is that from which an argument is drawn, that is, that in which an argument is located. So if there could be a Topic of a Topic and if what is in the thing at issue (taken as a Topic of a sort) could include the Topics *from the whole, from the parts, from a sign*, or *from related things*, these would not be Topics *from the whole, from the parts, from a sign*, and *from related things* but arguments since they would inhere in the Topic that (as we said previously) is in the very term at issue.[67] So there cannot be a Topic of a Topic. The division of Topics here occurs instead in the manner of the division of a genus into its species.

This point should not appear to contradict what was said above when we called both maximal propositions and their constitutive differentiae by the common name of Topics. Although maximal propositions insofar as they are maximal include other propositions and are called Topics, nevertheless because they are most known they can serve as an argument for things that are in doubt. Therefore the differentiae of these maximal propositions are rightly given the name 'Topics'. But things are different in the case of the species of Topics that certainly cannot be arguments. The Topic that inheres in the thing at issue is divided into Topics *from the whole, from the parts, from a sign*, and *from related things*, as if it were being divided into its "species." Every one of these Topics seems to bear the whole name of the first Topic. For as we say that a man is an animal and similarly we call a horse and a cow 'animals', so the Topic *from the whole* is said to be in the thing at issue, and similarly the Topics *from the parts, from a sign*, and *from related things* are in the things at issue. But though it is possible to draw arguments from these Topics, they themselves cannot be arguments.[68]

[2.9]

After the twofold division of Topics, namely, into those that are in the thing at issue and those that are external, Cicero separated the Topic in the thing at issue into four parts, that is, *from the whole, from the enumeration of parts, from a sign,* and *from related things.* Here before he divides the Topic that he declared to be from related things, he adds examples of the first three Topics, which for the time being in the first chapter he will not divide but will leave undivided; these are the Topics *from the whole, from the parts,* and *from a sign.*

He discusses the Topic *from the whole* in the following way. We draw the Topic of an argument from the whole, he says, when we encompass the whole that is in the question with a definition and use the definition to produce belief for the thing in doubt that is at issue. Now as was said above, every definition unwinds and unfolds what a name designates in an involuted way. Hence, it is not the term presented in the definition[69] but what is in the term that can furnish material for arguments. Moreover, there are appropriate definitions for every thing, for a definition is an expression signifying the substance of any individual thing. So since the appropriate substance does not leave each individual thing, neither does the definition. In the term at issue, then, there is a definition that must comprise the whole term, and it shows the substance of the whole term, not just part of the substance. Since belief for something in doubt arises from such a definition, an argument is drawn from a definition, which is in the term at issue and is the whole of that term. And so an argument drawn from definition is drawn from a Topic that is in the term located in the question, and (since there are many Topics in the thing at issue) this Topic is from the whole. For a definition comprises the whole term and unwinds and unveils what the name [288/1059] signified in an involuted way.

The pattern of an argument from the whole is this. Civil law is equity established among those who are of the same state for the sake of preserving what is theirs, but knowledge of this equity is useful; therefore civil law is a useful body of knowledge. Here *civil law* is the subject, and *useful body of knowledge* is the predicate.[70] So what is asked is whether the predicate can truly adhere to the subject. Therefore, I will not be able to call *civil law* itself to the argument, for it is a constituent of the question. So, I look to see what might be incorporated in *civil law.* I see that no definition is disjoined from what it defines, so that the appropriate definition cannot be disjoined from *civil law* either. So I define *civil law,* and I say, 'Civil law is equity established among those who are of the same state for the sake of preserving what is theirs'.

After this, I consider whether this definition can be conjoined to the remaining term, *useful body of knowledge*, that is, whether equity established among those who are of the same state for the sake of preserving what is theirs is a useful body of knowledge. I see that the equity mentioned above is a useful body of knowledge. And so I conclude, 'Therefore civil law is a useful body of knowledge.'[71]

This argument, then, is from the Topic that is in the thing at issue, that is, in civil law, which is a term in the question. The Topic is called *'from definition'*, and since a definition is a whole, the argument is from the whole. And every Topic from the whole is in the thing at issue. (We should not be troubled by any doubt because *civil law* and *useful body of knowledge* are a sort of phrase that we are classifying as terms; for not every term is expressed as a simple part of a phrase, but sometimes terms are constructed as entire phrases.) In this argumentation the proposition that is maximal and known per se is that by which we understand that all things conjoined to the definition of something are necessarily also united with the things defined. For since the definition of *civil law* can be joined to *useful body of knowledge*, it follows that *useful body of knowledge* can also be united with *civil law*. So this argument is drawn from a Topic that is in the thing at issue, for every definition is in the term that it defines. Among the Topics that are in the thing at issue, this is from the whole, for every definition shows and unveils a whole. The maximal proposition: things defined are necessarily suited to anything to which the definition of those things is joined.[72]

[2.10]

Suppose there is a question whether someone who indisputably was a slave is free. There are three parts to liberation. One is that someone is free as a result of being enrolled in the census, for in former times only Roman citizens were subject to the census.[73] So if in accordance with the consent or request of his master, anyone gave his name in to the census, he became a Roman citizen and was released from the bond of servitude; being liberated by being enrolled in the census was giving one's name in to the census with the consent of one's master and being made a Roman citizen. There was also another part to obtaining liberty, which was called 'with the manumission staff'. The manumission staff is a small stick of a sort with which the lictor touched the head of the slave who was to be freed, [289/1060] and speaking some ceremonial words in this way he liberated the slave. And therefore the small stick was called the manumission staff.[74] This is also a part of liberation: if someone in the course of his last will and testament bequeaths freedom to his slave.[75]

Since these are the parts of liberation, if someone wants to show that a person who has indisputably been a slave was not liberated, he will say, 'If he was not liberated by the census or the manumission staff or a will, he is not free; but he was not liberated by any of these parts; therefore he is not free.'[76] For if you detach all the parts of a whole from any thing, you have necessarily also separated the whole from that thing; since a whole consists of its parts, if something is not made up of any of the parts of a whole, it is separated from the whole as well.

We speak of parts in two ways, however, as species and as members. A species is what takes the entire name of the whole, as, for example, a man and a horse. Each of them respectively is called by the entire name of 'animal', for man is an animal, and a horse also is an animal. Again, members are what produce a whole and conjointly (but not individually) take the name of the whole. For example, because a foundation, wall, and roofs are the members of a house, all of them taken together are called a house; but neither foundations, walls, nor roofs taken alone are called a house.

So since species take the entire name of the whole, you cannot show that the whole is absent unless you detach all the parts one by one from that which is in doubt, for we said that each individual part takes the entire name of the whole. For example, since there are three species of liberation—by the census, the manumission staff, and a will—if you take away any two of the three but one still remained, you have necessarily confessed that the slave is free, for whether he is liberated only by the census or by the manumission staff or by a will, he is indisputably free. So in these cases, unless you take away all the species, you cannot argue destructively concerning what is presented in the question. But if you want to affirm and argue constructively concerning what is presented in the question, demonstrating any one species alone is enough. For example, if you want to show that the slave is free, you need only show that he was liberated by the manumission staff or by the census or by a will. But if you want to argue destructively, showing either that he was not liberated by the census or that he was not liberated by the manumission staff or that he was not liberated by a will is not enough; rather you must show that he has not achieved liberty by any of these methods. Thus as far as parts that are species are concerned, if you want to argue destructively, you must use all the parts; but if you want to argue constructively, one part is enough.

The opposite is the case for those parts that are members: if you want to argue destructively, disjoining one part will be enough; but if you want to argue constructively, you will have to prove that all the parts are present. For example, if you want to show that a house does not exist, saying that there are no foundations or no walls or no roofs is enough, for whatever lacks any of these cannot be called a house. But if you want to show that a house exists, you will not be able to argue constructively for your position unless you conjoin all the parts into one thing.

All these Topics[77] are derived from the enumeration of parts, because in the case of parts that are species, all the parts are enumerated in order to argue destructively; in the case of parts that are members, all the parts are enumerated in order to argue constructively.

In Cicero's example of an argument [290/1061] derived from the enumeration of parts, the question is whether someone who was indisputably a slave is free. *Someone who was indisputably a slave* is the subject term; *free* is the predicate. We will not be able to bring either of these terms to the argument, for things that are themselves in doubt cannot produce belief for something else that is in doubt. So I look to see what is incorporated in one or the other of the terms. Since all parts are in the thing whose parts they are and since the bestowal of liberty has appropriate parts, I take these parts and enumerate them; I consider whether any one of these parts seems to be incorporated in the subject, but none of them is. So I conclude that he is not free.

From this it is made more apparent that arguments can be taken not only from the subject term but also from the predicate term. For in the previous example in which Cicero demonstrated that civil law is a useful body of knowledge, he defined civil law, which was the subject; the argument that was based on the definition produced belief for what was in doubt. Here, however, he enumerates the parts of *being freed*, which is the predicate term.

So, as was said, the question is whether someone who indisputably was a slave is free. The term *someone who was indisputably a slave* is the subject; the predicate is *free*. The parts that are enumerated are in the thing at issue, that is, in the predicate;[78] when an argument is drawn from this enumeration, the argument arises in the thing at issue from an enumeration of parts. The maximal proposition: a thing to which none of the parts of something are united cannot have the whole conjoined to it either.

At this point we should perhaps wonder whether the Topics from the whole and from the parts are the same since if all the parts are conjoined, they produce the whole. But, we will answer, when an argument arises from an enumeration of parts, the whole is divided, not conjoined, for the argumentation advances by division. If anyone takes a part of something, from the very fact that he does so he seems to have partitioned that thing. Furthermore, someone who divides a thing does not assemble a whole but rather disperses it.

Nonetheless, we might still remain uncertain, for a definition also unfolds the involuted signification of a name by means of a kind of enumeration of substantial parts, and an enumeration of parts is a kind of dispersal of those parts. But it is one thing to enumerate the parts of a thing and another to enumerate the parts of a definition. The parts of a thing are always less than that thing of which they are part, as the head or chest or other members are less than the whole man; but if the parts of a definition are substantial, they are apparently greater than the whole they define. For example, *animal* is greater than *man*, and similarly *mortal* and *rational*, as greater, comprise *man*; these are the individual parts of the definition that is *mortal rational animal*. So a partition takes parts that are always less than the thing partitioned, but the parts that a definition takes are universal in their own right, whole, and constitutive of the thing defined, even though they are parts presented in a definition, as can be easily understood from the examples presented above. Hence it is apparent that the Topic *from a whole*, which concerns definition, and the Topic *from the enumeration of parts* are different.

[2.10]

The Topic *from designation* is established as the third of those Topics that are in the thing at issue. Designation is a sort of explanation of a name, and a name [291/1062] is always in the thing at issue. As a definition disentangles and spreads out what a name proclaims in an involuted way, so the name designates in an involuted and undifferentiated way what the definition expresses discursively. And so if a definition is in the thing at issue, a name undoubtedly is also. The Topic is called '*from designation*' because a name designates and signifies all of a thing.

A guarantor is someone who takes upon himself the guaranteeing of someone else's court case, just as do those whom we now call representatives.[79] The law associated with Aelius Sentius prescribes that a taxpayer be the guarantor for another taxpayer.[80] The question is whether, since the law associated with Aelius Sentius intends a taxpayer to be the guarantor for another taxpayer, it also intends a wealthy man to be guarantor for another wealthy man. Here the subject term is *the law associated with Aelius Sentius intending a taxpayer to be the guarantor for another taxpayer;* the predicate is *a wealthy man being the guarantor for another wealthy man.* I will not be able to base belief for the question on these terms themselves, for no belief can be produced from things that are themselves uncertain. So I ask what is incorporated in one or another of the terms, and I see that one of the terms (namely, the subject) is *the law associated with Aelius Sentius, which decrees that a taxpayer be the guarantor for another taxpayer.* I give an explanation for part of this phrase, namely, for *a taxpayer.* For what is a taxpayer except someone who pays money? But no one except a wealthy man can pay money,[81] so a taxpayer is a wealthy man. Therefore since the law associated with Aelius Sentius establishes that a taxpayer be the defender for another taxpayer, it prescribes that a wealthy man be the defender for another wealthy man; indeed a taxpayer is just a wealthy man who gets that designation because he pays money.

So this argument is drawn from a Topic that is in the thing at issue, namely, *from the explanation of a name;* for a name is in the thing whose name it is (and an explanation of the name is called a designation), but an argument is made from the explanation of this name.[82] This argument, then, is drawn from the Topic that is in the thing at issue, that is, from a name. With regard to those Topics in the thing at issue, it is drawn from designation, that is, from an explanation of the name. The maximal proposition is 'An explanation of a name has the same force as the name.'

But the argumentation given in a somewhat confused way by Cicero contains a sizable error, for it should have been expressed in this way. A taxpayer is someone who pays money, but someone who pays money is a wealthy man; therefore a taxpayer is a wealthy man. Now the law associated with Aelius Sentius prescribes that a taxpayer be the guarantor for another taxpayer; therefore, it dictates that a wealthy man be the guarantor for another wealthy man.[83] If the argumentation had been expressed in this way, it would have been clearer. In fact Cicero expressed it in this way: since the law associated with Aelius Sentius prescribes that a taxpayer be the guarantor for another taxpayer, it prescribes that a wealthy man be the guarantor for another wealthy man; he appended the rest to show that a wealthy man is a taxpayer. But Cicero's claim—that since the law associated with Aelius Sentius prescribed that a taxpayer be the guarantor for another taxpayer, it enjoined that a wealthy man be the guarantor for another wealthy man—is valid only if he also says that whoever is a taxpayer is a wealthy man. For unless everyone who is a taxpayer is also a wealthy man, it does not follow that since the law associated with Aelius Sentius prescribed that a taxpayer be the guarantor for another taxpayer, it prescribed that a wealthy man be the guarantor for another wealthy man. Cicero presented the conclusion of the argument first and appended the proof;[84] for the conclusion is that since the law associated with Aelius Sentius intends that a taxpayer be the guarantor for another taxpayer, it prescribes that a wealthy man be the guarantor for another wealthy man, and he put this first. The proof is that a taxpayer is just a wealthy man who gets that designation because he pays money, and this he [292/1064] added after the conclusion.

Of the Topics that are in the thing at issue, the Topic drawn from related things remains. Since the division of that Topic is various and complicated, let us defer its exposition and end the first book here.

BOOK II

[292/1063] In the course of so very difficult a task, my Patricius, I am aware that this work of ours, which we have undertaken at your urging, is easily attacked with various biting censures when it is made light of or put down in the opinion of the ignorant multitude.[1] Those who dislike this whole kind of discourse disdain it as a superfluous study in servile sophistry for perverse minds, and those who think very highly of the results of this body of knowledge measure others by their own sluggishness and judge us not equal to so great a task. The first sort of men are altogether intolerable, I think, since they do not have a low opinion because of envy at another man's work and none-theless still agree with the censorious judgment. I would very willingly turn the envy of such perverted opinion toward myself, and I would readily suffer such men to despair of my intellectual abilities rather than have them spurn the theory of so great a discipline. But, alas, God help us all, such is human perversity and such is the blindness of such great ignorance that these men practically condemn themselves by their own confession. For there is no one who does not want to appear very skilled at discourse. In fact, they even attempt themselves to bring and to refute charges; if this could be done easily, they would all rush together to the knowledge of the discipline of logic as if it were a public treasure of wisdom. But now can anything more absurd be imagined than their trying to argue that the study of dialectic is useless for arguments that are even in their own view readily believable? For what sense does it make to subvert the art of discourse by engaging in discourse, so that you despise the truth of the very art in which you seek a reputation? But as that musician directed his disciple to make music for himself and for the Muses,[2] so I too could also have sung for myself and for you, who are not a Muse but a protector of the Muses. And what I have gathered together with much work and study I will bring forth not only with rhetorical skill but also with dialectical subtlety.

The following passages are of this sort.

[3.11]

After Cicero divided the Topics from which arguments are drawn into two groups, saying that some inhere in the thing at issue and others [293/1064] are taken from without, and after he cleaved the Topic that inheres in the thing at issue into four species (namely, *from the whole, from the parts, from a sign,* and *from related things*), he appended examples for the first three species, which we set forth as carefully as possible in the first book. There remains the Topic that he presented as the fourth species, namely, *from related things.* Since this Topic has many species, he could not present an example for the whole undivided Topic, for things in need of division are clarified better with examples arranged according to their individual parts. Cicero divided this Topic in the following way. The Topic *from related things* derives from these: *from conjugates, from the genus, from a kind, from similarity, from a differentia, from a contrary, from conjoined things, from antecedents and consequents and incompatibles, from causes, from the effects of causes,* and *from comparison of greater, equal, or lesser things.* All these Cicero elucidates a little later with appropriate examples.

Here we should say something about the nature of related things and their characteristics. For related things are those that can somehow be traced back to something (namely, to the thing to which they are traced back). Moreover, all things that hark back to one another in a relationship are joined together either as congenial or as discordant. If as congenial, then either as congenial in substance (as, for example, genus, kind, antecedents, consequents, cause, effect)[3] or in quality (as, for example, a conjugate, a similar, a conjoined thing)[4] or in quantity (as, for example, equals). Those things which are joined together as discordant sometimes just differ from one another and sometimes are opposed to one another. Those which are opposed to one another are opposed partly in quality (as, for example, contraries and incompatibles)[5] and partly in quantity (as, for example, comparison of greater or lesser things). Hence, it is clear that those which are congenial are joined to one another by a relationship of an affinity and those which are discordant are compared to one another insofar as they are opposed to one another; for in the case of those which are congenial, each is congenial to the other, and in the case of those that are discordant, each is discordant to the other. In this way a genus is the genus of a kind, and a kind is the kind of a genus. Antecedents are the antecedents of consequents, and consequents are the consequents of antecedents. Causes are the causes of effects, and effects are the effects of causes. Conjugates are conjugated to conjugates. A similar is similar to a similar. A conjoined thing is conjoined to a conjoined thing. Equals are equal to equals. A differentia is a differentia for differing things. Greater things are greater than lesser things; lesser things are less than greater things. Contraries are contrary to contraries. And incompatibles are incompatible with incompatibles. Therefore, although related things are not identical with one another, they nevertheless are related to one another.

We will present definitions for all these things in the order in which Cicero described the Topics in the previous passage.

In Cicero's discussion the first of the Topics said to be related to one another is conjugates. I call conjugates all those things which are inflected in differing expressions derived from one name, as, for example, 'a just [man]', 'a just [thing]', and 'justly', derived from 'justice'. These are said to be conjugated among themselves and with 'justice', from which their names flow.

A genus is that which is predicated of many things differing in species in respect of what they are,[6] as *animal* is said of *man* and of *horse*, which differ in species, and is predicated in respect of what they are; for when we ask what a man or [294/1065] a horse is, the answer is 'an animal'. Although a genus must be different from that of which it is the genus, it is nevertheless connected to that of which it is the genus, because it is conjoined to it by a relation involving substance.

Species is that of which a higher genus is predicated; Cicero called it a kind, as man is a kind of animal.

Similarity is unity of quality, for two things that are similar to one another must have the same quality. Since nothing can be similar to itself, what is similar must be considered similar to something else, but there could not be something else unless it were different in some respect. And so things that are similar differ from one another in some respects but accord with one another in other respects. They are understood to be similar with respect to the quality in which they accord, and they are related to one another by the uniting of that very similarity.

A differentia is that by which every individual thing differs from another, as *man* diverges from *horse* by the differentia of *rationality*. So a differentia is related to those things whose differentia it is by the predication of its own nature, as *rationality* is related to *man*; but it is related by reason of a dissimilarity to those things from which the differentiated thing diverges, as *rationality* is related to *cow*.

Contraries are those things which are located in the same genus[7] and yet diverge very widely from one another. For example, *white* and *black* are located in the single genus of *quality*, and yet they are very widely distant from one another; there is no one who does not know that contraries also are related to one another. For it is one thing that these are and another thing that they are contraries. In that something is black, it has a quality; but in that it is a contrary, it diverges very greatly from a white thing.

Conjoined things are those which have a nature bordering on an individual thing, as, for example, pallor is associated with fear. The nature of these things is that though they often enough cohere with the things associated with them, nonetheless they are not compelled by necessity to be present to the things they border on. For pallor accompanies fear often but not always, as when apprehension is suppressed by dissimulation. And so verisimilar arguments arise from associated things, for conjoined things generally serve as evidence for the things to which they adhere.[8] But I will examine these things more carefully in the discussion that follows.

Antecedents are such that when they have been asserted, something else necessarily follows (as, for example, 'Since there is war, there are hostilities'). These things have necessity of succession, for consequents cannot be separated from their antecedents. A consequent is whatever follows an antecedent (as, for example, hostilities follow a war, for if there is a war, there must be hostilities). This Topic has the following remarkable and noteworthy feature, namely, that often things that are prior in nature are nonetheless consequents, though they often are both antecedent in nature and prior in the proposition. For generally hostilities exist before wars; but we cannot assert hostilities first in order to have a war as a consequent, for we cannot say truly, 'If there are hostilities, there is a war.' But we assert a war first, and hostilities, which are prior in nature, follow in this way: 'If there is a war, there are hostilities.' So here hostilities, which naturally precede a war, follow war in the proposition. But if I say, 'If he is arrogant, he is hateful,' arrogance precedes hatefulness both in nature and in the proposition; for arrogance is wont to exist first, and hatefulness is wont to follow after and as a result of that same arrogance. It makes no difference whether a given thing naturally precedes or follows something as long as we note in the proposition that the thing [295/1066] that is the antecedent (whether it is naturally prior or posterior) necessarily draws some other thing with it.

Incompatibles are understood to occur whenever something that is naturally joined to one of a pair of contraries is coupled to the other contrary. For example, since friendship and enmity are contraries and a will to injure follows from enmity, friendship and a will to injure are incompatibles. These things are also related to one another in the manner of contrariety.

A cause is a thing that precedes and produces something else, as, for example, the cause of day is the rising of the sun. An effect is what the preceding cause brings about, as, for example, day, which the rising of the sun brings forth.

A comparison of greater things occurs whenever that which is greater is compared to that which is lesser. For example, 'If no one who is innocent should be sent into exile, then it is even more the case that Cicero should not be sent into exile, since he was not only innocent but also a liberator of his country,' for being a liberator of his country is more than being innocent.[9] A comparison of equals occurs whenever equals are compared to one another; for example, 'If this innocent citizen should not be sent into exile because he is innocent, neither can this citizen, who is innocent, be justly cut off from his country.' A comparison of lesser things occurs whenever lesser things are compared to greater things; for example, 'If no one thought Cicero, the liberator of his country, worthy of a reward, no one should think worthy of a reward a man who was only innocent but did no special services for the republic.'

No one is ignorant of the fact that all these are connected to one another in this way and are mutually related to one another and hark directly back to one another. For (as we said in the beginning about conjugates) justice has to do with that which is just or that which can occur justly, and it also perfects the man who is just. The others too have not only a linguistic connection to one another but also a certain harmony of nature, although they are not identical with one another. Justice is not the same as a just man, for everything that is inflected from something differs from and yet is connected to the thing from which it is inflected. Genus is also undoubtedly connected to that of which it is a a genus, that is, to a species. (Cicero calls this 'a kind'.) For a genus is the genus of a species, and a species is the species of a genus; in this way they are mutually related to one another, although genus and species are not the same. (We should note well that what we call 'species' Cicero calls 'kinds'. And as long as I understand what he says, I gladly allow him to use whatever name he wishes. But I cannot be allowed the same leeway; for a person who promises an illuminating explanation must occupy himself with the very words that are customarily used, and it has become customary to call what is subordinated to a genus a species rather than a kind.) Again, a similar cannot be similar to anything except a similar, and what is different cannot differ from anything except a dissimilar. Contraries, too, are understood to be contrary to contraries, and conjoined things adhere to conjoined things. Antecedents are antecedent to something that can follow, and a consequent follows that which is an antecedent. Every incompatible, too, is understood to be mutually discordant with another incompatible. Also, a cause is the cause of its effect, for any cause is the cause of the thing it effects, and an effect is the effect of some cause. A comparison of greater things harks back to a lesser thing; a comparison of lesser things harks back to greater things; and a comparison of equal things harks back to other equal things.[10]

In all these things, one grasps a nature of this sort: although, when they are taken in their own right, certain things differ from the things to which they are connected, they are nevertheless [296/1067] seen to be related when they are brought into a comparison. The fact that nothing can be related to itself proves that they are different from the things to which they are related. Hence, they are rightly called 'related things'.

All these are species or kinds of the Topic called *from related things*, as Cicero himself also testifies, saying "But this genus is divided into many parts"; for since he called it a genus, he indicated that those things that he split off from the genus are species. Furthermore, all these things take both the name and the definition of the genus. For those things that can be connected to the thing to which they are related are related things with respect to it; but conjugates, genus, kind, and the rest are always connected to those things to which they are related.[11] The point made in the case of the preceding Topics that inhere in the thing at issue (that is, the Topics *from the whole, from the parts,* and *from a sign*)—namely, that these Topics should be understood to be from the whole term presented in the question, from its parts, or from its sign—applies in a similar way also in the case of related things. We will say that they are considered related to the term that is put as the subject or the predicate and that comprises the question.

It remains now to explain why related things are said to be in the thing at issue. For Cicero indicated that there are four Topics in the term at issue, namely, *from the whole, from the parts, from a sign,* and *from related things.* Of these, the first three clearly inhere in the term at issue. Because it is whole, the definition of any thing is in the thing it defines. Parts, too, are in the thing that they conjoin by being gathered together. A sign, too, is in the thing that it indicates with a name. But related things (that is, those that are connected to the things to which they are related) appear to be extrinsic, for unless they were understood as extrinsic, they would not be connected. Therefore we should explain why Cicero also numbered things that are related to what is at issue among the Topics that inhere in the term asked about, since what is said to inhere is not the same as the thing of which it is predicated as inhering.

Although related things are not identical with one another, they are nevertheless understood to be conjoined by a certain affinity. For example, a definition is not the same as the thing that is described by the definition; for if a definition makes what it defines clearer and if nothing can make itself clearer than it is, what is defined plainly differs from a definition. But we say that a definition inheres in what it defines because it is connected and conjoined to it; for as long as the definition signifies the nature of what is defined, it does not leave its substance. Parts and signs, too, are not identical with what they unite or designate. But because they conjoin or signify the term presented, having some affinity with the term presented, they are said to inhere in the thing at issue. Similarly also in the case of related things, although they are external: they are not the same as those things to which they are understood to be related; nevertheless, because they are considered to have some affinity with these things, they are necessarily said to inhere in the things to which they are related.

Although it can be explained more opportunely in the differentiae of Topics, I will append a description of the natural ordering of the Topics, their differentiae, and a different division among them when I set forth the examples Cicero adduced to explain these things.

[3.12]

[297/1068] The definition of conjugates offered by Cicero is this: "Conjugates are said to be those which are based on words of the same genus," that is, those which are inflected from one word in various ways. Words from the same genus are 'justice', 'just [man]', 'justly', 'the just', and any others that can be inflected into different species of words. Any words that originate from some one word and then are variously altered are called 'syzgia'[12] by the Greeks and 'conjugates' by the Romans, for what the Greeks call 'syzygia' we call 'conjugation'. Such are, for example, 'wise', 'wisely', 'wisdom', and any others that are drawn from one word and separated into various parts of speech and various inflections.

This is an example of an argument arising from conjugates. Suppose there is some doubt whether I and a neighbor may both pasture cattle at the same time in some field, that is, whether common pasturing is legal.[13] The subject is *field*; the predicate is *common pasturing*.[14] We will make an argument in this way. The field at issue is common pasturage, but one may pasture commonly in common pasturage; so one may pasture commonly in this field. Here the argument about the law of common pasturing is taken from common pasturage,[15] that is, from a conjugate, for *common pasturing* and *common pasturage* are conjugates. We adopt the argument that common pasturing is legal since the field is common pasturage. But *common pasturage* is conjugate to *common pasturing*, and so the argument is taken from conjugates. The conjugate is in the thing at issue, that is, in *common pasturing*,[16] for they all flow from the same thing and are constitutive of one another and hark back to one another. So the argument is made from what is in the thing at issue, from related things, that is, from conjugates. The maximal proposition: 'Conjugates, insofar as they are conjugates, have one and the same nature'—or also in this way: 'The conjugate of a thing can be associated with whatever that thing itself belongs to.'[17]

[3.13]

A genus is that which is predicated of some species in respect of what it is.[18] That which is given as a suitable answer to questions about a species and which shows the substance of the species being asked about is said to be predicated in respect of what it is. Moreover, a genus is always greater than its species and includes the species within the range of its predication.[19] So although a genus can also be partitioned into other things, it nonetheless does not in any way leave its species. For example, *animal* is predicated of *man* and shows the substance of *man*; for if we ask what *man* is, the answer is '*animal*'. The same genus can nonetheless be woven into other things, for example, into *horse* and *cow*, which are called 'animals'. But the genus is woven into different things in such a way that it does not leave any one of the species that it contains; for wherever there is a man, there an animal must be, for a man is an animal, and the same holds for cows and other animals. And so we have shown clearly that the name of the genus is in no way separated from the species. Hence, whenever the word for a genus is expressed universally, all the species of that genus must be designated. For example, if someone says 'every animal', he will designate man and cow and all the other species classified under [298/1069] the name 'animal'.

So a certain man had bequeathed all his silver to his wife in his will, and a question arises as to whether the coin was bequeathed to her also. In this question, then, *coin* is the subject, and *bequeathed* is the predicate. I consider, then, what is in one or the other of these terms, so that I may seek an argument from what is in the thing at issue. I see that the subject term *coin* has as its genus *silver*;[20] this genus is evidently related to its species, to which it is connected, for things that are mutually connected to one another are related. Therefore, since all the silver was bequeathed and since a genus does not leave its species, the coin must have been bequeathed also. Since the whole name of the genus was bequeathed, none of its species seem excluded. For example, if someone says that every animal lives, he does not say, I think, that *man* alone or *cow* or *horse* or any of the other species of animal taken individually (whether one species or more) lives, so that he in fact maintains that there are some things that are animals and yet lack the gift of life. Rather he asserts straightforwardly that whatever is an animal lives. Therefore, since the whole genus, that is, all the silver, was bequeathed, no species of silver is excluded. But coin is silver; therefore, coin can also be included by the word 'bequeathed'.

So the question, as was said, is whether the coin was bequeathed. The argument is from something that is in the thing at issue, that is, from the genus, which is in its species, and it is in the species in such a way that it is connected to the species. In this case the genus is *silver*. The argument is from related things, that is, from a genus; for *silver* is predicated of *coin* as its genus, since to those asking us what coin is, we correctly reply, 'silver'. The maximal proposition is 'Any species of a genus belongs to whatever the whole genus belongs to.'[21] Cicero also presented this maximal proposition with different words but the same meaning: "A kind is never disjoined from its genus as long as it keeps its proper name."[22]

[3.14]

A species is that which is informed by characteristic differentiae and classified under the predication of a genus. The characteristic differentiae separate and disjoin it from other species. For example, *man* is a species of *animal* and is informed by the characteristic differentiae of *rationality* and *mortality*; it is disjoined from those animals that are eternal, as the Platonists believe the sun to be,[23] and from those animals that are devoid of reason. Therefore, since all species are separated from one another by characteristic differentiae, what is said specifically of one species necessarily cannot be applied to another. For example, what is said of *man* specifically cannot be understood of *horse* and *cow*. Something is said of a species when its genus is "contracted" in a certain respect. For example, if someone says we ought to add *rational* and *mortal* to *animal*, we understand that this is said assuredly not of *horse* or *cow* or the rest but only of *man*. Therefore, just as a genus when it is said generally (as when someone says 'every animal') includes all its species, so any designated animal produces a species.

From a kind (that is, a species) belonging to a genus, an argument of the following sort arises. (Cicero often calls a kind belonging to a genus a part so that [299/1071] what is being said may be plainer, for 'part' is a more familiar word than 'kind'; but we have briefly discussed above the difference between a kind and parts, and it will be explained more fully by Cicero himself a little below. Now let us consider the example presented.) There are two species of wife; one is *materfamilias*,[24] and the other is *consort*, but they are called by the general name of the genus, 'wives'. Species are often called by the same names as their genera. A woman could not be a materfamilias unless she had come under her husband's authority. This was an established species of marriage, for there were three ways of taking a wife:[25] by common law,[26] by religious ceremony,[27] and by purchase.[28] The marriage by religious ceremony was in the jurisdiction of priests alone. A woman who came under the authority of her husband as a result of marriage by purchase was called a materfamilias; a woman who was married by common law or religious ceremony was not called a materfamilias.[29] Marriage by purchase was carried out by established ceremonies. The parties being married by purchase asked one another questions; the man asked whether the woman wanted to be a materfamilias, and she answered that she did. In the same way, the woman asked whether the man wanted to be a paterfamilias, and the man answered that he did. In this way, a woman came under the authority of her husband, and the marriage was called marriage by purchase. The woman was a materfamilias to her husband and had the status of a daughter of his. Ulpian describes this ceremony in his *Institutes*.[30]

Now a certain man in his last will bequeathed to his wife Fabia all his silver on the condition that Fabia would be not only his wife but in fact a definite species of wife, namely, a materfamilias. The question is whether the silver was bequeathed to the wife Fabia. *The wife Fabia* is the subject; *bequeathed silver* is the predicate.[31] So I ask myself what argument I can take from the things presented in the question, and I see that there are two kinds inhering in *wife*: one is only a wife and the other is a materfamilias, a status brought about by coming under the authority of the husband. If Fabia did not come under the authority of her husband, she was not a wife, that is, she was not that species of wife to whom all the silver was bequeathed. Consequently, since what is said of one species is not appropriately said of another,[32] and since Fabia is not included in that species of wife that has come under the authority of the husband (that is, the species that is a materfamilias) but her husband bequeathed the silver to a materfamilias, it appears that the silver was not bequeathed to Fabia.

So the question, as was said, is whether all the silver was bequeathed to the wife Fabia. The subject is *the wife Fabia;* the predicate is *bequeathed silver.* The argument is taken from something that is in the thing asked about, that is, from something that is in *wife,* which is being asked about; for a species of wife is in *wife,* which is being asked about, namely, the species that has not come under the authority of the husband. And this is related to *wife,* for every species (that is, every kind) is related to its genus. The argument is therefore made from something that is in the thing at issue, namely, from related things—from a kind belonging to a genus. The maximal proposition is 'What is said of a single species is not appropriate for another.'

[3.15]

Similars are things that have the same quality; from these an argument is taken in the following way. Someone in his will bequeathed the usufruct of a house, that is, he granted the use of the house to a certain man for the duration of that man's life. The [300/1072] house has begun to be in disrepair (that is, it is in danger of falling down) or has even in fact collapsed. So the man to whom the usufruct of the house was bequeathed demands that the heir make good the damage to the house bequeathed to him by the testator and that he restore the house that is in disrepair or collapsed.[33] The question is whether the heir is compelled to restore the disrepair or collapse of a house whose usufruct was bequeathed. Here a phrase, as if it were a term, is the subject: *the collapse or disrepair of a house whose usufruct was bequeathed;* a phrase, put in the place of a term, is the predicate: *restoration by the heir.*[34]

I take an argument from a similar in this way. If someone bequeathed the usufruct of a slave and that slave perished in some way, the heir is not compelled to restore the slave.[35] Therefore, neither in this case will the heir be compelled to restore the house whose usufruct was bequeathed and which is in a state of disrepair or collapse, for the bequeathal of the usufruct of a slave is similar to the bequeathal of the usufruct of a house. The cases are also similar: if a slave whose usufruct is bequeathed dies, he is not replaced by the heir; if a house whose usufruct was bequeathed is in disrepair or collapse, it is not repaired by the heir. The question is whether the heir is compelled to restore the disrepair or collapse of a house whose usufruct was bequeathed. The terms are these: the subject is *the disrepair or collapse of a house whose usufruct was bequeathed;* the predicate is *restoration by the heir.* The argument is from something that is in the thing at issue, that is, from something that is in the disrepair or the collapse of a house whose ususfruct was bequeathed. This is a related thing, that is, a similarity; for every similarity is considered to be in the thing that is similar, and the similarity is the usufruct of a bequeathed slave who perished and whom the heir is not compelled to restore. The maximal proposition: 'What is appropriate for one similar is appropriate for another.'[36]

[3.16]

With respect to things that are very different from one another, what is said of one does not seem appropriate for the other.

Now a certain man bequeathed all his silver to his wife. She claimed that the money that was owed him in debts was hers also, because all money was called 'silver'. What is asked is whether the silver that was owed as debts was also bequeathed. Here the subject term is *silver that is owed as debts;* the predicate is *bequeathed.* And so we will make an argumentation from differentia in this way. We cannot understand the same thing of things that are very different, but silver placed in a strongbox is very different from silver owed as debts. Money placed in a strongbox is in our power while money owed as debts is not ours; for what is given as a loan ceases to be mine and becomes the recipient's, and therefore the debtor is not compelled to restore to his creditor the very same money but only other money.[37]

Money placed in a strongbox and *money owed as debts,* however, are not species of silver or of money but rather differentiae, for the species of silver are said to be *coined* and *not coined.* But the quality *money possessed or not possessed but not altogether belonging to another* comprises these differentiae: some money is placed in a strongbox, and other money is owed as debts.[38] And I have spelled this out lest anyone think that the argumentation is drawn from a species rather than from differentiae, for a substantial quality [301/1073] is reckoned not among species but among differentiae.

So since the man bequeathed to his wife everything that was his silver and since it is clear that what was the testator's (that is, what was stored in a strongbox) now belongs to her, the bequest cannot be understood to include money owed as debts, since (as was said) money owed as debts is very different from money placed in a strongbox. The argumentation is made from something that was in the thing that was asked about, for silver owed as debts was asked about, and in this is the characteristic differentia by which it differs from other silver (namely, the silver that was placed in a strongbox). This is a related thing, that is, a differentia. The maximal proposition: 'We cannot understand the same thing of things that are very different.'[39]

[3.17]

What is said of one thing cannot be appropriate for its contrary, for the same thing cannot in any way be understood of two contraries. Now a certain man bequeathed the usufruct[40] of his goods to his wife in his last will. The woman claimed the usufruct of his full wine and oil cellars. What is asked is whether the ususfruct of the provisions was also bequeathed. So *usufruct of provisions* is the subject; *bequeathal* is the predicate. An argument is taken from a contrary in this way. We use those things which persist despite our use of them, but we consume those things which perish when we use them. Therefore, since to persist and to perish are contraries, use and consumption must also be judged contraries. Although other goods persist when they are used, wine and oil cellars are consumed when they are used. Of other things, then, there can be usufruct, but of provisions there can only be consumption and not use. Therefore, since the man bequeathed the usufruct of his goods to his wife, he could not have bequeathed the contrary, namely, the consumption of his goods. But wine and oil are consumed. So the woman cannot have a right to the usufruct of the wine and oil.

The argument is taken from what is in the thing at issue, namely, from the bequeathal of usufruct, and from a related thing, namely, a contrary. Contraries, however, are not in contraries as a definition is in what is defined but rather as a relation. For every relation is said to be in relative things, and all contraries are said to be in contraries, not because of what they are (namely, qualities) but rather because they are contraries, because contraries are compared to one another not with respect to their specific quality but with respect to the great distance between them. The maximal proposition: 'What is appropriate for a thing is not appropriate for its contrary.'

[4.18]

Associated things are those which occupy near and adjacent places, so that if one of the associated things exists in some way, the other apparently also has existed, exists, or will exist, for associated things "border" on one another. A thing that is near another in existence tends to occur before that thing (as love often occurs before intercourse), or it occurs simultaneously with that thing (as pallor occurs simultaneously with fear), or it occurs after that thing (as murder occurs after wrath). And it is the nature of associated things that, though they can be separated, they indicate one another. For it is not necessary that a man had the woman he loved, and often a man had a woman whom he did not love. It is also not necessary that someone who is pale be afraid, and often someone who is afraid is not pale. Nor is it necessary that someone who is enraged commits murder, and often a person who commits murder [302/1074] is not enraged. Nevertheless, if we ask about individual cases, it is likely that a man who loved a woman lay with her, and that a man who is afraid is pale, and that a man who was enraged committed murder, not that it is necessary for things to be this way, but we deduce neighboring things from one another.

As for an example of this sort of argument, this is an instance. Forfeiture of civil rights is an alteration of a previous status. This customarily occurs in several ways, to an extent that is great, moderate, or small.[41] The extent to which it occurs is great when both liberty and citizenship are lost, as in deportation. The extent is moderate when citizenship is lost but liberty is retained, as in migration to Latin colonies. And the extent is small when neither citizenship nor liberty is lost, but the status of a man's preceding condition is altered, as in adoption or in any other way in which a preceding status could be altered while citizenship was retained.

Under ancient law, women were always the wards of a guardian. Women who came under the authority of their husbands, however, left the power of their previous guardian; in this way, for such women who came under the authority of their husbands, there was an alteration of their preceding status and a loss of civil rights.[42] Now a certain woman who had never forfeited her civil rights in this way, that is, who had not come under the authority of her husband, made a will without the authorization of her guardian.[43] The question is whether possession of the inheritance in accordance with her will ought to be given by praetorian edict.[44] Here the subject term is this: *the will of a woman who has never forfeited her civil rights.* The predicate: *granting possession of the inheritance.*

The argument is taken from associated things in this way. If possession of the inheritance were given in accordance with the will of a woman who had never forfeited her civil rights, there is no reason why possession of an inheritance in accordance with the wills of children and of slaves should not also be allowed by praetorian edict.[45] For what can prevent conferring the possession of an inheritance in accordance with the will of a woman who has never forfeited her civil rights? Just the fact that the woman who made the will was not independent under law. And the same thing can be said of children and of slaves, for the age of children[46] and the status of slaves put them in the power of another.

And so these things are associated: if possession of an inheritance were given in accordance with the will of a woman who was not independent under law, possession of an inheritance would also be given in accordance with the wills of children and of slaves, who are not in any way independent under law since children are in the power of their guardian and slaves are in the power of their master. For what is consequent on the thing asked about and subsequent to it is also near to it, so that possession of goods would be granted in accordance with the wills of slaves and of children if we conceded what is at issue in the question. For the question is whether possession of an inheritance is given in accordance with the will of a woman who has never forfeited her civil rights; if this occurs, it follows that possession of an inheritance is conferred in accordance with the wills of slaves and of children. But because conferral in accordance with the wills of slaves and of children should not occur, the preceding parallel case ought not to occur either.

The sequence of the two cases nonetheless is not necessary but adjoined, for it is possible that we accept only giving possession of an inheritance in accordance with the will of a woman and not also granting possession of an inheritance in accordance with the wills of slaves or of children. But the latter case is near to the former case, so that someone who now accepts the former case may subsequently admit the latter case. And so the argument is from associated things, that is, from what inheres in the thing asked about. The question concerns the will of a woman who has never forfeited her [303/1075] civil rights. The argument is from related things, namely, from associated things. The maximal proposition: 'Associated things are judged on the same basis.'

[4.19]

Antecedents are such that when they have been asserted, something else necessarily follows, even though the antecedent is narrower[47] and subsequent. The antecedent is narrower, for example, in 'If a man is, an animal is,' for *man* is narrower than *animal*; nevertheless, once man is asserted, it follows that an animal is. It is subsequent, on the other hand, for example, in 'If she has borne a child, she has lain with a man,' for having borne a child is subsequent to having lain with a man. But sometimes something equal, something simultaneous, and something prior are asserted as antecedents. The antecedent is equal, for example, in 'If it is a man, it is risible'; it is simultaneous, for example, in 'If the earth is interposed, an eclipse of the moon occurs.' These convert with one another so that the consequents become the antecedents, as for example, 'If it is risible, it is a man,' and 'If an eclipse of the moon occurred, there would be an interposition of the earth.' The antecedent is prior, for example, in 'If he is arrogant, he is hateful,' for he is first arrogant and subsequently hateful. Nevertheless, what stays the same in all these cases is that once the antecedents have been asserted, the consequents are necessarily drawn.

The explanation of Cicero's example is this. Under Roman law children remain in their father's control (until they are set free by a third sale).[48] So when a divorce occurred and the woman was at fault, she was fined a certain part of her dowry in accordance with the number of the children.[49] Paul, in the chapter titled "On Dowries" in the second book of the *Institutes*,[50] gives the following discussion of this matter. If there is a divorce, and it is not the woman's fault that the divorce occurred, she will recover her entire dowry. But if it is the woman's fault that the divorce occurred, her husband keeps a sixth part of the dowry for each child, up to not more than half of the dowry. So since the portion of the dowry sought belongs to the children, who are in the power of their father, that portion must remain with him.[51]

Now in a certain divorce, contention arose over whether a part of the dowry should remain with the man for the children. Here the subject is *a divorce that has occurred and been initiated by the woman;* the predicate is *the man's retention of a sixth part of the dowry after the divorce.* The question is whether after a divorce initiated by the wife, the man ought to retain a sixth part of the dowry. If the argument is to be made from antecedents, I ask what the antecedent is and what the consequent is. If it is the man's fault that the divorce occurred, I see that the woman is not fined a part of her dowry, even if she initiated the divorce. For the antecedent, that it was the man's fault that the divorce occurred, does not allow the woman to lose a part of her dowry, even though she initiated the divorce. She is not to be fined a part of her dowry because she initiated the divorce, but rather she is absolved from loss because it was the man's fault and not hers that the divorce occurred. So the antecedent is *a divorce that has occurred as a result of the man's fault;* the consequent is *a part of the dowry is not retained;* for if the former is, the latter is also.

I will make an argumentation in this way. If it is the man's fault that the divorce occurred, even if the woman initiated the divorce, [304/1076] she is nevertheless not to be fined any part of her dowry. But it is the man's fault that the divorce occurred. Therefore, the woman will not be rightly fined part of her dowry. If she is not fined part of her dowry, the man will be owed none of the dowry for the children. But she is not fined part of her dowry. Therefore, the man will not be owed any of the dowry for the children. The conclusion of either syllogism is this: therefore if it is the man's fault that the divorce has occurred, nothing ought to be retained for the children. The argument is taken from what is in the thing at issue. The suit concerns part of the dowry and the man's retention of it after a divorce that the woman initiated. The fault of the man is antecedent to this, and because it goes before, it is a related thing; for everything that goes before must be related to what follows. The maximal proposition: 'Where the antecedent is, there the consequent will be also.'[52] But in this question the antecedent is (namely, a divorce that is the man's fault), therefore the consequent will also be (namely, that sixth parts of the dowry are not retained). The reason I have embroidered the argument above with conclusions in this way will become clearer when I discuss Cicero's fuller exposition of them.

[4.20]

Consequents are those things that follow when antecedents have been asserted; for example, if we say, 'If it is a man, it is an animal,' 'it is an animal' is the consequent. In the example presented, however, the argument does not seem to be really from consequents but rather from antecedents, as will be clear shortly.

Children who were not legitimately begotten were not in the power of their fathers but rather followed their mothers. The Romans did not count all unions wedlock, and unions that were entered into by partners who were not both Roman citizens or who were not persons to whom the ruler or the people had allowed citizenship or wedlock were not legally contracted wedlock—and particularly in this respect: that the children were not placed in the power of their progenitors.[53] And we should also notice that children begotten of such an inferior sort of marriage follow their mother, not their father.

Now a certain Roman woman united with a Latin man or a foreigner or a slave, with whom there was no legal wedlock, and brought a dowry with her. When they were divorced, contention arose over whether a part of the dowry of this woman (who was united with a man with whom there was no legal wedlock) should remain with the man after the divorce. Here the subject is *a woman who is united with a man with whom there was no wedlock;* the predicate is *the man's rightful continued retention of a part of the dowry after a divorce.*[54] An argument is taken from consequents in this way. Because she united with a man with whom there is no legal wedlock, it follows that the children do not follow their father. But if the children do not follow their father, they are not in their father's power either. And if they are not in their father's power and are joined to their mother, the man will not be able to keep part of the dowry. Here the antecedent is *union with a man with whom there was no legal wedlock;* the consequent is *none of the dowry ought to remain as owed the children.* The argumentation concludes: since the children who are begotten do not follow their father when wedlock was not allowed, a part of the dowry should not remain with the father for the children either, since the children [305/1077] follow their mother, not their father.

So we have proved that nothing ought to remain for the children from the fact that the woman united with a man with whom there was no legal wedlock, but this was the antecedent. Therefore we have detected that the argument is made not from a consequent but rather from an antecedent. If we had proved that she united with a man with whom there was no legal wedlock from the fact that none of the dowry should remain as owed the children, then the argument would correctly be said to be made from consequents. The argument would arise from consequents if it were put in this way: if any of the dowry should remain for the children on the grounds that the children follow their father, then the woman was united with a man with whom there was legal wedlock. I take the consequent as a premise: but the woman is not united to a man with whom there was legal wedlock. I conclude the antecedent: therefore, none of the dowry should remain for the children since the children do not follow their father. The argument is taken from what is in the thing asked about, for what is being asked about is those unions which were not legal wedlock. It is an argument from related things, for every consequent is related to what precedes it. The maximal proposition: 'Where the consequent is not, the antecedent cannot be either.'[55] There will be another place for discussing these things more fully.[56]

[4.21]

A substitute heir is someone who takes the place of the appointed heir.[57] For example, suppose someone appoints his son to be his heir and draws up his will in this way: if this son were to die young, a nephew (or someone else) should be the heir. Then the nephew (or whoever else it is) is called the substitute heir.

Incompatibles, as was said, are things that follow from contraries, if they are considered in relation to those contraries.

Now a certain man drew up a will making his son heir and appointing a substitute heir for him, and he bequeathed his wife the usufruct of maidservants as a proviso in the son's inheritance; although he said that his son was to allow his wife usufruct of the maidservants, he did not add that the substitute heir should also grant the woman the same usufruct. The son came into his inheritance and bestowed usufruct of the maidservants on the woman. The son having died young, the substitute heir goes to court and tries to deprive the woman of the usufruct of the maidservants, saying that the usufruct was bequeathed to the woman as a proviso of the son's inheritance but not as a proviso of his inheritance.[58]

What is asked is whether a woman can lose against her will a bequest that she received legally from a will. So here the subject is *bequest that she received legally and rightly from a will*; the predicate is *able to lose against her will*. So I take an argument from incompatibles. An incompatible is a thing that follows from one of a pair of contraries and is considered in relation to the other contrary. For instance, in the example we are discussing, receiving legally and not receiving legally are contraries. But losing against one's will accompanies not receiving legally, for he who does not receive legally justly loses against his will. So losing against one's will is incompatible with receiving legally.[59] So we will make an argument in this way. Someone who receives something in a will receives it legally. But what is received legally cannot at the same time be taken away against the will of the one who receives it legally.[60] The woman received the usufruct of maidservants in a will, however, and so this cannot be taken away from her against her will. The argument is from what is in the thing at issue, that is, [306/1078] what is received legally. And it is in the thing at issue as a thing related in the manner of contraries, as was said above. It is an argument from

an incompatible. The maximal proposition: 'Incompatibles cannot occur together.'[61]

[4.22]

There are many genera of causes, and Cicero shortly hereafter distinguishes among them. Here, however, he is discussing an argument
from efficient causes. An efficient cause is such that when it precedes
(not in time but in its particular nature) something is effected, as for
instance in the example we are clarifying here.

A guarantee against future harm is when someone guarantees that if
his work occasions any harm, he is obligated to make restitution.[62]

Now it is legal to conjoin another wall to a common wall whether it is
vaulted, that is, arched, or straight and solid. And a certain man joined
another wall to the outside of a common wall and gave security against
future harm. The common wall, however, was vaulted, that is, it had
arches or it consisted in Signinian work.[63] The man who had given
security adjoined his wall and in order to do so tore down part of the
wall where the juncture of the walls occurred; in this way the common
wall was damaged.[64] What is being asked is whether the guarantee
against future harm compels the man who gave the guarantee to make
restitution for the damage. The subject term is *guarantee against future
harm*; the predicate is *restitution for the damage*. We take an argument
from causes in this way. If the man who gave the guarantee against
future harm was the cause of the damage, he ought to make restitution
for the damage since it was his fault that it happened. But if the wall by
its own nature could not be supported and upheld (for a vaulted wall
by nature cannot be supported), then the damage will apparently have
been produced by the form of the wall rather than by the fault of the
man who tore down part of the wall. And thus the man who was
bound by the guarantee against future harm is not compelled to make
good the damage.

An argumentation will arise in this way. If the form of the wall
occasioned the damage when the man who gave the guarantee against
future harm adjoined a wall, then the man who gave the guarantee is
not compelled to make good that damage. Rather the cause of the
damage was the wall, which by nature could not be supported and
upheld. And so the man who gave the guarantee against future harm
is not obligated to make good the damage that the vault of the wall
produced. The argument is from what is in the thing at issue, that is, in
restitution for damage; it is from a related thing, that is, from a cause.[65]

For the cause of the damage is the form of the wall and not the fault of the man conjoining a wall.[66] It was made in such a way that the vault of the wall became damaged, and since the cause of the damage is absent from the man who joined the wall, restitution for this damage is absent from him also. The maximal proposition: 'A thing ought to be judged on the basis of its causes.'[67]

[4.23]

Effects are those things effected by causes that precede not in time but in nature, as for example, if we ask whether the goods of a dead wife who had come under the authority of her husband belong to her husband. In this question the subject is *goods of a dead wife who came under the authority of her husband;* the predicate is *belong to her husband.* I seek [307/1079] an argument from an effect: I perceive what coming under the authority of a husband brought about, and I draw an argument from that. This is that everything that belonged to the woman becomes her husband's under the designation of dowry.[68] And so not by the passage of time but just by the characteristic force of its nature, coming under the authority of her husband brought it about that everything that belonged to the woman was made over to her husband under the designation of dowry. For as soon as a woman comes under the authority of her husband, her goods come into the possession of her husband under the designation of dowry.

I make an argument in this way. If a woman who came under the authority of her husband has died and the goods of a such woman become the husband's under the designation of dowry, then the goods that are at issue are the husband's.[69] The argument is from what is contained in the thing at issue, for at issue are the goods of a woman who came under the authority of her husband. And so the argument is from related things, that is, from the effects of a cause, for the effect of coming under the authority of a husband is that everything belonging to the woman becomes her husband's under the designation of dowry.[70]

Here, however, the argument will be shown to have been made not from effects but from a cause, for the fact that everything belonging to the woman becomes her husband's under the designation of dowry was shown from the fact that the woman came under the authority of her husband; this, however, is a cause of the fact that everything belonging to the woman becomes her husband's under the designation of dowry.[71] But, someone might say, we prove that the goods of the

dead woman ought to belong to her husband from the fact that whatever belonged to the woman becomes her husband's under the designation of dowry.[72] But that the things belonging to the woman become
her husband's under the designation of dowry is either the same as
that her goods belong to her husband, or neither is the cause of the
other. Or if someone says the fact that the woman's goods were made
over to her husband under the designation of dowry as a result of her
coming under his authority is the cause of the fact that the woman's
goods ought to be granted to her husband,[73] he will again be reckoning
it as an argument from a cause (namely, the dowry) and not from
effects—an argument from effects proves nothing but a cause.

The argument would be from effects, and a cause would be proved
from it in the following way. If there were a question whether a woman
had come under the authority of her husband and it were known for
certain that everything that had belonged to the woman had been
made over to her husband under the designation of dowry, we would
speak in this way. If everything that belonged to the woman was made
over to her husband under the designation of dowry, the woman came
under the authority of her husband; but everything that belonged to
the woman was made over to her husband under the designation of
dowry, so the woman came under the authority of her husband. The
maximal proposition: 'Causes are not separated from their effects.'

[4.23]

The Topic said to be from comparison is split into three parts, for it
arises from comparison of greater, lesser, or equal things. It is from a
comparison of greater things when greater things are compared to
lesser things, in, for example, the following way: 'What is acceptable in
a greater thing should be acceptable in a lesser.'

Now a question arises whether one can exclude water in the city.[74]
In this question the subject term is *water in the city*, and the predicate is
the right to exclude. Boundaries are said to be regulated when each
individual field is limited by its own boundaries.[75] Also, a man who
excludes water is one who does not allow the water to pass through his
territory. And so we might make an argument in this way. Since regulating boundaries is greater and excluding water is lesser, if boundaries are not regulated in the city (and this is greater), what is lesser
(namely, that water be excluded in the city) will not occur either. Here
the argument is taken from what [308/1080] inheres in the thing asked
about, and what is being asked about is rightly excluding water. So the

argument is taken from a related thing, that is, from a greater thing, which is connected to what is lesser. Moreover, we should notice that Cicero included the maximal proposition in the argumentation, in this way: 'What is acceptable in a greater thing should be acceptable in a lesser'; then relying on the maximal proposition, he developed the argumentation. (And so what I recounted in the first book is clearer here, namely, that maximal propositions are sometimes included in argumentations, as is shown in the present example, and sometimes give force to argumentations, as in the previous examples for Topics.)

If we turn the same example around, we will say: 'What is acceptable in a lesser thing should be acceptable also in a greater. But water is excluded in the city; therefore, boundaries will be regulated.' Here, however, the question is altered in this way, that what is asked is whether boundaries in the city ought to be regulated. The argument then is taken from a lesser thing, that is, from the excluding of water, so that here also the argument is from what is in the thing at issue (that is, from what is in regulating boundaries). It is taken from a related thing, that is, a lesser thing, for a lesser thing is a related thing since it harks back to the thing to which it is compared. Here, too, Cicero presented a maximal proposition: 'What is acceptable in a lesser thing should be acceptable also in a greater.'

A comparison of equal things arises in the same sort of way, for equity, which wants equal laws for equal cases, must prevail.

Usucaption is the obtaining of ownership as a result of the lawful possession of something for an uninterrupted period of two years (or some such time).[76] For many things usucaption requires a period of one year, so that if anyone used them for an uninterrupted period of a year, his possession of them (movable property, for example) would have firm legal authority. Usucaption of a farm requires the space of a two-year period, but there is nothing in the law about houses. So what is asked is whether a one- or a two-year period is required for the usucaption of a house. We will make an argumentation from equals. Since all instances of possession of immovable pieces of property are equal and a house is an immovable piece of property, usucaption of a house should take the possessor two years just as usucaption of a farm takes two years, for equity wants equal laws for equal cases.

Cicero presented this maximal proposition most clearly,[77] but he gave a rather brief example, which is not very easy to understand, for he says, "Since use and warranty of a farm requires a period of two years, that of a house does also." Here, then, he thinks that the use and warranty of a house requires a two-year period; but he added, "Houses are not mentioned by name in the law, however, and are included with all the other things whose use extends for a one-year period." In this passage, he seems then to put houses among those things whose usucaption requires a one-year period. And he concludes saying nothing more precise than "Equity, which wants equal laws for equal cases, should prevail."

But it is as if he had spoken in this way. Since a house, like a farm, is an immovable piece of property and the usucaption of a farm requires a two-year period, the usucaption of a house will require a two-year period. And, on the other hand, he raises an objection against himself: but there is nothing written in the law of the XII Tables about houses, and because of the silence of the law houses are included among the things whose use extends over a one-year period.[78] For although the law prescribed a period of two years for the usucaption of a farm, it was silent about houses and [309/1081] by this silence joined houses rather to those things whose use extends over a one-year period. But Cicero answered his own objection in this way: equity wants equal law in equal cases; so since a farm and a house are equally immovable pieces of property, their usucaption equally requires a two-year period.

Here also the argument is made from what is in the thing at issue, that is, from a related thing, an equal, for since what is at issue is the possession of a house, the argument is taken from the usucaption of farms.

Since the Topics that inhered in the thing at issue have been explained, Cicero now presents an example of the Topic that he said is extrinsic. This Topic is taken from an authoritative judgment and is certainly readily believable even if it does not have the greatest necessity. For things that are necessary are considered on the basis of their own nature, but things that are readily believable depend on the judgment of the multitude. For things that are readily believable are those which seem true to everyone or to most people or to the most famous and distinguished or to the experts in any individual art and science (as, for example, a doctor in the field of medicine, a geometer in the field of geometry, and others experienced in the appropriate skill of their studies).[79] He speaks about this extrinsic Topic in the following way.

[4.24]

There are some arguments that an orator himself uncovers and that he gets for himself in some way on the basis of the designated Topics and that he procures by his own skill. There are other arguments that are located extrinsically and that the orator does not discover but that he takes ready-made and at hand for his use, such as testimonies, official documents, public opinion, and other things that Cicero will discuss at more length later. For an orator does not make testimonies for himself but rather he uses them ready-made; nor does he himself produce opinion, but rather he takes common talk that already exists and has arisen spontaneously and uses it for his case. Therefore the Greeks call these Topics 'atechnoi',[80] that is, unartful and (as Cicero said) devoid of art, for things that are not procured by the orator's own art but provided from without are rightly called devoid of art. The following is an example of this Topic.

[4.24]

The grounds belonging to the site[81] of a house are as much of the grounds as the site of the house encloses. Scaevola[82] said that the grounds belonging to the site of a house are what is covered by the extension of the roof, for plainly roofs are broadly extended and go beyond the walls in order that rainwater may fall further away.

Now a certain man labored to cover a common wall. What is asked is whether there is any law pertaining to such cases of covering. You, Trebatius, might reply (Cicero says) that the law pertaining to the covering of a common wall is that rainwater run onto some other roof belonging to the man covering the common wall and that otherwise it is not legal for someone to cover a wall, with rainwater flowing down onto the roofs of his neighbor.[83] For unless your neighbor is in agreement, there is nothing legal about subjecting him to additional runoff of rainwater.

But (Cicero says) if you object to this reply because it is not legal for a man to cover a common wall even in this way, since the grounds of a house are equal only to the area the walls enclose, and a man who covers a common wall extends his roof beyond his walls, you will strengthen your reply with the authority of Scaevola, saying that on Scaevola's view the grounds belonging to the site of a house [310/1082] are not the area the walls surround but rather the area over which the roof projected. So it is legal for a man to project a roof if his covering of the common wall remains within the site of his own house, but he must do so in such a way that water flows onto his own roof and does not injure his neighbor by subjecting him to additional water.

In this question the argument is drawn from neither the subject nor the predicate term, which is what we customarily consider in the case of those Topics inhering in the terms at issue, as we were careful to show in all the examples. Rather because the argument is taken from without, the authoritative opinion of someone is offered in opposition to a doubt (as, for example, in this case the authoritative opinion of Scaevola, whose authority is the basis of the reply). And so the argument is said to be taken from the Topic that is called extrinsic.

[5.25]

Every element is a principle of the thing whose element it is judged to be, since the elements must hold the place of a principle for the thing that arises from them. Therefore since the Topics designated above are "principles" of a sort for arguments (for they themselves contain arguments, and everything that contains something is a principle of what it contains), Cicero says that the Topics he presented above appear as if they were elements of a sort for arguments. And he added very cautiously, "as if they were elements of a sort," for the Topics adopted to produce arguments are not entirely elements but resemble elements in a way, since they seem to be principles of a sort for arguments. In general, every element is a minimal part of the thing of which it is an element, and it conjoins the thing produced from the elements as if it were a part, as, for example, letters conjoin a phrase. A Topic, however, is not a part of an argument but rather the whole of it. For it is a sort of indication and demonstration given in order to find an argument, so that if you gave your attention to the Topic, you would know where the argument is hiding and whence it should be drawn.

The rest of the discussion addressed to Trebatius is very brief, and Cicero even flatters him that the advantages of his keen mind can make up for the brief treatment, especially since he is occupied with legal business and does not have time for reading much. But since, as he says, he found Trebatius very greedy for learning when he received him at this banquet of ideas, he wants to leave him satisfied and not still hungry, so that Trebatius might lack nothing but in fact even have something left over from the abundance. (Cicero is making a pleasantry here by using an analogy with banqueting.)

Since all the Topics have been explained and their examples have been carefully set forth, I will say a few things about the force and ordering of the Topics, so that when they have been explicated with the fullest discussion, I may turn to the things that remain to be explained. But this should be done in a third book since the second book contains enough.

BOOK III

[311/1083] Before I begin Cicero's more detailed division of the Topics which were enumerated above, it seems to me that I should, as I promised,[1] discuss briefly the force and ordering of Topics, so that it will be easier to supply an abundance of arguments once the nature of Topics is better known.

Since all Topics are divided into those which inhere in the thing asked about and those taken from without, we should first consider which Topics are the ones that inhere in the thing asked about and how they differ from the things in which they are said to inhere. (I explained very clearly that by "things" here is meant the terms that occur in the question; of these, as the explanation above made evident, one is the predicate and the other is the subject.)[2]

How, then, does the Topic *from the whole* differ from the term at issue, since being the whole of something and being that thing itself are the same; for being a certain term presented in a question is nothing other than being the whole of that same term located in the question? We will make the same point concerning parts too; for if all the parts produce the thing whose parts they are and if a term presented in a question is produced by its parts, there can be no doubt that all the parts coming together are correctly understood to be the thing presented in the question. In the same way also designation is the thing presented in a question, for every name designates and denotes some one thing.[3] Hence, the whole, parts, and a sign seem to be the same as the thing asked about. Therefore, given so great a similarity among these things, we must provide a differentia. For if, as we said,[4] a Topic inheres in the thing asked about and an argument cannot be taken from the thing asked about, a Topic cannot possibly be the same as the thing asked about.

The differentia between a Topic and the thing asked about is this. The thing asked about is the thing understood as taken in isolation from other things and undifferentiated (for example, *man*); its whole, which is the definition, is in it. Our understanding separates the whole of a thing from the thing itself, because the thing itself is understood as taken in isolation; but the whole of the thing is shown by the enumeration of a genus and differentiae, for a definition divides, distributes, and reveals the whole that in the thing itself was understood in isolation from other things. The same reasoning applies also to parts, for if [312/1084] you were to compare the concept of a term taken in isolation to the multitude of its members or to the enumeration of all its species, you would immediately grasp the differentiae between the thing itself and its parts. A sign also is very different from the thing whose sign it is, because it is an utterance and a signification, but the thing itself is what underlies the signification. There are also undoubtedly differentiae between related things and those things to which they are shown to be related. For who would say that a conjugate is the same as that from which it is conjugated? Who would say that *justly* is the same as *justice?* Who would say that a genus is the same as a kind? Who would say that one contrary is the same as the other? Or that one of a pair of similars is the same as the other? A contrary cannot be contrary to itself; a similar cannot be similar to itself; a genus cannot be a genus of itself; and the same reasoning applies to the rest.

Now we must discuss a point for which all these things have been preliminary. When arguments are taken from the three Topics that were presented first (that is, *from a whole, from parts,* and *from a sign*), the very term for which we are seeking an argument to provide belief is contained within one of the things that are shown to be Topics when they have been brought to the argument. For example, when an argument arises from a whole, the term for which belief is adduced is comprised within a whole. This whole, which is a definition, is a thing (if we can call a phrase a thing); but if an argument is taken from it, it becomes a Topic. The thing at issue, then, is included within a whole; when an argument arises from this whole, the whole itself becomes a Topic. But since this whole includes the term used in the question, it seems to inhere in that term; hence, the Topic that is from the whole[5] also inheres in the same term that is in doubt in the question. The enumeration of parts also includes the very term that it conjoins by gathering the parts together. This enumeration of parts is itself a sort of thing (if a phrase is to be reckoned a thing), but if an argument is drawn from the enumeration of parts, that enumeration becomes a Topic. And since the multitude of parts is in the term that the parts conjoin by coming together, the Topic that is from the conjunction of parts must also inhere in the term asked about. Again, a sign designates a thing and by doing so in some way encompasses it, but if an argument is drawn from a sign, the sign becomes a Topic. And since every name is apparently present to the thing whose concept it signifies, the Topic that is from designation also inheres in the thing that is in contention.

The case of related things, which are divided into thirteen parts, is not the same. Since they are connected to a term in some way and yet are almost external to it, they are apparently not conjoined with a term in the same way in which the previously discussed Topics *from a whole, from enumeration of parts,* and *from a sign* are. Nonetheless, a related thing is said with respect to something. This something is always joined to a related thing, because it is produced in relationship to a related thing and cannot ever be without it since it comes into existence with it, and when one of the two has been said the other is in some way understood. If you consider what is being asked about and its related things, you should regard the things that are said to be related as outside the thing in doubt. For none of the things that exist with respect to something can exist on their own but always exist dependent on another since (as is shown in the *Categories*)[6] all things said with respect to something are opposite to one another. Nonetheless, they are not so disjoined that they are altogether divided from one another.[7] Rather since they are joined by a relative predication, they must in some way be in the thing to which they seem related. For every related thing [313/1085] takes its form from the thing to which it is related and cannot exist without that thing,[8] and when one of a pair of related things has been said, the concept of the other is immediately added. For example, when I say 'half', *double* is understood; when I mention a father, a child comes to mind. All things that exist with respect to something depend on one another and do not leave one another. Every related thing, then, harks back to the thing to which it is connected and is in that thing. It harks back to that thing because it is connected to its related thing in the way in which relatives are predicated of one another. But it is in that thing because the nature of related things is that they exist in dependence on one another and possess each other, since what is called a related thing belongs to the term to which it is considered related, and a term presented in a question is understood to be connected to its related thing.

Hence, when an argument is taken from conjugates, what is being asked about inheres in the externally located conjugate, since one of a pair of conjugates is related to the other. The Topic from which the argument is drawn, then, is produced from the other conjugate. For example, if the field is common pasturage, common pasturing is legal, and *common pasturing* and *common pasturage* are conjugates. What was asked is whether common pasturing was legal, but the argument was drawn from common pasturage. In this way the term questioned is found in one conjugate, namely, in *common pasturing;* but the Topic from which the argument is drawn is in the other conjugate, namely, in *common pasturage.*[9]

Similarly, when an argument is drawn from a genus, what is asked about must inhere in a species, as when it is shown that the coin was bequeathed because all the silver was bequeathed. For what is asked about is *coin,* which is a separate species of *silver,* and the argument is drawn from *silver,* that is, from a genus. And so the thing asked about was in a kind, that is, in a species, but the argument is drawn from a related thing, that is, a genus.[10] If the argument is from a kind of a genus, however, the situation is reversed. What is asked about is shown to be in a genus, but that from which the argument is taken is judged to be in a kind. For when we ask whether the silver was bequeathed to the wife, we show that it was not bequeathed because it was bequeathed not simply to a wife but to a wife who was a materfamilias. *Wife* is a genus, though, and *materfamilias* is a species of wife. So what is asked about is *wife,* that is, a genus, but the argument is produced from *materfamilias,* that is, from a kind.[11]

Moreover, when an argument is drawn from a similarity, since what is similar is judged to be similar not to itself but to something else, the thing asked about is located in one of the things that are similar, and the Topic is in the other. For example, when we ask whether the heir is compelled to make good the damage or collapse of a house whose usufruct was bequeathed, the question is in this. But the Topic is from similarity, because the heir need not make restitution for the house just as he need not make restitution for a slave who has perished for some reason. So since usufruct of a house and usufruct of a slave are similar, what is being asked about is located in the usufruct of a house, but the Topic is located in the usufruct of a slave.[12]

The case is the same for differentia. For what is asked about is located in one of a pair of things that differ, [314/1086] but that on the basis of which what is in doubt is proved is located in the other—as, for example, when it is asked whether the silver owed as debts was also bequeathed. This is what is in doubt here, but the Topic from which we show that the silver owed as debts was not bequeathed is in something different from this, because it makes a great difference whether the silver was in a strongbox or owed as debts.[13]

The same holds for the Topic *from a contrary,* as in the case where the question was whether the usufruct of provisions was bequeathed. The question concerns usufruct. But we prove that usufruct of provisions was not bequeathed because there cannot be use of things that perish when we use them; there can be only consumption. So the Topic is located in consumption, namely, in the other of the pair of contraries, since the question was located in use.[14]

The Topic *from associated things* also is separated in the same way from what is asked about: the question is in one of a pair of associated things and the Topic is in the other. For when we asked whether possession of an inheritance should be given in accordance with the will of a woman who has never forfeited her civil rights, the question is in this. But the Topic is in something associated with it, because we show that possession of the inheritance ought not to be given since granting possession of an inheritance in accordance with the wills of children and slaves is a neighboring case.[15]

In the case of the Topic *from antecedents*, the question is in consequents. For because the question is whether any of the dowry ought to remain as owed for the children, the argument that nothing at all should remain is taken from antecedents, because the divorce was the man's fault; so the Topic is in an antecedent but the question in a consequent. For the fact that nothing remains with the father for the children is a consequence of the fact that the divorce was the man's fault, since the man's fault preceded.[16]

If the argument is from consequents, however, the thing that is in doubt is found to be in antecedents—as, for example, when it is asked whether any of the dowry should remain as owed for the children when a woman has divorced a man with whom there was no wedlock. An argument arises in this way. If any of the dowry should have remained for the children in virtue of the fact that they followed their father, then the woman was married to a man with whom there was legal wedlock. Here the antecedent is *if any of the dowry should remain for the children,* and the question whether anything should remain is in the antecedent. The consequent, however, is *the woman was married to a man with whom there was legal wedlock* and the argument is taken from it, that is, from a consequent. For since it is clear that she was not married to a man with whom there was legal wedlock, it is shown that the children do not follow their father and that therefore nothing should remain for the children. Here, then, the thing that is in doubt is in the antecedent, namely, in this, *whether any of the dowry should remain for the children;* but the argument is in the Topic that is in consequents, that is, in *a woman who was married to a man with whom there was no legal wedlock.*[17]

Similarly, when arguments are taken from incompatibles, the thing in doubt is in one of the pair of incompatibles, and the Topic for the argument is in the other, as, for example, when one asks whether a woman can lose against her will a bequest that she at the same time received legally from a will. The Topic *from an incompatible:* not being able to lose against one's will what one received legally.[18] So the question is in the idea of losing against one's will, but the argument is in the other incompatible, that is, in the idea of receiving legally. For losing against one's will and receiving legally are incompatible with one another, but the question is in one of these and the Topic is in the other.[19]

When an argument is drawn from efficient causes, the question must be in effects, as in the [315/1087] example in which we ask whether someone who gave guarantees against future harm is compelled to make good the damage to a wall. The question is in this, that is, in *damage to a wall*, but the argument is drawn from a cause, for it is said that he is not obligated to make good the damage since the nature of the wall was the cause of the damage and not the man who had given guarantees about making good any damage to the wall. The effect of a cause, then, was damage to the wall, and in this way the question is in an effect, but the Topic is considered to be from a cause. On the other hand, if something is proved from effects, the Topic is in an effect and the question is located in a cause, as, for example, when we ask whether a certain woman, whose goods were made over to her husband under the designation of dowry, had come under the authority of her husband. Since coming under the authority of a husband brings it about that the husband obtains the woman's goods after her death, we draw the argument from effects, for what is effected by coming under the authority of the husband is that whatever belonged to the woman was made over to her husband under the designation of dowry. So since the man obtains the things that belonged to the woman under the designation of dowry, the woman must have come under the authority of her husband. And in this way the question is about the woman, whether she came under the authority of her husband; but the argument is from an effect of a cause, that is, an effect of coming under the authority of her husband, and this effect is that the man acquires the things that belonged to the woman. Hence, what is asked about is in a cause, but the Topic is in effects.[20]

If the argument was from a comparison of greater things, the question will be in lesser things—for example, if we ask whether water should be excluded in the city, and we maintain that it ought not to be, for boundaries are not regulated. In this way the question is in *excluding water*, which is a lesser thing, but the Topic is in *regulating boundaries*, which is greater. And on the other hand, if the argument is drawn from a lesser thing, what is in doubt will be in a greater thing.

For example, if there is some doubt whether boundaries in the city are regulated, we might reply that they are not since water is not excluded either. In this way, what is in doubt subsists in a greater thing, but that from which the argument is taken is in a lesser thing. Similar reasoning applies in the case of comparison of equals. For the question subsists in one of the things that are equals, and the Topic for the argument is understood to be in the other. For example, when it is asked whether usucaption of a house requires two years, we prove that it does since usucaption of a farm does also. Since a farm and a house are equals, the question concerns a house, but the argument is drawn from a farm.[21]

This discussion has concerned the force of the Topics and the way in which questions and Topics for arguments are distinguished from one another. Now I will very briefly relate their ordering. Our entire judgment about which Topic is to be regarded as prior and which as posterior arises from considering the terms used in the question presented, in the following way. The Topics that are nearer to these terms are rightly accounted prior, and those that are at a great distance from the terms presented are rightly accounted posterior. The following explanation will make this point clear.

First, the multitude of Topics is divided into those that are in the thing at issue and those that are taken from without; in this we understand that the Topics that are in the thing at issue are put before the Topics drawn from without. Moreover, the Topic that is in the thing at issue is divided into four primary parts, of which the first is definition, and this is called the Topic *from the whole*. *From the whole* is put first, because nothing is as close to a thing as its own definition. The enumeration of parts follows, because the parts that conjoin the whole whose parts they are said to be should have the nearest place after the definition. A sign is put next to these [316/1088] and is something like the converse of a definition; for as a definition unfolds what a sign designates involutedly, so a sign enfolds and indicates in an undifferentiated way what a definition reveals and explicates. And therefore a sign is third, because a definition contains the substance and a partition enumerates the things that join together the composite whole, but a sign only designates and does not produce anything.

After these Topics which principally inhere in the term themselves, related things are enumerated. Now they are not in the terms themselves; but located outside the terms, they follow from them. They are said to be in the terms themselves only because they cannot be without the terms.

The first of the related things are conjugates; for among related things, only that which is separated from the terms themselves by just a small inflection of a name is so close to the terms as to share both in their nature and their name. For what is just shares in justice and is also called by an inflected name of justice, and the same is true of other conjugates.

Genus is added after conjugates. A genus, which universally shows the substance of a thing and which is a substantial likeness of many things differing in species, is separated from the terms presented more than conjugates are, because although a genus shows the substance of a term, it is nevertheless not united in name with that term, not even by means of an inflected word, but rather is called by a name that is broadly and greatly different from the name of the term. Species (which Cicero called 'kind') is added after genus, because nothing is so near to a genus as a species. Species is a substantial likeness of individuals and is put under a genus.[22]

Similarity is located after species, for after that which is understood to be in substances, we rightly put that which is judged to be in a quality.[23] A thing begins to move away from similarity little by little and does not immediately arrive at its contrary but constructs first the Topic *from differentia*, for when similarity has been taken away, difference is the first thing to present itself. After differentia, Cicero draws the Topic *from a contrary*, that is, from the greatest difference.[24]

Next, related things are transformed into things that are congenial to one another, but they are not congenial in the same way in which similar things are congenial. For Cicero here presents associated things, which are not entirely similar; nonetheless, judgment concerning them is the same, and they have the sort of proximity pertaining to things that adhere to one another.[25]

After associated things, Cicero presented antecedents. For after that which is joined in some way, we must next understand something that is either antecedent or consequent. And in this way Cicero classified first an antecedent and then a consequent.[26]

After antecedents and consequents, Cicero discussed incompatibles,[27] so that in some ways a twofold ordering of contrarieties and similarities arose. For first he presented *from a similar, from a differentia,* and *from a contrary,* and this is a general ordering of similars and contraries. And next he presented *from associated things, from antecedents and consequents,* and *from incompatibles,* and this we perceive to be a second ordering of similars and contraries. But the first ordering is certainly more apparent than the second. For being similar is more than being associated; differing is more than being an antecedent or a consequent; and being a contrary is more than being an incompatible.[28] Within the ordering themselves, however, each retains the full form. For example, because similarity ought to have a sort of proximity, what is similar has a greater proximity to the thing to which it is considered to be similar than what is associated [317/1089] has to the thing to which it is conjoined by a natural nearness. Again, since differentia is the source of dissimilarity, that which differs from something else is more dissimilar than is that which is an antecedent or a consequent. Again, since one contrary ought to be as far away as possible from the other, one contrary is further away from the other contrary than one incompatible is from the other.

After these things, what could be left except to investigate the causes of effects? And after the causes of effects what could be left except to examine the effects of those causes? Finally, Topics from comparison have the last place in the ordering because they possess similarity or dissimilarity in quantity alone. And enough has been said about the ordering of the Topics.[29]

In addition, I think we should consider whether the Topics for arguments which inhere in the thing asked about could also be rightly included among related things since related things are called related just because they exist with respect to something and are bound in a relationship to the term presented.[30] For a definition is the definition of something, a whole is the whole of the parts, and a sign is the sign of what is signified. But we must examine the nature of the individual cases and see whether a definition, a whole, and a sign are related to something in the same way as related things are. For a definition in some ways unfolds and gives shape to the thing it defines. Similarly, by their conjoining, the parts produce the thing whose parts they are. And a sign has the general concept of the thing it signifies. But since the others, which are called related things, do not do these things, definition, whole, and sign are rightly not included among related things but are said to be in the thing at issue which they (as it were) make and shape. But since enough has been said about the force and ordering of Topics. let us now pass over to the following passages.

In addition to all the things said above, it is most important to notice that if something is used in arguments, it is not to be called a Topic for those arguments unless it not only is in the arguments but the arguments also arise from it. An example will make my point clearer. If there is an argument in which genus or species is used, that argument is not immediately said to be drawn from genus or from species unless the nature of a genus or of a species supplies the force for that argument. For suppose there is a question whether, for an animal, being is the same thing as living. An argumentation might arise in this way. For an animal, being is not the same as living, because neither is being the same as being dead for an inanimate thing; indeed many things are inanimate but are not dead, for it is apparent that things that never lived cannot die either. Here *inanimate* is the genus of rocks and molten metals, and it is used in an argument. The argument, however, is made not from a genus, even though genus seems to be included in it, but rather from a contrary. For *death* is contrary to *life* and *inanimate* is contrary to *animal*, but *being dead* does not follow from *inanimate* and therefore *living* does not follow from *animal* either.[31] Therefore, this Topic should not be said to be from a genus but rather from a contrary. An argument of the following sort might contain a genus, for the Topic would be from genus if the idea of the argument were drawn from the genus of animal or of living. For example, if an argument were to arise in this way: for an animal, being is a substance; living, however, is not a substance, although it enters into a substance; therefore, for an animal, living is not the same as being. [318/1090] So the argument is drawn from a substance, that is, from the genus of *animal*,[32] and hence this argument both contains a genus and is drawn from a genus. But although the previous argument contains a genus, we judge it to be drawn from a contrary, for we must always look to see not what is in an argument but from what the argument is drawn.

The same point holds also for the other Topics, but we should not linger over individual cases. For if people exercised care over the explanation developed above, they would easily work out in the remaining cases what is shown in this one example.

[5.26]

Although the Topics for arguments were presented briefly before, Cicero decided to partition the same Topics more minutely and plainly into their own parts and appropriate subdivisions; for we will consider the nature of all the Topics more carefully if we know them not only as they are when they are undifferentiated but also as they are when they are divided into their own parts. And Cicero gives here a great abundance for finding arguments. For example, we might say with regard to definition that if someone knows all the parts[33] of definition, he will be able to procure arguments for himself from them all, and he will find an abundance of arguments more easily than a man who does not know how many species of definition there are. For a man will devise arguments from as many parts of definitions as he knows there to be. The man from whom the diversity of definitions is not hid, then, will have greater skill at such Topics. So for this reason Cicero now partitions with more careful criteria the Topics that he presented before in an undifferentiated and unanalyzed way.

We must also give closer consideration to the fact that, as we said above,[34] the Topics themselves are things of a sort, too, but that they are understood to be Topics when an argument is drawn from them. Accordingly, Cicero here mainly divides not Topics but the things themselves, which become a species of Topics when they are brought to an argument. A definition, a part, and a sign are things of a sort, but when an argument is drawn from them, they become Topics. So when Cicero is partitioning the things themselves as they naturally are, he is at the same time dividing Topics. For if the thing from which an argument can be drawn is one, the Topic is also one; but if that thing is divided, there will be as many of that kind of Topics from which arguments arise as there were parts of that thing.

Since the first Topic of all is *from the whole*, that is, *from definition*, Cicero first shows with a definition what a definition is, so that once the nature of the thing has been revealed, its species and subdivisions may be partitioned and appropriately arranged. "A definition," he says, "is an expression that unfolds what the thing defined is,"[35] as the definition of *man* is *mortal rational animal*. Cicero's use of the word 'unfolds' was very circumspect, for what a name makes known in an undifferentiated way, the definition spreads out into substantial subdivisions of a sort. For example, what is shown in an undifferentiated way by the name 'man', the definition unveils and unfolds by saying that a man is a mortal rational animal. If Cicero had not spoken in this way, the definition of a definition would have been applicable to a genus also, in the following way: a definition is that which designates what the thing defined is; a genus, however, also designates what the thing of which it is predicated is—but it does not unfold it. Only a definition, which is produced by a phrase, unfolds what a thing is; a genus and the rest, which [319/1091] are expressed for the most part by a single name, do not *unfold* what a thing is.

A definition does not unfold what it defines in every possible way, though; that is, it does not unfold what it defines with respect to quality or quantity or any of the other categories. Rather, the definition shows what the thing defined is; that is, it shows its substance. A definition that consists in a genus and differentiae, however, does lay out a substance, for genus and differentiae indicate the substance of anything, as we said in the passages where we discussed genus and species, differentia, property, and accident.[36] Therefore, every definition unfolds what the thing that it defines is. (Aristotle delimited definition in almost exactly the same way: a definition is an expression signifying the being-what-it-is.)[37]

Cicero divides definition in this way.

[5.27]

It is apparent that every definition is said with respect to something, for it is always the definition of something. But things that are said with respect to something must take some characteristics from the things to which they are related. Hence, definitions transfer to themselves some characteristics from the things that a definition delimits. But because what is related to something cannot be the same as the thing with respect to which it is said, what is related to something else must also possess its own characteristic form. Therefore, in the case of definitions, each definition has its own form, but we also observe a form that definitions receive from the things they define. Cicero sees this and so divides definitions first in accordance with the things they define.

He claims that there are two genera of things that are defined, one genus of things that exist and another of things that are understood. He appears to have taken these differentiae of definitions from the things that are shown by a definition, for everything that is defined is either corporeal or incorporeal. All things to begin with are first divided into these two genera. Things that are corporeal Cicero says exist, and things that are incorporeal do not exist—not that things that are incorporeal do not exist entirely; otherwise they would not admit of a definition. If a definition is that which unfolds what is defined with respect to what it is, there cannot be any unfolding with respect to what it is for a thing that does not exist at all. But because mankind lives by its senses, it thinks that what really exists is what can be grasped by the senses. For who does not seem to himself to know a stone or a man more than justice or inheritance or anything else that is grasped not by the senses but by the understanding? Hence, because the knowledge of such things is evident, things subject to the senses seem more truly to exist; things grasped by the reasoning of the understanding seem to exist less truly.

We must understand, however, that Cicero expressed this thought with regard to the opinion of men and not with regard to the truth. As the best philosophers agree, the things that really exist are those which are thoroughly isolated from the senses, and those which supply beliefs for the senses exist less truly. Hence, even Cicero himself in his commentary on the *Timaeus* says, "What is it that is always and has not beginning and what is it that comes to be and never is? Of these, one is grasped by the reasoning of the understanding; the other, apart from reasoning, imparts sense impressions for belief."[38] Here, then, Cicero associated what is always with reasoning, but what [320/1093] never is he joined to the senses.

But, as we said, Cicero's statement that corporeal things exist and incorporeal things do not exist was made not with regard to the truth but with regard to the common opinion of ordinary men. As examples of things that exist, he presents certain kinds of corporeal things, as, for instance, a farm, a house, walls, rainwater, and things of this genus. His criterion for thinking that these are corporeal is that they can be seen and touched. As examples of things that do not exist, he presented usucaption, guardianship, a clan,[39] and other things that are incorporeal. He showed that they are incorporeal from the fact that, as he says, they cannot be touched or pointed to, but are grasped by the understanding and the mind; he added a reason for his saying that they do not exist, namely, that there is no body of any sort for these things nor any mass that might affect the senses. For what body can there be for usucaption? Those things which are acquired through usucaption are corporeal, but usucaption itself is not corporeal. For can there be any body for the confirmation of possession as a result of habitual use? Again, what someone governs by guardianship is corporeal, for it is a man, but the administration of guardianship and the legal authority of guardianship over another can have no body at all. Men, too, who are in the same clan, are corporeal, but the clan—that is, the association of free men having a common name, as, for example, the clan of Scipio, Valerius, and Brutus[40]—is certainly incorporeal. There is, however, a certain incorporeal mental conception and understanding of these things, which Cicero called an idea; for the mental image of usucaption or guardianship and the incorporeal understanding of a thing is said to be an idea (the Greeks call this *ennoia*).[41]

So Cicero divided definition into these two parts, in accordance, that is, with the differentiae of the subject of the definition. Hence, according to Cicero, there are some definitions of things that exist (that is, of corporeal things), and others[42] of things that do not exist (that is, of incorporeal things).

On the basis of this, it is possible to ask (as I explained briefly above)[43] why a definition should not be counted among related things since every definition seems to be with respect to something; for similarity, a contrary, and the others are said to be related things because they are always connected to something. And if definition too is connected to something and yet does not give a complete and appropriate presentation, then it too should be included among related things.

But one counters this objection by saying that as shadows cannot leave a body, so related things, which are external, cannot leave the thing to which they are shown to be related. And either they utterly fail to signify the substance of the things to which they are related (as in the case of a contrary, a similar, and others), or when they do designate the substance, it is understood to be some one part of the substance (as in the case of genus, species, and differentia). A genus is not the whole substance of a species since not only a genus but differentiae also form a species. Nor do differentiae contain the whole form of the substance since not only a differentia but also a genus produce a species. And a species itself is a certain part of a genus.[44] But although a definition is with respect to something, it shows the whole substance and is equivalent to the thing it defines and does produce the complete substance. And so a definition is not external like similarity and contraries, nor is it a part of the substance that it delimits by defining it, but rather it is the substance itself. And enough has been said about this subject.

The same point can be made about parts, for the conjoined parts produce the whole whose parts they are. A sign [321/1094] also indicates the whole that it designates. And these are all equivalent: a definition is equivalent to the thing it defines; parts are equivalent to their whole; and a sign is equivalent to the thing it shows by its signification (if the sign is not homonymous[45] or equivocal, or if the thing designated does not have synonyms).

We can certainly reasonably wonder why, when Cicero said there are two genera of definitions, he partitioned the things defined (that is, the corporeal and the incorporeal) and not the definitions themselves. His reason for doing so seems to be that since a definition is with respect to something, as was said, it takes a certain quality from the things whose substance it delimits.[46]

[5.28]

A definition takes characteristics from the underlying thing that it defines, but it does so in such a way that it does not lose its own characteristic form. For this reason, after drawing the differentiae of definitions from the things that are defined, Cicero propounds the differentiae of definitions taken from their own characteristic form. The characteristic form of any composite consists in its parts, and Cicero therefore teaches the following differentiae based on the parts of definitions: some definitions arise by division and some by partition, for a thing is defined when all its species or parts are enumerated. I will say a little later what the difference between a species and a part is.[47] Now I think I should set out Cicero's examples, for he gives the following example of partition.

Suppose we are given civil law to define. We will speak in this way. Civil law is what consists in laws, decrees of the senate, judicial decisions, the authority of jurists, edicts of the magistrates, custom, and equity.[48] Law is what the people have given assent to when they were voting in the assembly. Decrees of the senate are those things which have been decided by authority of the senate. Judicial decisions are things that the opinions of judges have settled when men were in contention about some thing, and their example sets a standard of judgment for other things. The authority of jurists belongs to those who have expounded civil law from the XII Tables or the edicts of the magistrates, with an opinion that is approved and accepted by the judgments of the citizens. Edicts of the magistrates are what praetors of the citizens or praetors of foreigners or curule aediles said is right. Custom is what is customarily done in the state. Equity is that to which natural reason persuades us. All these things, which are "parts," produce a single form of the law, just as the head, arms, chest, abdomen, legs, and feet produce a man. For partition, as Cicero says, rends a given individual thing into its "members."

Cicero shows the other part of definition which arises by means of a division of species with an example of the following sort. He defines alienation of a thing that is *mancipium*[49] by saying, "Alienation of a thing that is *mancipium* is either transfer to another with *nexum*[50] or cession at law[51] among those who can do these things in accordance with civil law," for only Roman citizens can do something in accordance with civil law, and for them civil law is what is contained in the XII Tables.[52] Now all things that can be alienated, that is, that can be transferred from our ownership to that of another, are either *mancipia* or not. The ancients called things *mancipia* [322/1095] that were alienated by means of the ceremony of *nexum*, and *nexum* is a certain legal ceremony that occurred in the way Gaius describes in his *Institutes*.[53] In the first book of Gaius's *Institutes*, there are these words about enacting *nexum*:[54] "Mancipation (as we also indicated above)[55] is a certain imaginary sale. This law pertains only to Roman citizens, and the thing is done in this way. No fewer than five adult Roman citizens are brought forward as witnesses, and also one other man of like legal status who holds the bronze balance and is called the balance holder. The person who is receiving the *mancipium* holds bronze money and speaks in this way: I declare this man to be mine by Roman law, and I have bought him with this bronze money and the bronze balance.[56] Then he strikes the balance with the money, which he gives as the price to the man from whom he receives the *mancipium*." By the law of the XII Tables, nothing could be alienated except by means of this ceremony.[57] But other things were called independent under law and not *mancipia*. These things, too, were ceded at law,[58] but the cession occurred in the following way, as Gaius explained in the second book.[59] "Cession at law arises in this way. In the presence of a magistrate of the Roman people, a praetor, or a provincial governor, the man to whom the thing is ceded at law takes hold of the thing and lays legal claim to it in this way: 'I say that this man is mine under Roman law.'[60] Then after he has laid legal claim to it, the praetor asks the man who is ceding the thing whether he makes a counterclaim to the thing. If he says no or is silent, then the praetor awards the thing to the man who laid legal claim to it; this is called an action of the law."[61]

So things that are *mancipia* are alienated either with *nexum* (as was said) or with cession at law; the preceding passages from Gaius show that these are judicial ceremonies of a sort. If a thing that is a *mancipium* is handed over to another without any intervening ceremony, it will not be able to be alienated, unless the person to whom it is handed over receives it by usucaption.[62] Hence, the alienation of a *mancipium* is rightly defined by division, namely, as that which is accomplished either by handing over with *nexum* or handing over by cession at law, for *alienation of a mancipium* is not exhausted by *handing over* alone. We understand that *nexum* and *cession at law* are species of *alienation* and not parts from the fact that if someone alienates a *mancipium* with *nexum*, he will have given over a thing that was his into the power of another in accordance with the complete law of alienation, and if someone cedes something at law, there will also be the complete law of alienation. But when the parts receive the complete name of the thing they divide, anyone imbued with even a little knowledge of dialectic understands that the parts are species and that the thing divided is a genus.

Hence, Cicero divided definition into two parts, one that occurs by the enumeration of parts and the other that occurs by means of a division of parts; each sort of definition enumerates parts, but the latter sort of definition divides species and the former divides members. And here a very difficult question arises, for if a definition is also a division, we might wonder how [323/1096] the Topic *from definition* differs from the Topic *from the enumeration of parts*. This subject occasions a great deal of confusion. In the enumeration of Topics above, one Topic was presented as *from definition* and another as *from enumeration of parts*, but now Cicero asserts that enumeration of parts and division are species of definition. Therefore, since an enumeration of parts is the same as a definition (for a species is the same as its genus), the Topic *from definition* is undoubtedly the same as the Topic *from the enumeration of parts.*

The resolution of this very difficult question is easier if we consider the kinds and diversities of definitions themselves, for a definition can arise in many ways. One of these ways is a true and complete mode of definition, which is also called 'substantial'; the rest are called definitions through an improper use of the word. I will make a complete division of all of these a little later;[63] here I will discuss them all in general in the following way. Every definition unfolds what the thing defined is, but the unfolding occurs in two ways: in one way when something clearer is adduced for something less well known, and in another way when the unfolding arises from a certain enumeration of parts. The first way we will discuss later.[64] Here, concerning enumeration of parts, we must say that every definition that arises by means of an enumeration of parts is rightly understood as a partitioning of a sort. For we said that what is signified in an undifferentiated way in a name is unveiled and unfolded in a definition that arises from an enumeration of parts, and this can occur only by naming certain parts, because nothing can be said all at once while it is in the process of being unfolded with a phrase. Because of this and the fact that every definition of this sort is a certain division of parts, it can arise in four ways: either we unfold substantial parts, or we speak of parts of the nature, or we enumerate the parts as members of the whole, or we divide the parts as species.

We unfold substantial parts when a definition is constructed of genus and differentiae. A genus that is predicated in isolation is a whole of the species, but when it is taken in a definition, it becomes a sort of part, because a genus extends beyond a species unless differentiae also are added. As for differentiae, the point made about genus applies to them as well. Although differentiae enclose the whole species when they are said in isolation, they become the parts of a species when they are taken in a definition, because they indicate not only that the species is but also that the genus is.[65] An example of this is 'A man is a mortal rational animal'. Since the whole definition is equivalent to *man* and the parts of the whole definition are *animal* and *rational* and *mortal*, the parts of man himself seem to be the individual things that are the parts of this definition. This is called 'definition' in the strict sense of the name.

Again, there is the sort of definition where accidents are gathered together into one thing and one thing is produced from them; it is a sort of enumeration of parts located not in substance but in a gathering together of accidents.[66] An example of this sort of definition is 'An animal is what can move by its own will.' For motion, will, and possibility are accidental to an animal, but these things produce an animal when they have been joined together, not because they are substantial constitutents of an animal but because they indicate an animal by certain accidents that are a sort of parts for an animal. This sort of definition is called a description.

If we are talking not about the accidents of a thing but rather about certain members [324/1097] from which a thing is composed and conjoined, and if we attempt to make a definition from such members, we speak in this way: 'A house is what consists in a foundation, walls, and a roof.' Here "members," from which the thing as a whole is conjoined, are used in the definition; this is called a definition by means of enumeration of parts.

If someone makes a definition by presenting species rather than members in the definition, it is called a definition from the division of species, as, for example, if someone maintains this: 'An animal is that which depends on either the senses alone or on the senses and reason.'[67]

It is clear that these four sorts of definition differ from one another. In the definition that is produced by means of substantial parts, the individual parts seem to be greater and more universal in substance than the thing that they define; for example, *animal* is greater than *man*.[68] Moreover, *mortal* and *rational*, taken individually, extend beyond the nature of man. But when these things come together into one, they become equivalent to the thing that they exceed when they are taken individually. Accidents used in a definition, however, are entirely disjoined from the nature of substance. In the definition produced from the enumeration of parts, too, the things enumerated are such that taken individually they cannot receive the name of the whole that is being defined, and therefore they are less than that whole. For example, foundations cannot be called by the name 'house', and they are less than a house; the same is true for the other parts of a house. In the definition that arises by means of division, however, although the individual parts are less than the whole that is being defined, they nevertheless take the whole name of the thing being defined. So, for example, *rational* receives the name 'animal', and in the same way *irrational* does also.

Since these definitions diverge from one another in this way, when an argumentation arises from a definition produced by substantial parts or a definition gathered together by the enumeration of accidents, the argument is said to be drawn from definition, that is, from a whole. But when an argumentation arises from a definition that is brought about by the enumeration of members or by the division of species, the argument is held to be drawn from the enumeration of parts. Because Cicero was engaged here in the partition of *definition*, he inserted this also, although it belongs to the Topic of enumeration of parts and not to the Topic of definition. An argument for this point is that when he subsequently discussed the same Topics more fully and spoke about the enumeration of parts, he presented just this very enumeration of parts that he here said is a species of definition.

We should not think, however, that every partition can take the place of a definition.[69] For example, if someone says, 'Foundations, walls, and a roof are a house,' this is not necessary. It can be a portico designed for public use; it can also be something else, such as a theater, which generally has a roof in order to amplify the sound. But what we ought to understand is this. A thing can often be defined by means of a partition when the collection of parts can produce only one thing. For example, if there were nothing other than a house which could have foundations, walls, and a roof, the definition 'A house is what foundations, walls, and a roof produce' would seem correct.

[6.28]

Victorinus undertook to expand this passage in the course of a single book and to enumerate all differentiae of definitions,[70] and so he inserted many things that almost everybody protests are not definitions. [325/1098] For he includes names also among definitions, although Aristotle, who was unusually skilled in every kind of learning, does not think this right and denies emphatically in the *Topics*[71] that a definition arises by means of a name. For example, if someone were to ask, 'What is silence?' and one were to reply 'Quiet,' we should by no means hold these to be definitions. This can be shown also by Cicero's own definition, according to which a definition shows what the thing defined is, for he said that a definition is a phrase that unfolds what the thing defined is. But since a name is not a phrase, a name clearly cannot constitute a definition, especially because not even all the things that are uttered as phrases and that manifest something are appropriately designated 'definitions', as, for example, descriptions and every other sort of definition that is not produced from substantial parts but from things conjoined in some other way.

Even Victorinus himself is not ignorant of this. Victorinus, however, seems to have taken as the subject of the discussion not a definition but just whatever can show the underlying thing in any way. For he included a name, too, among definitions, because often something that is obscure when it is expressed with a rather unfamiliar word becomes clearer when it is expressed with a more familiar word. For that reason, too, we said previously that an unfolding can occur in two ways—in one way, when something clearer is brought forward for something less well known, and in another way when the unfolding occurs by means of enumeration of parts. The unfolding in which something more familiar is brought forward belongs to a name, but the unfolding that arises by means of an enumeration of parts belongs to a phrase (although even in the case of phrases something clearer that makes the subject of the discussion more familiar is always brought forward).

Therefore, in order that our explanation may omit nothing and that the nature of definition may be so apparent that we might have knowledge of all these things, to the end that we do not fail to recognize a true definition but also include within our science what is not strictly and truly a definition, we must make the following differentia among definitions. Some definitions are definitions strictly speaking, and others are called 'definitions' by an improper use of the word. Definitions that consist of a genus and differentiae, such as 'A man is a mortal rational animal,' are definitions strictly speaking; for here *animal* is the genus and *rational* and *mortal* are the differentiae. As for definitions that are called definitions by an improper use of the word and are not definitions strictly speaking, some are specified by individual names, and others are unfolded and expressed by a phrase.

Among the definitions indicated by a name alone, there are some that arise *kata lexin*,[72] that is, a word for a word, when a name is given for another name, as, for example, if someone asks, 'What is silence?' and the reply is 'Quiet,' or 'What is bloodshed?' and the reply is 'Smiting.' There are others that are given by way of an example, as when we want to designate what a substance is and we say by way of an example, 'A man'. This is called *typos*[73] in Greek; as we said,[74] it is included among definitions because whatever designates something in some way seems to be a definition of some sort (even if not strictly speaking) of the thing it designates.

There are many different kinds of definitions that consist in a phrase but are nevertheless not definitions strictly speaking, but the common name for them all is 'description'. Some of these arise by a partition, and others by a division; these we discussed above [326/1099].[75] Others adopt substantial differentiae but do not add a genus. Victorinus called these *ennoematike*,[76] as if to say that they contain a certain common idea. For example, if someone says, 'A man is what lives by rational comprehension and is subject to mortality,' the genus is not presented here, only the substantial differentiae.

There are others that are designated by several qualities that are accidents, in such a way that the individual qualities can produce the thing they show even if they are not conjoined. For example, 'A man is where piety and equity are and again where malice and guile can be'; for even if we add nothing else, to show a man it is enough to say, 'Where piety or justice or the rest can inhere.' This is called *poiotes*.[77] There are others that are produced by several accidents being conjoined into one, for example, if someone wants to define an extravagant man and says, 'An extravagant man is a man who abounds in pleasures and rushes prodically into voluptuousness with many unnecessary expenses.' All of these conjoined seem to produce an extravagant man, although taken individually they do not. This is called *hypographike*.[78]

Again, others arise in this way: they are presented to indicate a differentia for things that are conjoined within a determinate boundary. For example, if someone is in doubt whether Nero was an emperor or a tyrant, he says that Nero was a tyrant because he was cruel and debauched, for the added differentia separates a tyrant from an emperor in this way. Or again, if someone is in doubt about what a tyrant and a king are, the addition of a differentia designates them both, as, for example, if moderation and piety are said to belong to a king but debauchery and cruelty to a tyrant. This is called *kata diaphoran*.[79]

Another sort of definition is said to occur by means of a metaphor; for example, 'Youth is the blossom of one's age.'[80] What arises from the privation of a contrary is also said to be a definition, for example, 'Good is what is not evil.'[81] Victorinus maintains that what can be furnished only with proper names is also a definition, and this is also called *hypotyposis;* for example, 'Aeneas is the son of Venus and Anchises.'[82] In addition, there is also a definition that arises as a result of a thing's not being complete, for example, 'One-fourth is that to which three-fourths is lacking, as in the case of a coin.'[83]

Victorinus also includes among the differentiae of definitions that a definition can arise by means of praise of a sort, as, for example, 'Law is the mind, soul, plan, and purpose of a state.'[84] This is especially unreasonable, because this mode, the mode of praise, will not produce a differentia, for we must consider the things maintained in a definition and not the spirit with which they are constructed. And if an inclination to praise were to be admitted among differentiae of definitions, why should an inclination to censure not also produce yet another differentia of definition?[85] But this seems obviously inappropriate and contrary to truth.

Definitions also arise by means of an analogy, as, for example, if someone says, 'Man is a smaller world.' For the world is governed by reason, and since man is made up of many parts and yet has reason as ruler over them all, man can in this way also be called a smaller world.[86] Definitions also arise from relations. When one asks, 'What is a father?' the answer is 'One who has a child.'[87] A cause also generally [327/1100] produces a definition. For example, when we ask, 'What is day?' the answer is 'The sun over the earth'; for we substituted a cause (that is, the sun) for the thing whose cause it is, and in this way we showed *day* with a definition.[88]

These are the differentiae of definitions that Victorinus enumerated in the book he published on definitions. Cicero omitted them because he did not think them necessary. But we have added even the things Cicero omitted so that nothing might be lacking to complete the work.

[6.29]

The nature of definition has now been presented and divided into its individual parts with respect to both matter and form—with respect to matter when Cicero said that a definition defines either corporeal or incorporeal things; with respect to form when he showed that definitions arise either by partitions or by divisions. And other things that do not pertain to the purpose of this work Cicero has omitted. Now therefore he goes on to describe what is most useful and most able to make known the whole concept of definitions, namely, the method for all definitions, whatever they are and no matter how they arise.

Common to all definitions is one formula for defining: a definition of a thing is gathered from common characteristics joined with one another and together making up one nature. For if something is added to any common and universal things, they are diminished by being bounded and are reduced to particularity, and they are confined by the boundry in which they enclose everything, as, for example, when a differentia is added to a genus and a species arises. For although in its own right a genus contains many species within its bounds, if you add a specific differentia to it, it is diminished and reduced in some way to a sort of particularity. For example, when we say 'animal', this name encloses many things; but if you add 'rational' to it and make 'rational animal', it will be less than *animal* in its unconditional form, for *rational animal* is less than *animal* taken unconditionally. Thus, the addition of a differentia confines and constrains what is greater into a sort of particularity.

Therefore, when some thing is to be defined, we take what it has in common with several other things. To this we add differentiae, and what before was common to several must directly be diminished. If as a result of this addition of a differentia it is decreased to such an extent that it becomes equal to the thing that is being defined, it will not be necessary to gather and apply other differentiae. Instead the thing that is so far decreased that it is equal to the thing being defined must be the definition. But if it is still broader than the thing being defined, we must seek another differentia, whose addition increases the number of differentiae but decreases the quantity of the common characteristics because of the addition of differentiae. We must continue in this way until (as we said) the things adopted in the definition are equal to the thing that is to be defined.

In order to make this clear by an appropriate example and not only by reasoning, let us undertake to define a very familiar thing, namely, *man*. We seek a definition of *man* in this way. We take what *man* has in common with several other things, namely, *animal*. So we say that man is an animal. This is not yet a definition, first because (as we said) a definition cannot be given by a name,[89] and then because *animal* is greater [328/1101] than *man*. So in order to diminish *animal* and make it equal to *man*, we add a differentia whose addition increases the number of things but decreases the force and breadth of the thing.[90] So I add *rational*, and I produce *rational animal*. *Rational animal*, then, is less than *animal* taken absolutely. So I say that man is a rational animal; but this is not yet equal to *man*, for there can be rational animals that are not men, as Plato believed the stars to be.[91] So I add yet another differentia to see if the definition might by any means be contracted to such an extent that it becomes equal to *man*, which is being defined. So I add *mortal*, and I say that a man is a mortal rational animal. This is equal to *man*; for whatever is a man is a mortal rational animal, and whatever is a mortal rational animal is a man. So I say that this is the definition of man, which produced some one thing proper to man and equal to him out of several characteristics, and the same point applies also to other definitions.

So definitions arise when common characteristics have been gathered together and united into one thing, although by that union the things that are common must be contracted and confined into a smaller measure, and from the conjoined common characteristics something specific and equal to the thing defined is made. Hence, as Cicero says, this is the method of definition: "when you have taken the characteristics that the thing you want to define has in common with other things, you should continue until you produce something specific that cannot be applied to anything else."[92] By these words and this opinion, then, Cicero seems to indicate concisely that a definition is what is made up of substantial common characteristics reduced to a lesser measure so that it is equal to the thing defined.

The examples he presents are of the following sort: one to define inheritance and the other to define a clan. Inheritance he defines in this way: 'Inheritance is property.' Property is common and applies to many other things that are not inheritances, such as gifts, stolen goods, and other things that are property but not inheritances. So he had to add something to *property*, namely, *which someone obtains at the death of another*, for inheritance is property that someone obtains as a result of a death. But not even this sets forth the full concept of inheritance; for this is still common, and the property of dead men can be obtained in several ways, as, for example, if someone is conquered in war and plundered. So something must be added, namely, *legally*, so that the definition is, 'Inheritance is property that someone obtains legally at the death of another,' for inheritances are received legally. Perhaps at this point it might appear that the definition can stand, but this is not at all the case. For if the property is a bequest, it cannot be called an inheritance although it is property legally received at the death of another.[93] For wills are legal, and property is legally bequeathed, too. So something by which bequests might be separated from inheritances must be added. And so we say that an inheritance is property that someone obtains legally at the death of another and that is not bequeathed. Is the definition now complete? Not at all. For what if I have ownership of a farm or some other piece of property, but someone else has the usufruct of it? At the death [329/1102] of the man to whom the usufruct belongs, the thing that I had owned legally without possessing it reverts to me; yet it cannot be an inheritance. So we must add that it is not held in another's possession, that is, that what someone obtains legally but not as a bequest at the death of another is not possessed by someone else as owner. It can be held in the possession of someone else if we own it and the usufruct belongs to the man who will have died.

So all these things conjoined into one will make a definition of inheritance in this way: 'An inheritance is property that someone obtains legally at the death of another and that is not bequeathed or held in someone else's possession.' This definition is equal to inheritance; for as an inheritance is property that someone obtains legally at the death of another and that is not bequeathed or held in someone else's possession, so any property that someone obtains legally at the death of another and that is not bequeathed or held in someone else's possession must be an inheritance.

But when Cicero has come as far in the process of defining an inheritance as saying that an inheritance is property that someone obtained legally at the death of another, he says, "Here the thing will appear separated from common characteristics, so that the definition is unfolded in this way: an inheritance is property that someone obtains legally at the death of another."[94] This passage suggests that the definition here is complete, for what is it for a definition to be unfolded and separated from common characteristics except to be complete and to lack nothing? But then, on the other hand, as if the definition were not unfolded or separated from common characteristics, Cicero adds, "But this is not yet sufficient; add: 'and this is neither bequeathed in a will nor held in someone else's possession.'"

The reason for Cicero's addition is this. He made the definition partly from associated things and partly from separated things. Thus he isolated the thing he defined from the common characteristics that it shares with other things both by means of the things he associated with it and by means of the things from which he separated it. For he said that an inheritance is property, and to this he added "which someone obtains at the death of another"; so he separated inheritance from property that someone obtains not at the death of another but by a contract with the living. He added "legally" in order to separate inheritance from property that someone obtains by force at the death of another. So by these two additions, "at death" and "legally," he produced property that is separated from other kinds of property by being legitimately acquired not by one living man from another but by a living man from a dead man. And so because he made this one separation of inheritance from other things, he says that the definition is unfolded and disjoined from common characteristics.

But since certain things that are not inheritances are incorporated in *property that someone obtains both legally and at the death of another*, the full definition of inheritance is produced by their separation. When he says that an inheritance is property and property that someone obtains at the death of another and property that is obtained legally, all these things are presented to produce the substance of inheritance. But since there were certain things in this group to which the criterion for inclusion in the group could be applied and yet that were not inheritances (such as a bequest or possession by someone else), when these things were removed, there remained *inheritance*, which can be understood as property obtained legally at the death of another.

[330/1103] *Bequest* and *possession by someone else* do not produce the substance of inheritance; indeed, unless they were taken away, they would be an obstacle to indicating the substance of inheritance. (But, then, a negation never produces the substance of anything; it only shows what it is not.) So since *bequest* and *possession by someone else* not only do not complete the substance of inheritance but even are an obstacle to it and undermine it unless they are separated and excluded from it, and since the negation of *bequest* and *possession by someone else* indicates nothing of the substance of inheritance but only shows what it is not, the preceding part (namely, *property that someone obtains legally at the death of another*) remains. It shows the substance of inheritance, and it is the definition unfolded and separated from other things. Since, however, there are certain things to which the concept of this definition can be diverted (as we said), the last part is added in order to indicate the complete distinction. Thus since *property that someone obtains legally at the death of another* shows *inheritance* and produces its substance, Cicero was right to say, "Here the thing appears separated from common characteristics, so that the definition is unfolded in this way: an inheritance is property that someone obtains legally at the death of another." Since, however, this concept could apply to many things that are included within it, he not unreasonably added, "This is not enough," and so forth, which disjoins *bequest* and and *possession by someone else* from the definition of inheritance. And let these be the things said about the first example concerning inheritance.

Cicero deals with the second example, which has to do with the definition of a clan, in a similar way. Clan kin are people who share the same name, as, for example, the clan of Scipio, the clan of Brutus, and others.[95] What if they are slaves? Can there be such a thing as a clan of slaves? Not at all. So we must add: *who are sprung from freeborn ancestors.* What if the descendants of freedmen are called by the same name as Roman citizens? Is there a clan in such a case? No, not in this case either, since the clan of the freeborn goes back to antiquity. So we add: *none of whose forefathers was enslaved.* What if someone becomes part of someone else's family as a result of adoption? Then, even if he is called by the name of the clan to which he has transferred, and although he is sprung from freeborn ancestors and from parents who were never enslaved, nevertheless since he does not remain in the family of his own clan, he cannot remain in *clan* either. So we must add: *and who have not forfeited their civil rights.*[96] In accordance with the definition of

Scaevola the pontiff,[97] Cicero says, this is probably sufficient; for Scaevola added nothing further, so that the definition of clan kin is this: clan kin are people who share the same name and are sprung from freeborn ancestors, none of whose forefathers was enslaved and where no forfeiture of civil rights has destroyed their ties with their clan. This definition, too, is made from many common characteristics flowing together into one thing and making one nature of the thing that was defined, namely, *clan*.

So this mode of definitions is acceptable in both genera of things, those which exist and those which do not (that is, corporeal and incorporeal things, for as we showed above,[98] Cicero says that what is corporeal exists and what is incorporeal does not). Finally, the mode of all definitions is that some nature arises from many common characteristics. But definitions differ from one another, because those which are called definitions strictly speaking are conjoined by common characteristics that are substantial, [331/1104] while those that are called definitions not correctly but by an improper use of the word are brought together by accidental common characteristics.

[6.30–8.32]

Because Cicero divides the kinds of definitions into partition and division, he gives differentiae for partition and division so that the reader might not be confused by a similarity between these things. First he shows that parts are one·thing and species another (for species are often called parts, but parts are never called species). Parts and species differ from one another, because a part conjoins members of a whole, but a species divides and distributes a genus. For (as we said above also[99]) parts do not receive the name of the whole that they unite; foundations or a roof cannot be said to be a house since the individual parts will not take the name of the whole unless all the parts that produce it are joined together. But species, even taken individually, receive the name of their genus, as, for example, *man* receives the name of *animal*. So, we can also recognize as a differentia between species and parts that parts are said to be parts of a whole, while species are said to be species not of a whole but of a universal thing, namely, a genus. A whole differs from a genus, because a genus is universal but a whole is not. This is proved in the following way. If what is said to be a whole, such as a house, were universal, its parts would also receive the name of that whole; but (as we have often shown) they do not receive the name of the whole, and therefore a whole is not universal. It is clear, however, that a genus is universal, because the kinds drawn from it receive its name.

Again, another differentia is this. A genus is always prior to its species, but a whole is found to be posterior to its parts, for a whole cannot be joined together unless its parts exist. Hence, if a genus is eliminated, its species are also taken away; but if a species is lost, the genus remains—and this is the contrary of what is the case for a whole and its parts. For if any one part is eliminated, the whole is necessarily lost; but if the whole that the parts joined together is dispersed, the parts that were divided from one another remain. For example, if the roofs, walls, and foundations of a house are understood as placed apart from one another, there will be no house because the conjoining of the parts is destroyed, and yet the parts will remain.

Using appropriate names, Cicero calls parts "members (as it were) of a whole," but he calls species "kinds," because the inflection of cases from the name 'species' does not seem to him sufficiently neat. Even though many men have made use of the name 'species', Cicero says, because the inflection of the word into its cases is hard (since we say 'speciei', 'specierum', and 'speciebus'), he thought (as he says) that convenience in speaking should not be neglected, and therefore he called species "forms," a word whose cases have no perceptible roughness.

Since a kind cannot exist without a genus (for nothing can exist without its source), Cicero added definitions of both genus and species and said that a genus is an idea relating to many differentiae. An idea, however, is a concept and a simple mental comprehension that is related to many things differing from one another. It is plain that this is what a genus is, and a perspicuous example will make it clear. The concept of *animal* is indeed related to many differentiae, [322/1106] namely, to *rational* and *irrational*, and also to *mortal* and *immortal*, to *capable-of-walking, creeping, flying*, and *capable-of-swimming*; it is the genus of all the things located under these differentiae. This definition of genus designates the same thing as the former definition, which is this:[100] a genus is what is predicated of many things differing in species in respect of what they are; for example, the genus *animal* is predicated of many things differing in species (namely, *man* and *horse*) in respect to what they are. For to those who ask us, 'What is a man?' or 'What is a horse?', we say, 'An animal.'

Similarly, Cicero gave this definition of a kind: a kind is an idea whose differentia can be related to a head and "fount" in the genus. And he was right to do so, for if kinds are drawn from a genus, the species must be related to the genus. So if a genus is a sort of source and "fount" of a kind, the concept of a kind must revert to its origin, namely, to the idea of the genus; for the concept of *man* (and also of *horse* and others) is related to *animal*.

Cicero calls an idea what the Greeks refer to as *ennoia* or *prolepsis*.[101] The definition of an idea is this: an idea is ingrafted and previously obtained cognizance of some form, which is in need of elucidation.[102] This definition is drawn from Plato's claim that there are certain forms, or incorporeal species, constituting substances and separate in their own right from other things by reason of their nature, such as *man* itself, and that other things become men or animals when they participate in these forms. Aristotle, however, thinks that there are no separate substances; rather he thinks that a genus or a species is a substantial similarity understood of many things differing from one another. For since a man and a horse differ in rationality and irrationality, the understood similarity between them produces a genus. The substantial similarity between horse and man is that each is a substance, each is animate, and each is sensitive;[103] these things conjoined produce *animal*, for an animal is a sensitive, animate substance. So the similarity between *man* and *horse* is *animal*, which is a genus. Again, since Plato and Cicero differ in number and accidents,[104] the similarity between them which is understood and formed by the mind (namely, humanity) is a species. So a sort of common characteristic and similarity among many things differing from one another is an idea; a genus is one sort of idea, and a kind is another.

Because every idea is an understanding of similar things and because there must be a distinction of differentiae among similar things, an idea still needs a certain elucidation and division, just as the concept of *animal* by itself is not self-sufficient; for as soon as the mind is brought to examine some animal, namely, a man or a horse, the idea of *man* is related to Cicero or Plato or some other individual person. Hence, when a genus is divided into kinds, no kind should be omitted, for excess or deficiency occurs if the divider neglects a kind. For example, if someone wants to divide *the legal system*, he must partition it into law, custom, and equity, for law, custom, and equity are individual things and yet are also subordinated under the general term 'legal system'. Furthermore, Cicero censures the ignorance of those who reckon species or kinds the same as parts; he says that ignorance confuses them, because from lack of skill and want of forethought [333/1107] they are not careful to distinguish and separate things that are very different from one another.

Because he was discussing definition, he adds another species of definition (which we mentioned above)[105] which is produced by a metaphor, not because of its appropriateness and truth but for the sake of splendor and ornament. Cicero avers that this pertains to poets and orators, whose concern is brilliance in language. He seeks an example of this sort of definition from civil law, and he says that unless necessity compels him to do otherwise, he will use only examples familiar to Trebatius. A definition by metaphor occurs, for example, in the case of Aquilius,[106] who, when he wanted to define a shore, used to say that a shore is a place where the waves play. 'Play' here is a metaphor taken from those who are in motion with some activity for the sake of play. Similarly, 'youth is the flower of a man's age'; this is taken from trees, whose flowers come before their fruit. And 'old age is the sunset of life'; this is taken from day, which ceases to be when the sun sets. These metaphors abandon their strict signification and indicate their subjects by a certain similarity, for a metaphor occurs whenever a thing that has a name has imposed on it another name taken from a similar thing on account of the similarity of that other thing. For example, motion has its proper name, and play too is called by its own name; but someone who says 'where the waves play' is making a metaphor, applying a word to the motion of waves from their similarity to the activity of play.

Ending his discussion of definitions, Cicero makes a transition to partitions. But now this is enough for a third volume; the rest we should defer to the subsequent volume.

BOOK IV

[333/1107] I cannot express, my Patricius, how much strength reflection on our friendship affords me in the course of this very difficult work, since we write with much zeal for those whom we cherish from the heart with a store of love and we supply a great abundance of material to please those who desire it. Besides, whatever has come to mind I have expressed without deliberation and even without correction, since there is no danger in saying what you think in private to a friend. And so when I think about your goodwill toward me, I find myself inclined and, I might even say, delighted to do all the work expended on this task that pleases you. But when I consider myself, I fear that I might not be able to be equal to the task you have set me and that the blame for my failure will become injurious to you, who have exhorted me to it. Hence, we must take great care for your sake, lest you, who are free from all fault in your ways, should bear the burden of some mistake of ours. I have known the bite of carping envy; I have known how readily ill will passes judgment on the most difficult matters. Therefore, I entreat you, who are zealous for this common undertaking of ours, to impose the finishing touches on our work—to curtail its excesses, [334/1107] fill its gaps, and correct its errors. I ask, in short, that you be the protector of both our work and your exhortation, especially since your performing this office (for which your dislike of the disgrace of a friend might render you more fit) will leave me free from care. But more along these lines another time. Now let us press on along the course of the work we have undertaken.

Some of the Topics inhering in the terms asked about are from the whole, some from the parts, some from a sign, and some from related things. The Topic that is from the whole and that consists in a definition Cicero investigated sufficiently in the preceding discussion. Now he begins to talk about the enumeration of parts, naturally pursuing the right path with respect to order, so that he might not only teach by example what the nature of enumeration of parts is but also show by

105

reasoning how enumeration of parts should be used in argumentations.

[8.33–8.34]

The sense of this passage is this. Some of the things that are conjoined by parts are few in number and readily understandable and comprehensible; others have parts that are many and difficult to understand. With regard to the parts that are few in number and readily grasped by the understanding, it is certainly a serious fault if any is omitted in the process of partition. But with regard to the parts that are more indefinite in number and less distinguishable from one another by observation, it is a less serious fault if the person who is making the division misses a part in his enumeration.

This is the case not only with regard to those things that consist of parts, but also often with regard to those parts that are being partitioned in the division into parts. For example, if we want to divide in a concept or idea the body of a man into its appropriate parts, we will proceed in this way: head, arms, hands, chest, abdomen, legs, and feet. Since we have taken rather large parts for our division, nothing seems to have been omitted. But if we were to press on after tiny parts, then we should also press on after eyes, lips, nose, ears, and their parts, and we should do this with regard to the whole body. In this way the partition will be more difficult since the number of parts is more indefinite. In addition, as we said, the things themselves are often composed of parts that are not easily examined, as, for example, if someone partitions the formulas for contracts and judical actions,[1] or again if we have to divide the figures of speech which the Greeks call *schemata*.[2] In these cases, if something is omitted, it will not be a fault on the part of the person doing the partitioning, because the complicated nature of the parts generally excuses the error.

But if someone divides a genus, it is ruinous if any kind is omitted since the number of kinds is limited. For since genera are always divided into contraries, there are always two or three species of a genus. (There are three species when the third species adopted is produced from a mixing together of contraries.)[3] For example, if we divide color, we should speak in this way: With regard to color, some is white, some is black, and some is intermediate. The intermediate is made up of a mixture of white and black colors, no matter what other species of color is referred to, whether purple, red, or green.[4] So if what you are dividing is of this sort and if the parts that you are adopting for the division are comprehensible by the understanding without difficulty, it will be a fault if you omit any, as, for example, if you partition guardianship. Guardianship occurs in approximately four [335/1109] ways, for a guardian is conferred in accordance with the degree of blood relationship or in accordance with the rights of a patron, or a guardian is chosen in a father's last will, or a guardian is arranged under the jurisdiction of the urban praetor.[5] (Perhaps there are more than these, but these are enough for now.)[6] In this case, then, the parts are few in number and readily comprehensible. But if you want to comprehend the formulas of contracts and judicial actions, you will not be at fault if you omit some, since there are many of these parts.

The example of parts given in connection with guardianship, however, is inappropriate, for guardianship is divided more as a genus into its kinds than as a whole into its parts.[7] For whether someone is a guardian as a result of blood relationship or in accordance with the rights of a patron or in the other ways, he has the entire rights of guardianship; but individual parts do not generally take the entire name of their whole. In order for the example to seem appropriate, we should look for parts of guardianship that are such that they can produce guardianship when they are joined together, not such that they are individually designated by the name of guardianship (and whether any of the professional jurists have set forth such parts of guardianship I do not know). The rhetorician Merobaudes[8] showed that Cicero's statement "You should use partition in such a way that you do not omit any part" should be understood as said about division, that is, about one part of the partition under consideration, for both division and distribution into parts are called partition. For in a division it is a fault to omit anything, but in a partition into parts it is not. And so Cicero gave an example with regard to guardianship which is appropriate to the partition that is division.[9]

If you do make a division (that is, a partition of kinds from a genus), the worst fault is to omit any, because since there is a limited number of kinds, the omission of any is a result of ignorance. For example, if we want to divide oratorical questions into kinds, we will say that every rhetorical question has to do either with a deed or with the nature of a deed or with the name of a deed.[10] If I distribute figures of speech and thought, however, then (as we said[11]) passing over something will not be a fault since there are many figures of speech and thought, and they differ among themselves in a variety of ways. In this case also, the parts of figures of speech and thought apparently cannot be taken as parts of a whole but must be taken as species of a genus. For every one of these figures, which are indefinite in number, is like a species of the genus *figure*. We can understand this from the books of the rhetoricians where oratorical delivery is discussed, for there are no parts of figures that join together to make figures in such a way that the individual figures cannot receive the general name 'figure.'

Someone might say in objection to us, however, "In what way are figures indefinite in number if there are species of figure? " But I will have an easy answer: when the oral delivery is altered, the figure is altered also[12] and therefore it is in the power of the speaker to make figures that the theoretician is able to recognize only with difficulty before they occur. Moreover, these figures are not constituted by any substantial differentiae but are rather set forth by accidents.[13] Hence, the case of the division of *figure* seems more like the partition of a common name into its significations than like the partition of a genus into its species; it is difficult to include all the significata of a name in a division, because new ones are frequently formed. Even this, however, is not permitted by the nature of these things, because the name and definition of the genus *figure* apply to each individual figure[14]; [336/1110] for no matter how we define *figure*, that will be the definition also of each individual figure. And this fact shows that each individual figure is a species of the universal *figure*, for a species and its genus share a name.

But what is closer to the truth is that Cicero related the partition of figures to oral delivery; figure is a part, not a species, of oral delivery, for a brilliant delivery is shot through with various and manifold figures. If someone wants to partition oral delivery into figures, then he will be cleaving a whole into its parts, not a genus into its species. Hence, from this the difference between division and partition is also clear: in a partition it sometimes occasions no fault if something is omitted in the partition, but in a division of kinds nothing can be passed over in the division without blame. And so because the things themselves are different, diverse words were imposed on these things which are distinct from one another.

[8.35–8.37]

Cicero considers designation in the right order, after the enumeration of parts. Designation occurs when an argument is taken from a sign of the thing that is in doubt. A sign is that which designates any thing. Hence, every name is a sign because it makes known the thing of which it is predicated.[15] (Aristotle named this '*symbolon*.'[16]) And an argument is taken from designation when something is inferred from the explanation of a name. An explanation of a name is called 'etymologia' in Greek and 'veriloquium' in Latin, for the Greek 'etymon' signifies 'verum' and 'logos' signifies 'oratio'. But because 'veriloquium' is less commonly used in ordinary Latin discourse, Cicero calls the explanation of a name 'designation'.

Designation is of this sort. Suppose, for example, that someone asks, "What is postliminium?"[17] With this question we are evidently not searching for a list of things that return with postliminium, for this would fall under division; that is, it would require an enumeration of all those things that come back with postliminium.[18] For example, if we were to speak in this way: a man, a ship, a pack mule, a stallion, a mare accustomed to the bridle (that is, a mare that is broken in), we are in this case enumerating things that return with postliminium.

But since the question is what the right of postliminium itself is, that can be understood from an explanation of the name. Anyone who has been captured by enemies and then returned home to his native land comes back with postliminium, for during his captivity with the enemy he loses his civil rights, but he takes up all his rights again if he returns with postliminium. So from the designation of the name the right of postliminium can be made clear in this way. For example, because 'post' always signifies that which is left behind, the word 'postliminium' signifies a sort of return, as Servius shows.[19] He explains the force of the name 'postliminium' from the adverb 'post' and asserts that the remaining part of the word is only an extension of 'post', for he takes the explanation of the name 'postliminium' from 'post' and reckons 'liminium' to be a nonessential lengthening. He illustrates the form of such names with 'meditullium' (for the first part signifies a middle, but 'tullium' signifies [337/1112] nothing), 'legitimum', and 'aeditimum' (for 'lex' in the first case and 'aedes' in the second both designate something, but 'timum' designates nothing at all). Scaevola, the son of Publius,[20] on the other hand, reckons 'postliminium' to be composed of the adverb 'post' and 'limen'. Because the man who comes back with postliminium returns afterward (post) to the same threshold (limen) that he left behind, Scaevola thinks that the name 'postliminium' is made up by the joining together of both significations. For since they went out from our thresholds, all things that are taken from us and fall to the enemy come back with postliminium if they afterward (post) return to their same threshold (limen).

The case of Mancinus can also be defended in this way.[21] The Roman people had given him over to the enemy because he had concluded an unfavorable treaty with them, but the enemy would not accept him. When Mancinus returned, it seemed that he had come back with postliminium for the following reason. If the enemy had taken him when the citizens had given him over to them, Mancinus would apparently not have returned with postliminum, even if he had in some way escaped from the enemy, since he had been stripped of all the rights of a freeman by the decision of the citizens. But since it is apparently impossible for there to be a giving over or a giving up or a giving to without acceptance, someone who was not accepted cannot be understood to have been given over either. And so Mancinus was correctly defended as having rightly come back with postliminium when he returned home to his native land, since he came into the power of the enemy (if they wanted to use it) without having been given over.

[9.38]

Since Cicero previously divided the Topic that inheres in the things asked about into four differentiae—*from the whole, from the enumeration of parts, from a sign,* and *from related things*—and since he discussed the first three differentiae in detail in the preceding passages, he now continues with the fourth Topic, that is, related things. And because the Topic from related things is broken up into many differentiae, the first of which is said to be *from conjugates,* Cicero first talks about conjugates.

Conjugates do not differ much from designation; for since designation is drawn from the force of a name and conjugation is likewise comprised of linguistic similarity, designation and conjugation seem to overlap. But the difference between them is that designation is produced by the exposition of a name, while conjugation is produced by linguistic similarity and derivation.

Since this Topic is easy both to understand and to discuss, it is enough simply to present an example of this sort. Rainwater is what has risen and collected from rain. Now 'rainwater' ('*pluvia*') and 'rain' ('*pluendo*') are conjugates, for with regard to one and the same word a different ending of the names produces a differentia. Now it is legal to exclude rainwater; that is, for example, if rainwater collects in the field of one man and flows down into the field of another man, and the rainwater rises and is about to harm the produce of the latter, the man who reckons it will make a difference to his produce may exclude the rainwater from his borders so that it does not flow down into his field. So if a stream has arisen because of rain, a question arises as to whether it may be excluded.[22] The answer, Mucius says,[23] is that, since 'rainwater' is derived from 'rain', a stream that has arisen because of rain is also rainwater and should be excluded.

[9.39]

The nature of genera and species is understood to be this: when they are gathered together and also when they are divided, it is possible to ascend by means of species and genera from individuals [338/1113] to the highest genera; again from the highest genera by means of the genera and species located below them there can be a descent to individuals. An example will make this clear. Cicero is an individual. He belongs to the species *man*; man belongs to the genus *animal*; *animal* belongs to the higher genus *animate body*; and if you ascend further, you will find the higher genus *body*. If you mount up higher, you encounter *substance* in the place of the final genus.[24]

So since there are many genera, if a genus is to be assigned for some species, Cicero says that it will not be necessary always to ascertain the highest, principal genera; rather it will also be appropriate to employ one of the intermediate genera, though these should be obtained by reason so that the genus is always higher than that of which it is predicated as a genus. Indeed, it is the worst ignorance if something that is located further down is classified as a genus, when a genus by nature is always put above its species. For that reason, it is a fault if someone says that the genus of *body* is *animate body*. So if we are to apply a genus to a species, we should apply one of those genera which are above, but it will not be necessary always to employ the ultimate genus. For example, if we want to subsume *man* under his proper genus, we subsume him not necessarily under *substance*, but rather under *body* or *animate body* or (what is most appropriate of all) under *animal*. For we should always adopt those genera that are closest to their kinds; these are the genera that are most needed for a definition.[25]

But it makes no difference in argumentations whether you choose a proximate genus or a higher one, for since an argumentation arises from something that comprises, a higher genus comprises more. Therefore, if something having to do with man is in doubt and the Topic for arguing is taken from a genus, whatever is said of *animal* will also be predicated of *man*. And so if something is also predicated of *animate body*, the same thing can be said of *man*. Therefore, just as argumentations arise from proximate genera, so they also arise from genera located further away.

With regard to all these things, however, what we should evidently bear in mind most is that something that is higher should not be subsumed under something that is lower as its genus. This is Cicero's point. As for his example, we will illuminate that in the following way. Let rainwater be water that collects from showers that have come down from the heavens. There are two species of this: one is harmful rainwater, and the other is nonharmful rainwater. There are also two species of harmful rainwater: one is rainwater that is harmful because of the work of man, and the other is rainwater that is harmful because of a fault in the land. Rainwater harmful because of the work of man is water that runs off from a particular place in such a way that it flows forth from that place and harms a neighbor, when the place in question is not naturally so constituted but the work of man prepared it for the runoff of water. Rainwater harmful because of a fault in the land is when a place is naturally so constituted that water can run off and harm a neighbor. So if someone wants to ascertain the genus of the water coming from his neighbor, which he wants to exclude lest it be harmful to him, he does not need to go all the way back to the ultimate genus and say that the genus of the water he wants to exclude is rainwater. Rather he can find the genus he seeks a little further down and say that the genus of the water he desires to exclude is harmful rainwater. And if he seeks the proximate genus, he will be able to add this, namely, *rainwater harmful because of the work of man*. For a person is urged to exclude what is hurtful because of the work of man, but no one is urged to exclude what carries with it some damage because of the form or fault of the land.

Furthermore, what we [339/1114] have claimed to be the genus of rainwater which should be excluded—*rainwater harmful because of the work of man*—must be understood with the condition that the water that ought to be excluded has many, similar individual waters subsumed under it, for only in that case can *rainwater harmful because of the work of man* be the genus of the water that ought to be excluded.[26] But if the water that ought to be excluded is not sundered into any individuals, it is itself an individual, and *rainwater harmful because of the work of man* is not its genus but its species. Should this seem somewhat obscure to anyone, then if such a person will examine the commentaries arranged in five books that we wrote on genus, species, differentia, property, and accident,[27] none of the things that now darken his vision will be able to obstruct him.

[9.40]

We have discussed the way in which a genus should be fitted to a species, and in this regard we prescribed that nothing be employed as a genus unless it is higher. Here we are adding the way in which the Topic *from a genus* can be quite opportunely used in argumentations.

For if we have made a division of a genus when something is in doubt and are able to include the thing in contention under some part of that genus, then the argument is evidently drawn from genus, in the following way. Let fraud occur when a man does one thing and pretends to do another.[28] If the species of fraud are divided, and if we are able to join to one of the species drawn from fraud the deed that we are arguing was done, then however a person regards fraud, he must judge the thing we are arguing about in the same way also. The argument is made from a genus, for what is asked about is a species, and the argument is taken from a genus (that is, if fraud occurred in this way).

This Topic is different from the Topic that is from the enumeration of parts. Although we enumerate parts (that is, kinds or species), the argument is not therefore drawn from the enumeration of parts rather than from a genus. For when we make use of the enumerating of parts for an argumentation, we say that the argument in that case is drawn from that very partition—for example, in the following way. If a place has foundations, walls, and a roof and is intended for habitation,[29] then it is a house. So by using this very partition, we have proved that it is a house. But when something is to be classified under a genus, and we divide the parts of the genus and lump the things asked about with one of the parts drawn from the genus (for example, in this way: if we are showing that Cicero is an animal, we will say, 'Every animal is either rational or irrational, but Cicero is rational; therefore, Cicero is an animal'[30]), then we are not using principally partition to construct the argument. Rather we divided the genus so that what we were trying to show could be included within one division, that is, so that the thing in doubt might be brought within the compass of the genus adopted and that belief concerning the thing in doubt might arise from the nature of the genus. And so in this way an argumentation will rightly be said to be made from a genus.[31]

Furthermore, an enumeration of parts generally produces the substance of the whole, whether it be a universal, such as a genus, or united by the conjunction of parts, such as a whole. But the division of a genus, in some part of which we are to include the thing in contention, does not produce the substance of the whole; rather it places within the genus the thing that we seek to prove. Cicero asserts that this mode of argumentation is highly effective, for the rule 'Whatever things are predicated of a genus are certainly predicated of the species' is most true and [340/1115] necessary.

But when something concerning individual things is proved on the basis of the proximate species located above them (as, for example, if we prove that Socrates is rational since he is a man, given that man is rational), it is worth asking whether we think the argument is drawn from a genus or from a kind. We might say it is drawn from a genus, but a genus is not a lowest species. And we might say it is drawn from a species, but the species always needs to show a genus located above it, and although *man* furnishes belief that Socrates is rational, Socrates is not a species of man. But what we should say is that the argument seems as if it were drawn from a genus. For belief is drawn from a genus as from something that encompasses and is broader and is predicated of the substance, and no one doubts that a species plays this role with respect to its individuals, for it both encompasses its individuals and is predicated of their substance.[32]

[10.41–10.45]

Cicero discussed the Topic *from similarity* in a clear and uncomplicated way. He divided the kinds of similarity and revealed the entire concept, and he recorded very plainly for whom arguments from similarity are most appropriate, namely, for philosophers and orators. And indeed similarity seems especially suited for persuasion, for one can easily believe that what generally occurs in one or more cases other than the case in question is also appropriate for the case in contention. Therefore, argumentations drawn from similarity are very useful for orators. Similarity among things is often to be sought after by philosophers also, since they do not use demonstration for all questions but sometimes draw conclusions from verisimilar premises in order that what they are trying to show may be more readily believed. And therefore the Topic *from similarity* is chiefly profitable to orators and philosophers, but not exclusively to them; for all the Topics are common to every sort of subject matter, but they occur more abundantly in some subjects and are more restricted in others. So when the Topics are grasped and known in advance, the questions under discussion will themselves be able to suggest to an adroit mind which Topics should be used.

All similarity is twofold; for either the similarity is gathered from several things and is called an induction (to which the Greeks give the name 'epagoge'),[33] or individual things are compared to one another with regard to similarity.

The first kind of similarity is of this sort. If honesty is required of a guardian, a partner,[34] a mandatary,[35] and a trustee,[36] it is required also of an agent.[37] For since honesty is required in several cases, and since a guardian, a partner, a mandatary, and a trustee are similar in that honesty is required of them, this same similarity ought also to apply to an agent. (A trustee is a person to whom some property is transferred so that he may transfer it back again to the person who originally transfered it to him, as, for example, if someone who fears difficult times transfers a farm to a more powerful friend so that the friend might return the farm to him when the critical time has passed. This is called transfer of property to a trustee, because trust in the restoration of the property is established.) Socrates is said to have used such gathering of similarity commonly, as we find in the writings of Plato and others of his school.

But when one individual thing is compared to another with regard to similarity, [341/1117] an argument is produced in this way. Judges for regulating boundaries are said to be those who settle boundary disputes,[38] so that if contention concerning boundaries arose, their judgment would settle the dispute. But the term 'boundaries' is used only of the borders of fields; there cannot be judges for regulating boundaries with respect to the city. In the same way, the phrase 'excluding water' is used only in the case of fields, where if rainwater collects in one place and flows down into the fields of a neighbor, it damages the pastures and produce, and therefore the magistrates established judges for excluding water.[39] So there is a question whether we can compel arbitration to exclude water in the city, and the argument is taken from a similarity. If you cannot compel arbitration to regulate boundaries in the city because boundaries pertain only to fields, then you cannot compel arbitration to exclude water in the city either, because this too evidently pertains only to fields. So here one individual thing is conjoined to another on the basis of similarity.

Cicero maintains that those things called examples are also taken from this same Topic of similarity. Crassus,[40] for instance, used examples in the case concerning Curius,[41] which was of this sort. A certain man who was dying while his wife was pregnant made the child to be born after his death his heir. And he appointed a substitute heir, named Curius, with the following condition: if within a ten-month period after his death a child were born and if that child were to die before he came of age (that is, before he reached the age at which he himself could legally make a will), the substitute heir would inherit; but if the child lived till the time at which he had come of age and could with sound judgment and in accordance with civil law dismiss the appointed heir, the secondary heir (that is, Curius) would not inherit. (This is called the appointment of a substitute for a minor.)[42] What was in question was whether the plan established in this way is valid.

Crassus presented many examples in which the substitute heir appointed in this way received the inheritance, and the recital of these
examples moved the judges.

Cicero also says that lawyers themselves frequently use examples,
for instance, when an imaginary premise or case is thought up in order
that we might understand the case at issue on the basis of the similarity
between it and the imaginary case, in the following way. Suppose a
legal expert were to claim that a contract that was not legally made has
no weight,[43] and he were to use an example of this sort: if someone has
transferred by mancipation property that cannot be so conveyed,[44] has
he therefore succeeded in transferring the property, or could he have
indebted and obligated himself? Not at all. For a contract that is not
legally made has no force. And other instances of this sort are found
among legal experts, though they are of most use for orators, among
whom it is so acceptable to construct cases that are imaginary that often
the dead are even roused up from the underworld in their speeches.
(Cicero himself does this in the speech in which he defends Caelius.)[45]
But orators, Cicero says, have a wider field; it is acceptable for them to
be expansive and digress. It does not therefore follow, however, that
similarities are less useful for the other disciplines,[46] since the same
arguments are appropriate for both important and insignificant cases.
Hence, the Topics for argument are suited to questions in a variety of
arts.

[11.46]

The recognition of similarities and the recognition of differentiae are
part of the same skill, for whoever knows what is the same will also be
able to know what is different. Every similarity establishes that something is the same, for what is the same in quality must be similar.
Indeed, all things [342/1118] are the same in substance or in quality or
in the other categories.[47] And if this is the case, the mind can also
understand this sameness in several categories. When it observes this
sameness in the categories, however, it also perceives in the same way
and in the same categories what is different. But something is the same
by means of a similar and different by means of a differentia. Therefore, the same mind and intelligence recognize both a similarity and a
differentia.

There are many species of differentiae.[48] Some are substantial (as,
for example *rational* is a substantial differentia for *man*); some are not
substantial but are nonetheless inseparable (as, for example, *black* is a

nonsubstantial but inseparable differentia for *Ethiopian* and *raven*);[49] others are changeable and unstable (as, for example, *sitting, standing,* and others of this sort, by which we differ from other men and often from ourselves as well[50]). Again, some differentiae are in one way divisive of genera and in another way constitutive of species.[51] But if an argument is drawn from constitutive differentiae, it is as if it were drawn from a genus; for as a genus encompasses a species, so differentiae encompass species.[52] Certainly, if constitutive differentiae are understood as genera, the belief they furnish will be suited to the things the differentiae constitute, for these things are (as it were) kinds of a sort for such differentiae. But if those differentiae that divide a genus into contrary parts are brought to bear on the things to be proved, then the argument seems to arise from a differentia properly speaking, because contraries are related to one another as differentiae.[53]

As for Cicero's example, it is of the following sort. In former times women were always under a guardian, and in the same way minors were subject to guardians. If there were any debts owed to women, however, they could be discharged without the authorization of the guardian; this was not the case for minors.[54] So if one asks whether a debt owed to a minor can be discharged against the will of the guardian, an argument is taken from a differentia in this way. You cannot discharge a debt you owe to a minor if the guardian does not give his authorization in the way in which you can discharge a debt owed to a woman without the authorization of her guardian, for women are always under a guardian even when they have arrived at an advanced age, but a certain number of years puts an end to guardianship for minors. Therefore, one cannot discharge a debt to a minor without the authorization of the guardian, for the standing of women differs from the standing of minors, either because minors are not always governed by a guardian and women are, or because a minor is incapable of judgment about the advantages in the conducting of his business, while women have some ability to make choices, though it is not strong, when it comes to mapping out the advantages concerning their affairs.[55]

[11.47–11.49]

With the Topic *from a differentia* divided, Cicero now discusses contraries. And to clarify the order of things a little more, I should take up a few points that Aristotle, that most learned of all men, made concerning this division, for although Cicero agrees almost entirely with Aristotle as far as content goes, he differs from him on the explanation of names. Those things which Aristotle calls 'opposites' (that is, '*anti-keimena*') Cicero names 'contraries', but more about this a little later. Now let us consider Aristotle's division.[56]

According to Aristotle, some opposites are contraries, some consist in privation [343/1119] and possession, some are relatives, and some are contradictories. Black and white are examples of contraries. Sight and blindness, nobility and baseness, are examples of possession and privation. Father and son, master and slave, are examples of relatives. And 'It is day' and 'It is not day' are examples of contradictories. There are the following sorts of differentiae among all these opposites.

Some contraries admit of an intermediate and some lack an intermediate. Those that admit of an intermediate are, for example, black and white, for there is some other color intermediate between them, such as red or gray. And it is not necessary that one or the other of these contraries always be in bodies, for it is not the case that every body is either white or black; sometimes it is intermediate between these, as when it is red or gray. Exclusive contraries are those for which no intermediate can be found, such as weightiness and lightness, for there is no intermediate for these. Those things which are light are borne upward, and those things which are weighty are borne downward, but it is not possible to find something that is a body and is borne neither upward nor downward.[57] Exclusive contraries are such that one or the other of them always inheres in that to which it can belong, as in the example presented above; for every body must be either light or weighty, because weightiness and lightness have no intermediate that can also be in bodies.

Opposites that consist in privation and possession, such as blindness and sight, differ from those contraries which include an intermediate, because they themselves have no intermediate; they also differ from exclusive contraries, since one or another of those contraries must always be in a subject (such as weightiness or lightness in a body), but privation and possession need not always be in a subject.[58] For example, when sight is the possession and blindness the privation, not everything that can see either sees or is blind; for a baby that is not yet born neither sees, since it has not yet come forth into the light, nor is it blind, since it has not yet had sight that it could have lost. The same can be said of the young of animals which are not able to see as soon as they are born, for we are not able to say that they are then either blind or seeing.[59] Finally, contraries are always observed in their own qualities, but privations are obtained from the absence of the possession and not because the privations themselves are anything, for blindness is not anything but is understood from the absence of sight.

Both privation and contrariety differ from the opposition of a relation in that neither contraries nor privatives can exist at the same time, for the same thing cannot be white and black, or seeing and blind, at one and the same time in one and the same place; but relatives cannot be separated from one another,[60] for there cannot be a son without a father, nor can there be a slave if there is not a master. Moreover, contraries and privatives do not hark back to one another, for no one says that a white thing is of a black thing or that a black thing is of a white thing, or that blindness is of sight or that sight is of blindness. Those things which are in a relation, however, exist just in the predication of the relation, as double is double of a half, a master is a master of a slave, and so on.

Contraries as well as relatives also differ from contradictories, because contradictories always consist in sentences, and truth is found in one of the contradictories and falsity in the other. Contraries, privatives, and relatives, on the other hand, are found in simple parts of sentences, and neither truth nor falsity is in them. For when I say 'white', 'black', 'blindness', 'sight', 'master', 'slave', these are simple parts of sentences and contain neither what is true nor what is untrue, [344/1120] for there is no truth or falsity in simple parts of sentences. But when I say, 'It is day,' 'It is not day,' both propositions (one presented as an affirmation and the other as a negation) are sentences.

Cicero, however, does not use names that are both appropriate and familiar, for he says that there are some contraries that are called adverse, others that are privating, others that have to do with a comparison, and others that are named 'asserting' and 'negating'. What Cicero names 'contraries' are more truly said to be opposites; those which Cicero says are adverse are better referred to by the name 'contraries', and those for which he uses the name 'comparison' should really be called 'relatives' (or 'with respect to something'). But let him use the names however he wants to, as long as the things themselves are designated in accordance with the real character of their nature. (In certain books we published,[61] however, we ourselves name them in the way attributed above to Aristotle's division.) According to Cicero, then, some contraries are adverse (such as wisdom and folly); some are privating (such as nobility and baseness); some are compared to something (such as double and single); and some are called 'negating' and consist in the contrary of those that are asserting (such as 'If this is, this is not').

Adverse contraries are those which are located within one genus and yet differ very much from one another, as, for example, white and black are very different from one another and yet are located within one genus, namely, *color*. Similarly, slowness is adverse to swiftness, and yet they are both located within *motion*; for infirmity is not opposed to swiftness, because the contrary to infirmity is good health. (Cicero omitted this in his division, but he taught it in his example.) Those things that lie in different genera and are understood to diverge widely from one another, such as wisdom and folly, are also said to be adverse contraries, for wisdom is under the genus of *the good* and folly is under the genus of *the bad*. (An example of this sort seems to pertain rather to privation, though, for folly is the privation of wisdom, and in fact folly is nothing other than the absence of wisdom and reason; but I will show the nature of those things Cicero calls "privating" later). Arguments will be taken from adverse contraries in this way. If we flee folly, we should pursue wisdom; if we long for goodness, we should flee evil. (In the same way as that mentioned above, though, evil can also be associated with privation).

According to Cicero, privating contraries are those which the Greeks call *steretika*; these have as a prefix a part of speech whose addition to a word nearly always removes something. This is the prefix 'in', for the addition of this syllable usually takes away something of the force that a thing would have had if it had not had 'in' prefixed, such as 'humanity' and 'inhumanity' (for when 'in' is prefixed, that of which it is said is deprived of humanity), or 'dignity' and 'indignity'. Cicero maintains that only those words in which the syllable 'in' is prefixed are privating contraries; indeed, according to Cicero, the nature of privating contraries is defined by the expression of this syllable. But from the Peripatetics we have received the idea that privations are expressed sometimes by simple names and sometimes with privative syllables—by simple names, as, for example, 'blindness', and with privative syllables, as, for example, 'indignity' and 'inhumanity'. According to Cicero, then, blindness will not be the privation of sight but rather an adverse contrary of it; perhaps he counted folly among the adverse contraries because it does not have the syllable 'in', by means of which he thinks privations are generated.

Arguments are drawn from privating contraries in the same way as from the adverse contraries presented above: if [345/1121] humanity is to be striven after, we should recoil from inhumanity.

According to Cicero, the contraries that are compared with something are of this sort: for example, double of a single (this is as if he were to say 'double of a half', for a single is half of a double) and father of a son. These always reciprocate, sometimes in the instrumental case and sometimes in the genitive case; for a son is the son of a father and a father is the father of a son (this is a conversion according to the genitive case), and double is double in relation with a single (this is according to the instrumental case). There are also those which reciprocate in the accusative case, such as few with respect to many and great with respect to small.

Again, negating contraries are those which are presented in affirmations and negations, as, for example, 'If this is, that is not,' or 'If it is day, it is not night.' Cicero says that this opposition is especially contrary.

From all these there is an abundance of arguments, in the way mentioned above. For we take an argument from relative contraries in this way: 'If a father exists, this cannot happen unless he has a child.' And we take an argument from negating contraries (which, as Cicero says, the Greeks call 'apophatika') in this way: 'If the sun was over the earth, it could not be night,' for the former affirmation destroys the latter negation.[62] But why he maintained these to be negating contraries is a puzzle, for negating contraries are opposed to those that are asserting and cannot exist simultaneously with them, as, for example, that it is day and that it is not day.[63] But *this* is the consequent when we speak in this way: 'If this is, that is not,' or 'If day is, night is not.' And Cicero says that affirmation and negation are especially contrary, but in this inference they cannot be contraries because the consequent is not a contrary.

[11.50–12.52]

Cicero showed above what the Topic *from associated things* is with a brief example, namely, with the example in which he said that if possession of goods were given in accordance with the will of a woman who had never forfeited her civil rights, it would follow that possession of goods in accordance with the wills of children and of slaves would also be allowed.[64] Here, however, Cicero proposes to show the very form and "substance" of this Topic, which is of this sort. The Topic *from associated things* occurs when in an argumentation we infer from what is asserted that something else is or was or will be, as, for instance, in the example he just presented. For he proved that we should not give possession of goods in accordance with the will of a woman who had never forfeited her civil rights because if this were asserted, it would also be the case that possession of goods in accordance with the wills of children and slaves would be allowed. Things called associated are such that they are generally found in the vicinity of the thing asked about, but it is nevertheless not necessary that they always adhere to that thing. The form of this Topic is such that it can also admit of this definition: the Topic *from associated things* occurs when, from things that are near to the things asked about, we show that the thing asked about was or is or will be.

This Topic is most indispensable to conjectural cases.[65] When the question concerning a deed is whether the deed in doubt was done, we generally consider what was or is or will be the case, for there are many things that [346/1123] are inferred as associated with a thing in the course of various times. Therefore, in connection with conjectural cases we ask what happened before the deed, what happened simultaneous with the deed, and what happened after the deed. These things are discussed only by orators; jurists do not share with the rhetorical discipline in legal actions of this sort, for a legal expert gives an opinion only about the quality of a deed and not also about the truth concerning that deed. Hence, when a question about a deed was brought to the legal expert Gallus, he used to say, "This is not a matter for us," and he used to send those consulting him to Cicero instead, that is, to a rhetorician. Here Cicero wittily added a jest for Trebatius, saying, "Although•this Topic from associated things is most useful for conjectural cases and is of no aid to the art of jurisprudence, you will nonetheless permit me," he says, "not to omit any part of the work I have undertaken lest I appear to be a slave only to your favor if I include in this book nothing but examples pertaining to your art."

The Topic *from associated things* (which extends only to orators and not to jurists or philosophers either) must be discussed with respect to three different times, for if we ask about a deed, we must inquire what occurred before it, simultaneous with it, or after it. [Something occurred] before a thing, in this way: preparations (for it is likely that someone did something, given that he made preparations before the thing that was done), conversations (for it could be the case that a man who was frequently in conversation with a woman loved her), place (as when someone chooses a place that is opportune for doing something), the arranging of a banquet (for example, if we argue that someone did something in a banquet arranged before the deed and we make conjectures about the deed from the fact that the banquet was arranged). All of these are examples of things that are before the thing in question. [Something occurred] simultaneous with a thing, in this way: the noise of footsteps (for example, if someone is accused of having walked in some place, from the noise of footsteps we will prove that he is found out; or if an adulterer is accused of having been in a bedroom, we will indicate this from the shadow of his body). These things, which are observed together with the things in question, are understood to be associated with those things. [Something occurred] after a thing: if pallor, blushing, or faltering has betrayed any stains on the conscience; an extinguished fire (for example, if we want to show that something was done secretly because the fire was extinguished so that the deed might be more safely committed with the shadows preventing knowledge of it; similarly, a bloody sword shows that a crime was committed). All these which are after a thing are understood to be associated with a deed.

'Before a thing', 'simultaneous with a thing', and 'after a thing' are always to be understood as having to do with time, and not in the manner of antecedents and consequents. For in the case of antecedents and consequents we consider the logical character of their nature; indeed, they are all simultaneous, for if the antecedent is asserted, the consequent immediately is. For example, if you assert *man*, *animal* must immediately be; we cannot say that *man* is before with respect to time or that *animal* follows after, as something is prepared before with respect to time and brought to pass afterward. And so in the earlier case they are called 'before a thing', 'simultaneous with a thing', and 'after a thing', but in this latter case they are called 'antecedents and consequents', because in this latter case a thing is said to be antecedent not with respect to time but with respect to the priority of its nature which simultaneously draws something with it, and what follows the antecedent is said to be a consequent. But those which are considered associated with respect to the prior or subsequent character of time got the designation 'before a thing, simultaneous with a thing, and after a thing' for that reason.

[12.53]

[347/1124] With the Topic *from associated things* explained, Cicero now discusses antecedents, consequents, and incompatibles. Although this is one Topic, it is divided into three "parts." Cicero is silent about the designation for this Topic, but it seems to me that the whole Topic should be called 'conditional'. When the nature of this Topic has become perfectly clear, this name which we have proposed will also more plainly appear correctly imposed on the Topic.

First we should provide a definition of the individual parts of the Topic. An antecedent is such that when it has been asserted, something else must follow. Similarly, a consequent of something is what must be if the thing whose consequent it is has definitely gone before. An incompatible is that which cannot exist simultaneously with the thing with which it is said to be incompatible.

As we said before, the Topic *from antecedents, consequents, and incompatibles* is one Topic; here I will show briefly the way in which it is one. First of all, when there was a question how the Topic *from consequents, antecedents, and incompatibles* is one Topic, we said that this Topic appears to be one because the same intellectual faculties and understanding provide both things that agree with one another and things that are discordant with one another. With regard to things that agree with one another, there are two parts: one is the antecedent, and the other is the consequent. They must agree with one another in a succession of nature since when one precedes, the other follows. With regard to incompatibles, there are two parts and yet only one designation for them both, for they are both given the name 'incompatible', although there is no one who does not recognize that things that are incompatible and discordant with one another are two. But they differ from antecedents and consequents in virtue of the fact that there are two names for antecedents and consequents, even though there is one agreement between them both. So the same intellectual faculties and the same reasoning of the understanding understand what precedes and what follows; for it cannot happen that we understand something to be an antecedent unless at the same time we consider what the consequent is, and in the same way we cannot understand something to be a consequent unless it is clear what the antecedent is. Similarly, no one can understand something to be an incompatible unless he understands what it is incompatible with. So since the same reason can perceive similars and dissimilars, and since there is a certain agreement and harmony as a result of a similarity of natures in the case of antecedents and consequents, and discord and dissimilarity in the case of incompatibles, one and the same reason must see both the nature of antecedents and consequents and the nature of incompatibles. And what is grasped by one understanding is also one Topic.

But here there was an objection: why then did Cicero mention above one Topic *from similarity* and another *from a contrary*, for according to the point just made there should have been one Topic *from similars and contraries* since one understanding considers similarity and contrariety. But there was this reply: because antecedents and consequents are not said to agree with one another in the same way as the things called similars agree with one another. In the case of similars, we find only one quality, and the things are said to be similar in accordance with that same quality; but in the case of antecedents and consequents, there is a certain agreement of natures and not a similarity of quality. Also, those things that are similars can exist without one another, but antecedents and consequents cannot exist without one another. For that reason antecedents and consequents do not seem to have a nature in common with similarity. But this reasoning does not seem very apt, nor does it explain what it is attempting to show.[66]

It [348/1125] is definitely most solidly established that the treatment of this Topic is always suited to conditional propositions. A conditional proposition is one that maintains with a condition that something is if something else has been (as, for example, when we say, 'If it is day, it is light'). This inference of things is easily turned into an incompatibility; for if a negation is inserted among the things that are consequents, the consequents are turned into incompatibles, in the following way. 'If it is day, it is light'; incompatibles arise in this way: 'If it is day, it is not light,' for that it is day and that it is not light are incompatible with one another. This incompatibility consists in a condition; for we say, 'If it is day, it is not light,' because the contrary of day is night and a consequent of night is that it is not light, and therefore that it is day and that it is not light are incompatible with one another.

That this incompatibility consists in a condition is proved from the fact that if the condition is lacking, there is no incompatibility, in the following way. 'It is day'; 'It is not light.' Both of these disjoined propositions carry their own meanings, and they are not understood to have anything common to them both; so taken with respect to different times, they are true, and they are not incompatible. Just as in the propositions 'It is day,' 'It is light,' there is no inference because the condition that makes a connected proposition is lacking and instead each proposition is disjoined from the other and contains its own meaning, so in the same way in the propositions that were asserted— 'It is day,' 'It is not light'—there is no incompatibility since each is separate from the other and keeps its own meaning. But if a condition is interposed between these propositions, the meanings of the former pair of propositions are united in such a way that they become a consequence, and the meanings of the latter pair are united in such a way that they become incompatibles, in the following way. 'If it is day, it is light'; this is a single consequence produced from two propositions by means of a mediating condition. But if it is produced in this way, 'If it is day, it is not light,' it is incompatible; for when the consequent has been negated, it necessarily becomes incompatible.

Furthermore, an argument that arises from antecedents and consequents is produced from the parts of one connected proposition, for one part of a connected conditional proposition is the antecedent and the other is the consequent. If an argument arises from incompatibles, such an argument will again be properly produced from the members of one proposition. Therefore, there cannot be one proposition from the propositions 'It is day' and 'It is light' unless they are united by a condition in such a way that one is the antecedent and the other is the consequent; hence in these cases an argument cannot be from an antecedent and from a consequent, since these are two. Furthermore, there cannot be one proposition from the propositions 'It is day' and 'It is not light' unless by the adding of a condition they are somehow drawn into the meaning of one proposition whose parts are incompatible; for just as in a connected proposition in which one part is the antecedent and the other the consequent, so in an incompatible proposition each part of the proposition is incompatible and discordant with the other.

Furthermore, an incompatible proposition has a part contrary to the connected proposition; for as in a connected proposition the antecedent draws the consequent with it, so in an incompatible proposition the parts cannot exist at the same time. Contrary differentiae, however, are customarily placed under the same genus. So if a connected proposition consists in a condition, an incompatible proposition also consists in a condition. But if a condition produced both the consequence and the incompatibility of propositions, this Topic is undoubtedly correctly called conditional and is one Topic located in a condition but divided into parts, namely, into [349/1126] antecedent, consequent, and incompatible; for one part of a connected proposition is the antecedent and the other is the consequent, and each part of an incompatible proposition is incompatible and discordant with the other. So the parts of a connected proposition are the antecedent and the consequent, and the parts of an incompatible proposition are the incompatibles. The fact that "It is day' and 'It is light' agree with one another in a certain nature and that 'It is day' and 'It is not light' "disagree" and are at variance with one another should not trouble our understanding. For a proposition is connected if something follows when something else has gone before. Similarly, a proposition is an incompatible if something is inferred falsely when something else is asserted; but this could not happen unless the force of a condition brought it about. Therefore, I think it has been clearly shown that this Topic is rightly called conditional and that Cicero rightly maintains it to be one Topic. Later I will discuss how an argument arises from antecedents, consequents, and incompatibles.

Since it belongs to no art save to dialectic alone, which professes the greatest expertise in this matter, to consider what follows from a thing or what is incompatible with a thing, Cicero says that this Topic belongs altogether to dialecticians.

Furthermore, this Topic is very different from associated things. First of all, associated things can reveal one another and make one another known, but they cannot bring about or complete the nature of one another,[67] as, for example, the noise of footsteps can herald and indicate walking, but it cannot produce walking. For the noise of footsteps does not produce the walking, nor is walking necessarily the cause of the noise of footsteps.[68] On the contrary, a person often walks in such a way that no noise of footsteps is heard, and often without a person's changing his location he can move his feet and make a noise without walking. Associated things are therefore not always found together; often arguments from associated things for the proposed term that we are trying to prove fail, because the things themselves also sometimes apparently fail to be associated. But antecedents, consequents, and incompatibles are never wanting, for everything whatever that exists among things has something that naturally follows or precedes it, and there is also something with which it is discordant as a result of a difference in their natures. For example, *animal* follows from *man* but precedes *substance*, for we say, 'If it is a man, it is an animal,' but *animal* precedes *substance* when we maintain, 'If it is an animal, if is a substance.' And *animal* is incompatible with *a dead thing* when we declare, 'If it is an animal, it is not a dead thing.'

Furthermore, associated things are distributed across times; that is, they are before a thing, simultaneous with a thing, and after a thing. But it makes no difference in what way antecedents, consequents, and incompatibles occur in time; for often those that are prior in time follow and those that are later in time precede, and those that are simultaneous in time sometimes precede and sometimes follow (as we have also often said above[69]).

In addition, antecedents and consequents cannot leave one another, and incompatibles cannot adhere to one another; they are necessarily either connected or disconnected with one another. But associated things have no necessity, because they can be both joined to one another and separated from one another.

In virtue of this, an exceedingly difficult question arises, for to those without much insight this Topic does not seem at all different from the Topics that are said to be from a genus, from a species, or from contraries. [350/1127] For a genus always follows from a species, a species always precedes a genus,[70] and contraries cannot exist simultaneously.

This difficulty should be resolved in the following way. First of all, not every consequent is a genus, nor is every antecedent a species;[71] incompatibles are not themselves contraries but rather the consequents of contraries (as we showed in our exposition of the Topics presented by Cicero[72]). Next, when an argument arises from a genus, the genus itself is taken in the argument, and the same thing holds for species, when we want to prove something on the basis of a species. But when we are trying to show something on the basis of antecedents and consequents, we use what preceded in the conditional proposition as a premise in our argument, even if it was not a genus. Similarly, if an argument arises from a consequent, the argument is drawn from the consequent part of the conditional proposition, even if it is not a species.[73] For example, when we speak in this way, 'If fire is, a light thing is,' *fire* precedes and *lightness* follows; but neither of these is a genus or a species with respect to the other.[74] I make the minor premise in this way: 'But fire is.' So here I have made what preceded the minor premise, and from this I prove the conclusion: 'Therefore, a light thing is.' If, however, the minor premise is 'But a light thing is not,' then I have made what followed the minor premise. And so I conclude and prove, 'Therefore, fire is not.'

So you see that we are here talking about the antecedents and consequents that are located in a conditional proposition and are understood either to precede or to follow. But when an argument arises from a genus, we intend to prove something about a species;[75] we take the genus in the minor premise not as something preceding but as something containing, so that whatever is observed to be in the genus should also be applied to the species, for as long as a genus persists, it does not leave its species. And when we take an argument from species, it is a genus about which there is some question, and we exert ourselves in order that what we are trying to show about the genus might be more readily known on the basis of the species. For example, when the wife Fabia was left a legacy on the condition that she be materfamilias, then since she had not come under the authority of her husband, we evidently correctly disjoin *wife* (which is the genus of *materfamilias*) from *the legacy*, on the basis of *coming under the authority of husband* (which is a species of *wife*). And we attach *the legacy* to the species, namely, to *materfamilias*.[76]

Whether the Topic *from antecedents and consequents* might be seen as wholly superfluous seems to need deeper investigation, however, because in whatever way arguments are constructed on the basis of this Topic, they do not diverge from the other Topics that we described above.[77] For any argument that is drawn from antecedents and consequents is considered to be drawn from a whole, from parts, from conjugates, or from one of the rest, in the following way. If equity established for the sake of preserving what is one's own is useful, civil law is useful; but what precedes is the case; therefore what follows is also useful. This is an argument from definition, namely, from taking the antecedent as minor premise. But if I speak in this way: 'But civil law is not useful; therefore the equity established for the sake of preserving what is one's own is not useful,' then the argument here is taken from the Topic of definition by taking the consequent as minor premise. Similarly from the enumeration of parts: 'If [351/1128] someone is not free as a result of being enrolled in the census or in the other ways, he is not free; but he is enrolled in the census (or in the other ways), and therefore he is free'; 'but he is not free, and therefore he was not liberated by being enrolled in the census or in the other ways.'

We should notice, however, what the force of each argument is and how it is expressed. There are arguments that are suited to categorical syllogisms, as, for example, from definition in this way: 'Civil law is equity established, etc.; but this is useful; therefore, civil law is useful.' Similarly, from parts: 'A man who was not liberated by being enrolled in the census, by the manumission staff, or by a will, has not been freed from slavery; but Stichus was not liberated by a will, by being enrolled in the census, or by the manumission staff; therefore, Stichus is not free.' And in the same way in other cases.

Now everything that can be expressed by means of a categorical syllogism can also be said by means of a conditional syllogism, for every predicative proposition can be turned into a conditional, in the following way. 'Every man is an animal' is predicative; this is easily turned into conditional in this way: 'If it is a man, it is an animal.' But it is not the case that every conditional proposition can be turned into a predicative proposition, as, for example, in this case: 'If she has borne a child, she has lain with a man,' for no one can say that having borne a child is that thing which is lying with a man, in the way that we say a man is that thing which is an animal.

For there is a different idea in those propositions which are expressed in this way: 'She who has borne a child has lain with a man,' for this is similar to the proposition that says, 'If she has borne a child, she has lain with a man.' But the predicative proposition says that the subject is that thing that is the predicate, while a conditional proposition maintains that if the antecedent is, then the consequent necessarily follows. And so when a predicative proposition is turned into a conditional, it is indisputably rendered a different proposition.[78] For when we say 'Every man is an animal,' we assert that man himself is animal; but when we say 'If a man is, an animal is,' this does not mean that he who is a man is an animal, but rather than when we assert that a man is, it follows that an animal is.

Therefore, whether a conditional syllogism, which is formulated in terms of preceding and following, arises by means of a definition, enumeration of parts, conjugation, or in any other way. it nevertheless has its own form specific to it and is conditional (that is, it uses a condition, which is specific to it), so that in a certain way a conditional syllogism seems to have the other arguments subordinated to its own "nature." Hence, when an argument is from a definition, if the syllogism was constructed with a categorical form, the argument is said to be drawn from definition. If, however, the argumentation was made with a hypothesis, the syllogism is conditional, and the minor premise determines whether it is an argument produced from an antecedent or from a consequent. So even if a conditional argument might be obtained by means of the other Topics, it nevertheless has a certain form of its own since it is constructed in terms of preceding and following. For when definition, parts, conjugation, and the rest enter into a condition, they become "things" in their own right and not Topics;[79] if there is a condition, the argument will appear to have been completed by those things. And if a condition has united a proposition, those things which are included in the propositions are parts of a sort of the argument, but the Topic consists in the condition.

The point of these remarks is not that [352/1130] this conditional Topic could not be used without one of the Topics mentioned above, for in fact this Topic can often be found apart from them, as when we say, 'If it is a man, it is a risible thing,' or 'If it is a raven, it is a black thing,' for here the argument does not contain a definition, parts, or any of the other Topics enumerated above.[80] Moreover, in individual cases it is easy to provide the differentiae separating these Topics. The Topic *from the whole* is drawn from substance, and the Topic *from parts* is drawn from the composition of a thing, for we cannot find an argument of this sort consisting in simple terms. The Topic *from a sign* is drawn from explanation; *from conjugates*, from one of a group that is sundered from one and the same thing; *from a genus*, from something that contains; *from a kind*, from something that is contained; *from a differentia*, from something that diverges; *from similars*, from one and the same quality; *from contraries*, from the fact that contraries are very different from one another; *from efficient causes*, *from effects*, from things that have received the force of another's efficient power; *from associated things*, from the nearness of natures; and *from a comparison of greater, equal, or lesser things*, from a relation to an equal or unequal quantity. But the Topic *from antecedents* is of a very different kind, for it consists in the fact that if a proposed thing is, then something else (which is called 'the consequent') certainly is. And the idea of this Topic consists in the fact that when one thing precedes, something else follows. The idea of incompatibles, however, consists not only in the fact that they cannot precede or follow, but also in the fact that they cannot exist simultaneously; this undoubtedly consists in a condition.

Now that these things have been explained, since Cicero clearly described the character of this Topic (as best he could in passing), he here adds the way in which it is appropriate to use the Topic. And since this part of his *Topica* must be explained very carefully, I will make an end of the fourth book and present the rest in the fifth book.

BOOK V

[352/1129] We have analyzed all hypothetical syllogisms fully and copiously, Patricius, most skilled of rhetoricians, in the books we wrote on the basic elements of hypothetical syllogisms;[1] the reader who has leisure for reading these books will receive entire and complete instruction from them. But because we have undertaken to expound Cicero's *Topica* here and because Cicero in this work mentions some of the modes of hypothetical syllogisms, I think I should briefly say something about the seven conditional syllogisms[2] and about their nature [353/1129] and the arrangement of their propositions, so that when these things have been digested and have in due course become known, Cicero's examples may be more readily understood.

Everything that is in doubt in a question will be proved either by verisimilar or by necessary arguments. Every argument will either fall into the arrangement of a syllogism or take its force from a syllogism. And every syllogism consists of propositions.

All propositions are either simple or composite. Simple propositions are those which are made up of simple parts of an expression. Simple parts of an expression—a name and a verb—unite a noncomposite proposition, as when we say, 'Day has come' (*dies est*), or 'The day is vernal,' or 'The day is fair'; for here the name and the verb bind together the whole force of the proposition.

Every simple proposition consists of a subject and a predicate; a subject is what a predicate is said of, and a predicate is what is said of a subject. Sometimes a verb is joined to a predicated name, and sometimes it is itself predicated. It is joined to a predicated name in the proposition 'The day is fair,' for 'day' is the subject, 'fair' is the predicate, and the verb 'is' is joined to 'fair', which we said is predicated. But if the proposition is such that it consists only in a name and a verb, as when we say, 'Day has come,' then 'day' is the subject and the verb 'has come' is undoubtedly predicated. But there is no proposition without a verb, for every proposition is either true or false; but unless

132

one adds some verb on the basis of which something is said to be or not to be, no truth or falsity is found in propositions.

Propositions also often consist of entire expressions, as, for example, if we say, 'Crossing over into Africa is advantageous for the Romans'; for here the subject is 'crossing over into Africa', 'advantageous for the Romans' is the predicate, and 'is' is conjoined to the predicate.

All propositions of this sort are said to be predicative. (They are called 'predicative' because they predicate one thing of another.) And all syllogisms that arise from these propositions are called predicative in accordance with the form of the statements in them.

From these predicative propositions composite propositions come into being. Some composite propositions are bound together by a copulative conjunction, such as, 'It is day, and it is light.' Others arise by means of a condition, and these are also called conditional statements; these are made into an inference and a condition by the insertion of a conjunction among their parts.[3] For suppose there are two predicative propositions, one that says, 'It is an animal,' and the other that asserts, 'It is a man.' If a conjunction is interposed among these propositions, it will produce this: 'If it is a man, it is an animal.' And so you see that the conjunction has united the two predicative propositions into one condition. Hence, all these propositions are called hypothetical or conditional, and syllogisms named 'hypothetical' or 'conditional' come into being from these propositions.

Every hypothetical proposition arises either by means of a connection or by means of a disjunction—by means of a connection in this way, 'If it is day, it is light'; and by means of a disjunction thus, 'Either it is day or it is night.' Some of those arising by means of a connection are united out of two affirmatives, such as, 'If it is day, it is light,' for both 'It is day' and 'It is light' affirm something. Others are united out of two negatives, such as, 'If it is not light, it is not day,' for [354/1131] that it is not light and that it is not day are each a negation. Others are conjoined out of an affirmative and a negative, such as, 'If it is day, it is not night.' And still others are united out of a negative and an affirmative, such as, 'If it is not day, it is night.' All these propositions are nonetheless formulated with a connection, for an affirmation follows from an affirmation, or a negation follows from a negation and is connected to it, or a negation follows from an affirmation, or an affirmation follows from a negation.

It is clear that incompatibles are produced from connected propositions; for if a mediating negation is inserted among affirmations when one affirmation follows from another, it produces incompatibility in the following way.[4] 'If it is day, it is light'—here an affirmation follows from an affirmation. But when I say, 'If it is day, it is not light,' with the inserted negation the parts of the connected proposition are incompatible with one another. Similarly, if a negative adverb is removed from the latter part of the proposition when a negation follows from a negation, incompatibles arise in the following way. 'If it is not an animal, it is not a man'—this is a connected proposition made up of two negative propositions. But if the negative adverb is withdrawn from the latter part, 'It is not a man,' it will become, 'If it is not an animal, it is a man'; this is incompatible. If an affirmation follows from a negation, incompatibles arise either when a negation is joined to the latter part of the proposition or when a negation is taken away from the former part, in the following way. 'If it is not day, it is night'—here an affirmation follows from a negation. When a negation is united to the latter part, 'It is night,' so that the proposition becomes 'If it is not day, it is not night,' or when it is taken away from the former part so that the proposition becomes 'If it is day, it is night,' in either case the proposition necessarily becomes an incompatible. If a negation follows from an affirmation and a negative adverb is subtracted from the latter part, the parts of the connected proposition fall into incompatibility in the following way. 'If he is awake, he is not snoring'—here a negation follows from an affirmation. But if a negation is removed from the latter part (namely, from 'He is not snoring'), the proposition will become, 'If he is awake, he is snoring,' and it will be incompatible.

With regard to connected and disjoined propositions, we must understand that the force both of the question and of the argument is included in their parts. For suppose that there is some doubt whether it is light and we are to prove that it is light from the fact that it is day. So if there is a proposition of this sort, 'If it is day, it is light,' the part of the whole proposition that is the consequent (namely, 'It is light') pertains to the question, for the question is whether it is light, but the former part of the proposition (namely, 'It is day') contains the force of the argument, for we will prove that it is light from the fact that it is day. And the same point applies to the rest, whether they are connected or disjoined.

With regard to all these, since a syllogism and an argumentation are adapted in such a way as to demonstrate one or another part of a question and since every question is something in doubt, syllogisms, which are adapted to the uncertainty in a question, should be evident and free from doubt. In order to be so, syllogisms must consist of propositions that are clear, manifest, and obviously true. But some propositions are known per se, and others will need some proofs. Now when a statement has been asserted, every syllogism has a part of that statement as its minor premise in order to conclude what is in the question.[5] For example, 'If it is day, it is light'—in order to demonstrate that it is light, I will take as a minor premise one part of this proposition, [355/1132] and I will say, 'But it is day'; then I will conclude what is in the question, 'Therefore, it is light.' So since we should use an entire statement in the major premise and a part of that statement in the minor premise in order to obtain the conclusion of a syllogism, the propositions that we use must be free from doubt if they are to provide belief for things that are uncertain.

But since propositions are sometimes known per se and evident and sometimes are found in need of proof, a minor premise will also sometimes be known per se to be true and sometimes stand in need of support for proof. Hence, if both the major and the minor premises need to be demonstrated, there will be a five-part syllogism (as Cicero in fact produced in his Rhetorics[6]) consisting of the major premise and its proof, the minor premise and its proof, and the conclusion. But if neither the major nor the minor premise needs proof, the syllogism will be three-part, consisting of the major premise, the minor premise, and the conclusion. And if one or the other of the premises needs to be demonstrated, the syllogism will be four-part, consisting of the major premise, the minor premise, the proof of one of them, and the conclusion. The proof of the conclusion itself, however, is produced by the preceding major and minor premises.

Since these things are so and since all hypothetical propositions are divided into those that are connected and those that are disjoined, with regard to connected propositions we say that the antecedent is one thing and the consequent is another. We call the same thing the consequent and what is connected, as in this proposition 'If it is day, it is light,' 'it is day' precedes and 'it is light' is annexed. The same point, however, does not apply with regard to disjoined propositions, because they are in no way said to be connected since the propositions asserted cannot hold simultaneously.[7] Rather the antecedent and the consequent are determined in this way: what is asserted first is rightly called the antecedent and what is asserted second is rightly said to be the consequent.

The first and second modes of hypothetical syllogisms arise from propositions that are connected. When a negation is added to a connected proposition composed of two affirmations and the whole proposition is negated, the third mode arises.[8] The fourth and fifth modes arise from disjoined propositions with the minor premise made in different ways. And the sixth and seventh modes arise when the disjoined propositions are each constructed with a negation.[9] These are the seven hypothetical conclusions that Cicero mentions in his *Topica*, and the arrangement of each of these modes and examples for them should be appended next.

The first mode occurs when there is a connected proposition whose antecedent has been taken as a minor premise and we want to show that what follows must be as it is expressed in the connection. In this case, if we take as the minor premise that part of the proposition which is connected and which follows, absolutely no syllogism will arise. An example of this is the following. 'If it is day, it is light.' If we are showing that it is light, we must take as the minor premise that it is day, in this way, 'But it is day'; it therefore necessarily follows that it is light. But if we take as a minor premise that it is light and speak in this way, 'But it is light,' that it is day is not necessary; therefore no necessity with regard to the conclusion occurs. But where there is no necessity, no syllogism can be understood either.[10] So the first mode is in this form:

If it is day, it is light.
But it is day.
Therefore, it is light.

Cases are found, nevertheless, in which the minor premise is acceptable in either way, with either the antecedent or the consequent taken as the minor premise, as, for example, in the case of *man* and *risible*:

If it is a man, it is a risible thing.
But it is a man.
Therefore, it is a risible thing [356/1133].

But it is a risible thing.
Therefore, it is a man.

The reason for these cases is that *man* and *risible* are equal terms, and therefore when one is asserted the other must follow. But because this is not so in all cases, we say that it is not a general rule that when the latter part is taken as the minor premise, the part that precedes is proved.[11]

The second mode occurs when we have taken the latter and consequent part as the minor premise and the antecedent is taken away, in the following way. 'If it is day, it is light.' Here if we take as a minor premise that it is not light, we take the minor premise in a way contrary to the way in which it is expressed in the proposition, saying, 'But it is not light.' It then follows in this case that it is not day. But if we deny that it is day, that is, if we express the antecedent in the minor premise in a way contrary to the way in which it is asserted in the proposition, what is connected is not removed. For example, if we say, 'But it is not day,' it does not then follow that it is not light; for it is possible that it is not day and that it is nevertheless light. So the form of the second mode is of this sort:

If it is day, it is light.
But it is not light.
Therefore, it is not day.

Hence, the first mode takes the antecedent as the minor premise in order to prove what is connected, but it cannot take what is connected as the minor premise in order to prove the antecedent. The second mode, in the contrary way, takes the consequent as the minor premise in order to subvert the antecedent, but it cannot in the contrary way take the antecedent as the minor premise in order to take away what is connected.[12]

The third mode occurs when a negation is inserted among the parts of a connected proposition composed of two affirmations and the negation itself is negated. (This proposition is called 'hyperapophatike' in Greek.)[13] For example, if a negation is interposed among the parts of the proposition that we presented above—'If it is day, it is light'—it will become 'If it is day, it is not light.'[14] If we negate it further, it will be this, 'It is not the case that if it is day, it is not light'; the meaning of this proposition is that if it is day, it is not possible that it is not light.[15] This proposition is called 'supernegative'; all propositions in which a negation is prefixed to a negation are supernegative, such as 'It is not the case that it is not day,' and also 'It is not the case that the Ausonians are not the Trojan people sent as colonists.'[16]

In this case, if we assert in the minor premise the former part of this supernegative proposition, namely, that it is day, it also follows that it is light, in the following way:

It is not the case that if it is day, it is not light.
But it is day.
Therefore, it is light.

This mode differs a great deal from the previous modes, because in the mode that arises from antecedents, the antecedent is asserted in order to support the consequent, and in the mode that arises from consequences, the consequent is destroyed in order to remove the antecedent; but in this mode neither of these things occurs. The antecedent is not asserted to corroborate the consequent, nor is the consequent destroyed in order to subvert the antecedent; rather the antecedent is asserted in order to destroy the consequent.[17]

Moreover, this mode contains parts of a proposition which are incompatible with each other; that it is not light is in fact opposite to and incompatible with 'if it is day'. But the proposition is made true because the incompatibility of the consequent that is produced by the mediating negation is destroyed by the other negation, and the whole proposition regains the force of an affirmation.[18] For because it is understood to follow and to be true that if it is day, it is light, it is incompatible and [357/1134] false that if it is day, it is not light. When this is itself in turn negated, it is true, in this way: 'It is not the case that if it is day, it is not light.' And it becomes similar to the affirmation 'If it is day, it is light,' because a double negation produces an affirmation.

Similarly, arguments arise from incompatible parts of a proposition if they are made up of two negations, a negation and an affirmation, or an affirmation and a negation. (We have said above how incompatibles might arise from connected propositions of this sort.)[19] An argument from an incompatible arises from a proposition that is made up of two negatives in the following way. Suppose the proposition is 'If it is not light, it is not day.' Let an incompatible arise in this way: 'If it is not light, it is day'; let us add a negation to this so that it becomes true, in this way:

It is not the case that if it is not light, it is day;
but it is not light;
therefore, it is not day.

Again, suppose there is this proposition composed of a negation and an affirmation: 'If it is not day, it is night.' Let a negation be added to the latter part of this, so that it becomes this: 'If it is not day, it is not night'; it becomes an incompatible. Let this proposition then be denied so that it is true: 'It is not the case that if it is not day, it is not night.' We then take as a minor premise, 'But it is not day'; we conclude, 'Therefore, it is night.'

Again, if a negation is subtracted from the former part of a proposition which is made up of a negative and an affirmative and which says 'If it is not day, it is night,' an incompatible will arise in this way: 'If it is day, it is night.'[20] Let a negation be put next to this proposition so that it can be true, in the following way: 'It is not the case that if it is day, it is night.' And let us take as the minor premise 'But it is day.' We conclude: 'Therefore, it is not night.'

If a proposition is made up of an affirmation and a negation, such as this, 'If he is awake, he is not snoring,' a negation is removed from the latter part of this proposition so that it becomes this, 'If he is awake, he is snoring.' But this is an incompatible. Let the whole proposition in turn be negated so that it becomes true in the following way: 'It is not the case that if he is awake, he is snoring.' We take as the minor premise 'But he is awake'; we must conclude, 'Therefore, he is not snoring.'

These four conclusions from incompatibles are understood to be subsumed under the third mode. Cicero mentioned three of these conclusions. One he taught by giving a rule for it (namely, the conclusion that a proposition made up of two affirmatives produces),[21] and two he taught by giving examples of them (namely, the conclusion that arises from a proposition united out of two negations,[22] and the conclusion that is generated from a connected proposition consisting of an affirmation and a negation[23]). He passed over the remaining conclusion because in virtue of its similarity to these conclusions it too seemed to be subsumed under the third mode of conclusion.

The fourth mode consists in a disjunction in the following way:

Either it is day or it is night;
but it is day;
therefore, it is not night.

The reasoning of the fourth mode is this: when a disjunctive statement has been asserted, the former part of that statement is taken affirmatively in the minor premise, in order that the subsequent part of the statement might be taken away. In the case of the proposition, 'Either it is day or it is night,' we take as the minor premise 'But it is day' (that is, we affirm that it is day); that it is not night follows from the affirmation of this minor premise.

The fifth mode occurs when the former part of the same disjunctive proposition is taken negatively in the minor premise, in order that the latter part of the proposition might be inferred in the following way: 'Either it is day or it is night; but it is not day' (the minor premise, you see, is made by means of a negation); it follows that it is night.

[358/1135] The sixth and seventh modes are derived from[24] the disjunctive proposition of the fourth and fifth modes by adjoining a negation, withdrawing the disjunction from the proposition, and adding a conjunction to those propositions which were asserted previously in the disjunctive proposition, in the following way. 'It is not the case that it is day and that it is night'; this was formerly a disjunction of this sort: 'Either it is day or it is night.'[25] When the conjunction 'or' was removed from this proposition which was disjunctive, we added 'and', which is copulative, and we asserted a negation. In this way from the united parts of a disjunctive proposition with the addition of a negation we made a proposition of the sixth and seventh modes, and it is this: 'It is not the case that it is day and that it is night.' In this case if we take as the minor premise that it is day, it follows that it is not night in this way: 'But it is day; therefore, it is not night.' The seventh mode occurs when the first part of the proposition is taken negatively in the minor premise so that the latter part may follow in this way:

> It is not the case that it is day and that it is night;
> but it is not day;
> therefore, it is night.

This mode of propositions can be found only in those cases in which one or the other must be, as, for example, day or night, sickness or health, and whatever does not have an intermediate.

In the books we wrote on hypothetical syllogisms we explicated carefully the way in which conditional syllogisms are true.[26] Here, however, we have presented only what was appropriate for explaining Cicero's thought and not what could be considered a rather complete treatment of conditional syllogisms. Here, then, is a brief summary of all the things we have said.

1. The first mode occurs when the part placed first in a connected proposition is taken as the minor premise in order that the part placed second might follow in the following way:

> If it is day, it is light;
> but it is day;
> therefore it is light.

2. The second mode occurs when the second part of a connected proposition is taken in the minor premise in a way contrary to the way in which it is put in the connected proposition, so that the part that is first might be taken away in the following way:

> If it is day, it is light;
> but it is not light;
> therefore, it is not day.

3. The third mode occurs when the parts of a connected proposition made up of affirmations are divided by a negation, and a negation is also added to the whole proposition, and the former part of the connected proposition is taken as the minor premise in the way in which it is stated in that proposition, in order that the second part might be taken as the conclusion in a way contrary to the way in which it is expressed in the connected proposition, in the following way:

> It is not the case that if it is day, it is not light;
> but it is day;
> therefore, it is light.

Here when the antecedent, that it is day, has been asserted; the consequent, that it is not light, is overturned. Indeed, every affirmation overturns a negation—either when a negation is withdrawn from the second part of a connected proposition made up of negations, and the whole proposition is negated, and the consequent is destroyed when the former part of the connected proposition has been asserted (as in this example: 'It is not the case that if it is not light, it is day; but it is not light; therefore, it is not day'[27]); or when a negation is added to the second part of a connected proposition constructed of a negation and an affirmation, and the whole proposition is negated, and the former part of the connected proposition is asserted so that the consequent might be taken away (as in this example: 'It is not the case that if it is not day, it is not night; but it is not day; therefore it is night'[28]); or when a negation is subtracted from the former part of the same proposition composed of a negation and an affirmation, and the proposition is negated, and the first part of the connected proposition is asserted so that the consequent might be taken away (as in this example: 'It is not the case that if it is day, it is night; [359/1136] but it is day; therefore, it is not night'); or when a negation is removed from the latter part of a connected proposition united out of an affirmation and a negation, and the whole proposition is negated, and the consequent is destroyed when the former part of the connected proposition has been asserted (as in this example: 'It is not the case that if he is awake, he is snoring; but he is awake; therefore, he is not snoring'[29]).

All these are understood to be in the third mode. They arise from incompatibles, and the antecedent is always asserted in order that the consequent might be taken away.[30] The minor premise does not present the former part of the conditional proposition that becomes true when the incompatibility of its parts is negated, in the same way in which that part is presented (whether affirmatively or negatively) in the conditional proposition.[31] But the second part of the conditional proposition is stated in the conclusion in a way contrary to the way in which the first part was taken in the minor premise; for if the minor premise was affirmative, the conclusion will be negative, and if the minor premise was negative, the conclusion will be affirmative.[32]

4. The fourth mode occurs when the first part of a disjunctive proposition is asserted so that the second part might be taken away in the following way:

> Either it is day or it is night;
> but it is day;
> therefore, it is not night.

5. The fifth mode occurs when the former part of a disjunctive proposition is taken away so that the second part might be asserted in the following way:

> Either it is day or it is night;
> but it is not day;
> therefore, it is night.

6. The sixth mode occurs when a negation is prefixed to the things that can enter into a disjunction (that is, to contraries or incompatibles lacking an intermediate[33]), and copulative conjunctions are added, and the first part is asserted so that the consequent might be taken away in the following way:

> It is not the case that it is day and that it is night;
> but it is day;
> therefore, it is not night.

7. The seventh mode occurs when the antecedent of the same proposition is taken away so that the consequent might be asserted, in the following way:

> It is not the case that it is day and that it is night;
> but it is not day;
> therefore, it is night.

Now that we have said these things in advance, let us turn to Cicero's words.

[13.53]

We have explained above that the Topic which is from antecedents and consequents and incompatibles correctly appears to be one Topic and that it consists in a condition, but that it is divided into three parts. Cicero indicates this fairly clearly, saying that the thought and consideration of this Topic are one and consist in a condition but that it is divided into three parts by the treatment of argumentation. With regard to this point, as we said shortly before, Cicero appended examples from the first, second, and third modes of hypothetical syllogisms. Since these seem too complicated to be grasped immediately at first hearing, I thought it good to spend a little time imbuing the mind of the reader with more perspicuous examples so that when the reader has exercised his understanding on easier matters, he may consider more difficult things without much trouble.

An argumentation arises from antecedents when we take the antecedent of a stated conditional proposition in order that we may infer the consequent, in the following way. Suppose that there is some doubt whether Cicero is an animal, and that it is granted that Cicero is a man, and that this proposition is sure: 'If Cicero is a man, he is an animal.' *Man* precedes and *animal* follows.[34] So if I want to make an argumentation from an antecedent, I take the antecedent as the minor premise in the following way: 'But Cicero is a man.' It follows that Cicero is an animal. And this is the first mode, which we discussed above.

Again, an argumentation arises from a consequent [360/1137] when the minor premise removes the consequent in the asserted conditional proposition in order to destroy the antecedent in the following way. 'If Cicero is a man, he is an animal.' *Man* precedes and *animal* follows. So if I want to make an argument from a consequent, I might say, 'But he is not an animal.' It follows that he is not a man either. This is clearly false, however, for it is indisputable that he is a man, and so it is false that he is not an animal; hence, Cicero is an animal.[35] This is the second mode of those discussed above.

If an argumentation arises from incompatibles, we will make the argumentation in the third mode of the conclusions analyzed above, in this way. 'It is not the case that if Cicero is a man, he is not an animal,' for that he is a man and that he is not an animal are incompatible. In this case, if we take as the minor premise that he is a man, we conclude with correct reasoning that he is also an animal, in the following way: 'But he is a man; therefore, he is an animal.' This mode is a transformation of the connected proposition made up of two affirmatives.

In these three ways, then, we have shown that Cicero, who is a man, is also an animal: first, when the antecedent (namely that he is a man) is taken as the minor premise; second, when we negate the consequent in the minor premise (namely, that he is not an animal); and third, when we negate the incompatibility of the things that follow from one another, assert the antecedent, and then infer the consequent.

Now that we have understood these things, we will next deal with Cicero's examples. For after having said that the conception of the Topic from consequents, antecedents, and incompatibles is simple when it comes to the discovery of arguments but tripartite when it comes to their formulation, Cicero added: "For when you have undertaken to demonstrate that the woman to whom all the silver was bequeathed is also owed the coin, what difference does it make whether you prove this from antecedents, from consequents, or from incompatibles?" For the same thought is inferred in the conclusion,[36] and the diversity of the argumentations consists not in the matter itself but in the formulation of antecedents, consequents, and incompatibles.

So first suppose that someone bequeathed all his silver to his wife in his will, and there is a question whether the coin was also bequeathed to the wife; let it be granted that coin is also called silver.[37] We devise an argument in the first mode from antecedents with the following sort of reasoning. We take as the major premise, 'If coined money is silver, that coined money was bequeathed to the wife.' Here that coined money is silver is the antecedent, and that it was bequeathed to the wife is the consequent. We take the antecedent as the minor premise and say, 'But coined money is silver.' We conclude that coined money was bequeathed to the wife. The construction of the entire argumentation will be this:

If coined money is silver, it was bequeathed to the wife;
but coined money is silver;
therefore, it was bequeathed to the wife.

With regard to this case, if the reader turns his mind to the things previously presented and elucidated with many examples above, he will see that this argumentation is constructed in the first mode from antecedents.

The argumentation is constructed from consequents, however, in the following way: 'If the coin was not bequeathed to the wife to whom all the silver was bequeathed, the coin is not silver.'[38] Here that the coin [361/1138] was not bequeathed when all the silver was bequeathed is the antecedent; that coin is not silver is the consequent. And so if we take away what was second (namely, that coin is not silver), we will say, 'But coin is silver,' for an affirmation destroys a negation. And so it follows that the first part is taken away, namely, that the coin was not bequeathed to the wife when all the silver was bequeathed to her. But since every negation is annihilated by an affirmation, we will say in the conclusion, 'Therefore, the coin was bequeathed to the wife when all the silver was bequeathed to her.' The argumentation will be of this sort:

> If the coin was not bequeathed to the wife when all the silver was
>   bequeathed to her, the coin is not silver;
> but coin is silver;
> therefore, the coin was bequeathed to the wife when all the silver was
>   bequeathed to her.

(For the sake of brevity Cicero omitted the part of the proposition that says, 'when all the silver was bequeathed to the wife'; but for the sake of clearer understanding we have appended it.[39])

It should not disturb the reader either that we have here produced both the minor premise and the conclusion with an affirmation, although in the examples above in the second mode we always produced the minor premise with a negation and drew the conclusion in turn as a negation. The reason for this fact is most apparent. Since the first proposition in the examples above consisted of affirmations, and since in the second mode the minor premise takes away the consequent in such a way that it destroys the antecedent, we had to annihilate the two affirmations with two negations, in the following way. 'If it is day, it is light'; both of these consist of affirmations. And so to destroy the second part, which is an affirmation (namely, 'it is light'), we must negate it; so I will say, 'But it is not light.' Hence, we also remove by means of a negation the first part, which is clearly an affirmation (namely, 'it is day'), and we conclude, 'Therefore, it is not day.' But in this example of Cicero's, both parts of the first hypothetical proposition are stated with negations, which cannot be taken away in the minor premise or in the conclusion except with affirmations, in the following way. Cicero's example is of this sort: 'If the coin was not bequeathed to the wife, the coin is not silver.' You see that both are negations, for both that the coin was not bequeathed to the wife and that the coin is not silver consist in negations. But because 'the coin is not silver' is a negation, if we are to take away the consequent part of the proposition by means of the minor premise, we must say that the coin is silver. And if in the conclusion we are to take away the antecedent part, which is a negation (namely, that the coin was not bequeathed to the wife), we must say, 'Therefore, the coin was bequeathed to the wife.' And the second mode rightly made from consequents is of this sort.

We should, however, take rather careful note of the fact that when Cicero previously drew up brief examples for all the Topics, [362/1139] he appended an example for this Topic which is drawn from consequents which is inappropriate for the second mode of conditional syllogisms and more appropriate for the first mode, which produces a conclusion from antecedents rather than from consequents. In fact, he presented an argument from consequents in this way: 'If a woman who was united with a man with whom wedlock was not permitted sent him a letter of divorce, nothing should remain for the children since the children who were begotten do not follow their father.'[40] And so here where there is a question about whether a part of the dowry should remain with the man, we take the antecedent as the minor premise in order to confirm the conclusion in the following way, 'But the woman was united with a man with whom there was no wedlock'[41]; we conclude, 'Therefore, nothing should remain for the children, since the children who were begotten do not follow their father.' And thus the argument is not from consequents since the antecedent, not the consequent, was taken as the minor premise.[42] In fact, *a woman united without legal wedlock* was the antecedent; that none of the dowry is retained for the children since they do not follow their father is the consequent. And so in this way Cicero gave an example of an argument from antecedents instead of an argument from consequents.

The argument can become an argument from consequents if the thing being asked about is asserted first and what should be taken as the minor premise is asserted second, in the following way:[43] 'If any of the dowry should remain for the children because they follow their father, the woman was united with a man with whom there was legal wedlock.' And so I take the consequent with a negation in this way: 'But the woman was not united with a man with whom there was legal wedlock; for that reason the children who were begotten do not follow their father.' And so the antecedent of the proposition is destroyed in the conclusion, in this way: 'Therefore, nothing should remain for the children.'[44]

This is enough about the second mode, for nothing, I think, has been omitted.

The third mode is very clear, in the following way. 'It is not the case that if all the silver was bequeathed, the coin was not bequeathed to the wife.' In this case it followed that the coin had also been bequeathed if all the silver was bequeathed. To make this an incompatible, we inserted a negation in the consequence, and we said, 'If all the silver was bequeathed, the coin was not bequeathed.' Because this is an incompatible and false, it is brought back to the truth with another negation, in this way: 'It is not the case that if the silver was bequeathed, the coin was not bequeathed.' In other words, it is equivalent to the affirmation, 'If the silver was bequeathed, the coin was bequeathed.' So we take as a minor premise for this proposition the claim that all the silver was bequeathed, and it follows that all the coin was bequeathed to the wife; thus the argumentation has this form:

It is not the case that if the silver was bequeathed, the coin was not
  bequeathed;
but the silver was bequeathed;
therefore, the coin was bequeathed.

Cicero himself, however, formulated the proposition in this way: 'It is not the case that the silver was bequeathed and the coin was not bequeathed'; but we added the causal conjunction 'if' in order to show the genus of such a proposition. For an incompatible arises from a connected proposition with the addition of a negation.[45] But no conjunction can show [363/1140] a connected proposition as well as 'if', although even a copulative conjunction might produce the same proposition[46] since things that are connected are also understood to be conjoined, given what we said shortly before. And this argument is produced from the proposition that was united out of two affirmations and that was itself negated with the addition of a negation.

In all these cases we have proved that the wife is owed the coin since all the silver was bequeathed; but with regard to the propositions described above we take as the minor premise sometimes the antecedent, sometimes the consequent, and sometimes an incompatible. And this is enough, I think, to explain Cicero's examples.

But here a doubt can arise. If someone who is not thoroughly versed in these matters considers Cicero's examples, he will think that the Topic which we said was from antecedents, consequents, and incompatibles is the same as the Topic *from genus*, falling into this error because of the fact that Cicero uses the same example (namely, of silver and coin) for both Topics. To a more careful observer, however, it will be apparent that the argumentations on the same subject are formulated differently. It is one thing to say that since coin is a species of silver, the species was bequeathed if the genus was bequeathed, because the species is never separated from its genus. And it is another thing to assert a statement with a condition and, by taking its parts as minor premises, to formulate argumentations with different forms of reasoning (as we showed previously),[47] especially since argumentations of this sort, from consequents, antecedents, and incompatibles, can arise even apart from genera and species.[48] This we indicated above with regard to the example involving day and light;[49] for day is neither a species nor a genus of light, and light is neither a species nor a genus of day. Instead, with regard to argumentations from antecedents, consequents, and incompatibles, the only thing we should consider is that when one has been asserted, the other follows by necessary reasoning. Hence, the Topics *from a genus* or *from a species* differ from the Topic that consists in a condition since the former are drawn from the idea of a universal and a part, but the latter deals with the order of a consequence and an incompatibility.

After these things, Cicero enumerates the modes and conclusions of hypothetical syllogisms, in the following way.

[13.54–14.57]

Although we have analyzed all these things many times before and although a discussion so often repeated needs no exposition, nonetheless it will be worthwhile if, as briefly as I can, I shed some light on Cicero's concise words with a commentary. Cicero enumerates seven hypothetical modes and says, "When the first part of a connected proposition is taken in the minor premise in order to show the second part, the dialecticians call this the first mode," in the following way. 'If this is, that is'; *this* is the first part, and *that* is the second part. We take the first part as the minor premise: 'But this is'; we conclude the second part: 'Therefore, that is.' Again, with regard to these examples 'If he is a man, he is an animal,' we take as the minor premise, 'But he is a man'; we conclude, 'Therefore, he is an animal.'

The second mode, Cicero says, is an arrangement of connected propositions according to which it follows that when the second part is negated, [364/1142] the first part is also negated, in the following way:

> If this is, that is;
> but that is not;
> therefore, this is not either.

With regard to examples, in this way: 'If he is a man, he is an animal; but he is not an animal; therefore, he is not a man.' Cicero said it in this way: if a connected proposition is made up of affirmative parts, then when you negate what was connected in order also to negate that to which it was connected, this is the second mode.[50] In general, however, he would have spoken more correctly if he had said this: when what is connected (that is, the second part) is destroyed, that to which it is connected (that is, the first part) is also destroyed, so that if what is connected is affirmative, it will be destroyed with negation, and if it is negative, it will be destroyed with an affirmation. The same point holds for that to which it is connected (that is, the first part): if the first part is affirmed in the connected proposition, it will be negated in the conclusion (as in the example Cicero presented here); but if the first part of the proposition is negative, it will be destroyed in the conclusion by the contrary affirmation.

The third mode, Cicero says, occurs when things that are conjoined are negated, and another negation is in turn added to these. For example, since *animal* is conjoined to *man*, suppose we speak in this way: 'It is not the case both that he is a man and that he is not an animal.' Of these, one is asserted so that the remaining one may be taken away, in the following way. We assert that he is a man, saying 'But he is a man.' Hence, we take away the remaining part, 'he is not an animal'; we conclude 'Therefore, he is an animal.' The argumentation, then, will arise in this way:

It is not the case both that he is a man and that he is not an animal;
but he is a man;
therefore, he is an animal.

From these, Cicero says, enthymemes arise which are inferred from contraries and which are for the most part generally used by rhetoricians. Although every discovery can be called an enthymeme (for an enthymeme is a conception of the mind,[51] and this can apply to all discoveries), these are called enthymemes because the things discovered, which are concisely deduced from contraries, are especially pointed. Therefore, they have appropriated the common name 'enthymeme' on account of the excellence and elegance of their discovery, so that the rhetoricians call them 'enthymemes' as if that were a proper name, just as the Greek poet Homer is also called simply 'the poet'. And whoever quotes something from Homer customarily says, 'This line is from the poet'; then no one but Homer is understood, not because the rest are not poets but because Homer's excellence turns the common name into a proper one. These enthymemes arise in the following way, constructed from contraries:

Fear this man and do not be fearful of the other;

(for example, if one were speaking of Lentulus and Cethegus and the rest[52]).

> You fear lest a few citizens be killed, but you make no effort to avoid the destruction of the republic

(for it is connected: someone who was unwilling that a few citizens be destroyed is much more unwilling that the republic be annihilated[53]).

When a negation is inserted among these, an argument from incompatibles arises. But Cicero stated this concisely. We, on the other hand, should reduce the argument to a syllogism, namely, from incompatibles, from which enthymemes generally arise in the following way. Suppose there is this connected proposition: 'If someone fears lest a few citizens be killed, he fears lest the republic be destroyed.' A negation is inserted in this way: 'If someone fears lest a few citizens be killed, he does not fear lest the republic be destroyed.' Another negation is added: 'It is not the case that if someone fears lest a few citizens be killed, he does not fear lest the republic be destroyed.' These two negations are equivalent to one affirmation that says, 'If someone fears this, he fears that also.' The minor premise [365/1143] for this connected proposition is 'But he fears this.' The conclusion follows: 'Therefore, he fears that.'

This conclusion is effective only if the question is posed negatively, in this way: 'You fear this; do you not fear that?' Because in these argumentations we present not the whole proposition (as we presented above) but only the major proposition,[54] whose minor premise and conclusion are known, it is therefore said to be an enthymeme, that is, a concise conception of the mind. And the mode is the same for other examples.

We understand Cicero's example here to contain an argument not only from incompatibles but also from contraries. Certainly, *to fear* and *not to fear* are contraries—unless the particular expression of the words reduces the argument from contraries to incompatibility, for the expression 'fear this man and do not be fearful of the other' is such that they appear to be incompatibles. For *to fear* and *not to fear* are truly contraries; but in the particular expression 'do not be fearful' and 'fear', they are understood to be incompatibles as well as contraries, although the thought is shown to be the same.[55]

To these, Cicero added yet other examples.

'Do you condemn the woman whom you accuse of nothing?' The complete syllogism for this enthymeme is of this sort:

It is not the case that if you accuse her of nothing, you condemn her;
but you accuse her of nothing;
therefore, you do not condemn her.

This argument comes from a connected proposition constructed of two negatives, in this way, 'If you accuse of nothing, you do not condemn.' A negation is withdrawn from the second part, and the whole proposition is entirely negated in the following way: 'It is not the case that if you accuse of nothing, you condemn.' From this proposition we make the argument that produces this enthymeme when the argument is turned into a question: 'Do you condemn the woman whom you accuse of nothing?'

'Do you claim that the woman whom you believe to deserve reward deserves punishment?' The reasoning for this enthymeme is of this sort:

It is not the case that you believe that she deserves reward and that she deserves punishment;
but you believe that she deserves reward;
therefore, she does not deserve punishment.

This enthymeme is obtained from a connected proposition consisting of an affirmation and a negation in this way, 'If you believe that she deserves reward, she does not deserve punishment.'[56] When a negation has been removed from the second part of this proposition, and the whole proposition has been negated, this proposition arises: 'It is not the case that if you believe that she deserves reward, she deserves punishment.' When this has been cast in the form of a question, it produces an enthymeme: 'Is she whom you believe deserving of reward deserving of punishment?'

Again: 'What you know is useful; is what you do not know no hindrance?' This enthymeme also is connected to a syllogism of this sort:

It is not the case that what you know is useful and that what you do not know is not a hindrance;
but what you know is useful;
therefore, what you do not know is a hindrance.

This argument is constructed from a proposition that was made up of two affirmations but then received an inserted negation and was itself in addition entirely negated. Put in the form of a question, it becomes an enthymeme in the following way: 'What you know is useful; is what you do not know no hindrance?'

This is the meaning of all the examples presented above. Whoever accuses a woman of nothing cannot rightly condemn her either; it is disgraceful for a man to claim that a woman is deserving of punishment whom he believes deserving of reward; if what a man knows with regard to a case is useful, what he does not know—if it is the contrary—will be a hindrance. Cicero says that this Topic is common to orators and philosophers but that philosophers call it 'the third mode', [366/1144] while rhetoricians call it 'enthymemes'.

According to Cicero, many other modes remain. Although he enumerated three modes above, he added four and said there are more. These consist in disjunctions in the following way.

> Either this or that;
> but this;
> therefore, not that.

This is the fourth mode, which we also presented above in this way:

> Either it is day or it is night;
> but it is day;
> therefore, it is not night.

In every case, what Cicero is calling 'this' refers to the antecedent, and what he is calling 'that' refers to the consequent, whether it is with regard to connected or disjunctive propositions.

Again:

> Either this or that;
> but not this;
> therefore, that.

This is also the fifth mode, as in these examples:

> Either it is day or it is night;
> but it is not day;
> therefore, it is night.

Cicero says that the necessity of these conclusions is a result of the fact that the things asserted in the disjunction do not seem to admit of an intermediate, so that there could be something else besides one or the other of the things in the disjunction.[57] Therefore, when one of the disjuncts is removed, we conclude that the other disjunct is; when one of the disjuncts is asserted, we conclude that the other disjunct is not. But if there is an intermediate that can exist in addition to one or the other of the disjuncts, the proposition is not true, and the conclusion is not confirmed—as, for example, in this case: 'Either it is white or it is black.' This is false, for in addition to these colors a thing can be red. If we then assert or deny that a thing is white, it will not be necessary either that it is not black or that it is black, because it can be red, which is intermediate.[58]

Next, according to Cicero, they add the negation of a conjunction, in the case of disjunctive propositions, that is, in the following way:

> It is not the case that both this and that;
> but not this;
> therefore, that

That is,

> It is not the case both that it is night and that it is day;
> but it is night;
> therefore, it is not day.

As we said before, this is the sixth mode.

The seventh mode comes from the same proposition in the following way:

> It is not the case that both this and that;
> but not this;
> therefore, that;

as if we were to speak in this way:

> It is not the case both that it is night and that it is day;
> but it is not night;
> therefore, it is day.

These propositions cannot have a confirmed conclusion except with regard to things that are disjoined and that lack an intermediate. For suppose we were to speak in this way: 'It is not the case that it is white and that it is black'; suppose we assert that it is not white. It does not follow that it is black, for there can be an intermediate. Hence, a proposition of this sort, made (as Cicero says) by the negation of a conjunction, should be applied to things that are disjoined and that lack an intermediate if it is going to confirm the conclusions; otherwise the conclusion will not be confirmed.[60]

A proposition of the third mode is distinguished from a proposition of the sixth and seventh modes because a proposition of the third mode originates from conjoined terms but a proposition of the sixth and seventh modes arises from disjoined terms as is clear in the examples above.[61]

And so Cicero says that innumerable conclusions arise from these modes, for any one of these modes can be adapted to an infinite number of conclusions. For example, the first and second modes can be adapted to all those things that are connected with one another, and they are numberless, if anyone wants to pursue them. Again, there is an infinite multitude of incompatibles, for which the third mode is useful. Again, there are many disjoined things, for which the fourth, fifth, sixth, and seventh modes are exceedingly effective. Dialectic, Cicero says, consists almost entirely in these modes; but the first three modes, which contain antecedence, consequence, and incompatibility, are necessary for the Topics.[62] The remaining modes seem added more for the sake of making the discussion exhaustive than because they were necessary for the subject of this work.

[14.58–15.59]

[367/1145] The Topic that was observed to be from causes follows after the Topic that consists in a condition; after it, the Topic that furnishes arguments from the effects of causes is described. Cicero did present examples for these Topics above, but here he discusses the nature of these Topics more extensively.

Aristotle maintained that there are four causes by which any individual thing is made.[63] The first is the source of motion; the second is that from which something comes to be, which Aristotle calls the matter; the third is the nature and fashion in accordance with which any individual thing is formed; and the fourth is the end for the sake of which a thing is produced. Cicero, however, makes the principal division of causes between those which produce something and those without which something cannot be produced.[64] The cause that produces something is equivalent to the cause consisting in the source of motion. But the cause without which something does not come to be sometimes is reduced to the idea of matter or to the idea of those things which are conjoined with matter and aid the power of an efficient cause, and sometimes it is equivalent to the remaining causes, as will be apparent a little later.

Cicero presents this example of a cause that by its own force produces the effect subject to it: 'Fire burns'; for fire is the cause of burning and can produce it, and fire moves and changes that which is burned. The cause without which the thing to be made cannot arise, however, Cicero designates by one of its parts, as when he says that bronze is the cause of a statue since the statue cannot exist without bronze. As the division to be produced makes clear, this is not itself the cause without which a thing is not produced; rather, it will be shown to be one of the parts of that cause.[65]

Cicero divides the cause without which what is made cannot be produced in the following way. Some instances of this cause are quiet, inactive, inert (in a way), and immobile in themselves until an external impulse for activity has been added to them; examples of these causes are, for instance, place, time, material, and instruments. For everything that comes to be must have a place in which it is comprised,[66] and unless something comes to be in that place, the place itself cannot move to develop anything. In the same way, unless material and instruments are moved by a skilled hand, they themselves by nature accomplish nothing. Time, too, is subject to action; if there is no action, time itself, in virtue of its own nature, produces nothing. And these are things that accomplish nothing by themselves but nonetheless are causes if an efficient action is imposed on them.

There are other causes, however, that consist in motion and seem to impart a sort of preparation and precondition for effecting something, as, for example, meeting (which precedes) is a cause of love, and love is a cause of outrageous conduct. Stoic reasoning, Cicero says, weaves Fate from such causes, for the Stoics say that Fate is a certain intricate interweaving and chainlike connection of antecedent causes and consequent events, in the following manner. He left home to go abroad because he could not bear the wrath of his parents; he would not bear the rage of his parents because he was occupied with the love of a woman; he loved that woman because he had often met her before; and he had met her because something else had gone before which had the result that he met her. And thus, as Cicero says, from the order of antecedent and consequent events, the Stoics weave Fate.[67]

[368/1146] Again, he divides causes that produce something by their own force into causes that are sufficient by themselves to produce something and causes that need external assistance. An example of a cause sufficient by itself to produce something is wisdom, which by itself and entirely unaided is wont to make men wise. (But whether wisdom alone can make men happy or whether external aids, such as the goods of fortune or the body, need to be added to wisdom is a different question.[68]) Thus, causes that produce something by their own force are either such that they need no external aid or such that for them we need to seek external aids, like the tools of an artisan by means of which he develops and fashions the thing he wants to make.

Of all the causes that Cicero places in one or another division of causes, all those causes that by their own force develop the things whose causes they are (including the causes able to produce something by themselves as well as the causes that need external aid) are equivalent to the cause that, in the Aristotelian division of causes, is the source of motion. (Wisdom, however, is not an appropriate example for this sort of cause; rather, it pertains more to nature and form, for wisdom produces wise men by means of a certain nature and form.) With regard to the cause presented by Cicero without which something does not come to be, on the other hand, matter, time, and place are the causes from which something comes to be or in which something comes to be. These causes are subordinated to the nature of an efficient cause; to comprise them in one concept, they are either matter or something put in the place of matter. Implements, however, belong to the cause that pertains to the end of something. Implements are not themselves the end of a thing, because the end does not aim at the implements, but rather the implements aim at the end, for implements are provided for the sake of some end.[69]

Someone might wonder why Cicero did not number meeting, which is the cause of love, among the causes that have the power of producing something, but reckoned it instead among the causes without which something cannot be produced, although meeting does accomplish something and does put something into motion. For meeting itself does apparently produce something, and it is similar to the causes that have the power to produce something but cannot do so without assistance (as, for example, when we ask whether wisdom by itself can make a man happy).[70] The rhetorician Merobaudes[71] discusses the matter in this way. Causes that have the power to produce something have the virtue that, even if they need external aids, their effects nonetheless are referred to the thing to be produced. But as for causes that are preconditions, even if something comes into being from those antecedent preconditions, the preconditions do not principally

effect the thing understood to come into being. The preconditions
themselves occur, at an "opportune" moment, but the things said to
come into being arise from other things acting efficiently. This happens
customarily in the case of meeting; for perhaps a man does not meet a
woman because he loves her, but rather love, which was not the main
purpose of the meeting, arises because of the preceding meeting.
Thus, since the love could not arise apart from the meeting, the meeting seems correctly included among the causes without which a thing
is not produced. On the other hand, because it does not produce a
thing by its own force (since producing something is not its main aim,
but rather it just precedes the thing that comes to be), it is correctly
classified among the preconditions and not among the efficient causes.

[15.60–16.61]

[369/1148] According to Cicero, the first division of causes was into
causes that produce something and causes without which something
cannot be produced. Causes that produce something are similarly divided into two groups, namely, into causes that possess the power
necessary to produce something and need no external aid, and causes
that cannot act efficiently or effect something unless other things aid
them. And Cicero discusses the cause that has the power of producing
something first. The subdivision of this cause that necessarily produces
something immediately implies the conclusion associated with it; for
when the cause that necessarily produces something has been stated,
the effect must also follow. For example, if someone says that the sun
was present, he also shows that light was present; or when we say that
wisdom is present in someone, we must also acknowledge him to be a
wise man.

But the same point does not apply to those efficient causes that need
external aids, for it is not the case that an effect must follow when a
cause of this sort is stated. A cause of this sort does not necessarily
produce what it wants to produce unless it is aided by external assistance. The same is true of the cause that does not itself have the
power of producing but without which the cause does not arise. As
Cicero himself points out, this cause has no necessity with regard to
the things to be produced; therefore when the cause has been stated,
the effect does not immediately follow. For it is not the case that if a
man met a woman, he straightway loved her; nor is it the case that if a
lump of bronze existed, a statue necessarily also existed.

From this, another partition of causes arises: some causes are necessary, and others are not.[72] Some causes that are not necessary are efficient causes,[73] and others are causes without which a thing is not produced. A conclusion based on necessary causes does not generally give rise to confusion, for when the cause is stated, the effects immediately follow in the conclusion. Those causes that are not necessary and that are efficient to some extent do not have a subsequent conclusion concerning the thing effected. (Cicero says nothing about these causes here, but he discussed them a little before.)[74] For children do not exist without parents, but it is not therefore the case that there was a necessary cause of producing in the parents since we see that men have the power not to beget children.[75] That cause, however, which does not itself produce something but without which something cannot be produced is of the sort described by a line of Ennius's: "Unless the beams of fir had fallen to the earth, the Argo would not have been built."[76] For the Argo was built of beams, but there was no necessity in the beams for a ship to arise from them. But the cause that is efficient and has its necessity in itself is like the furrowing fiery bolt that struck the ship of Ajax.[77] It was necessary that the ship be straightway enflamed, because fire is a necessary cause of enflaming.

This is the sense of what Cicero says, but the form in which he says it is a little more confused, for he speaks in the following way: "And the genus of causes which has a necessary power of producing something does not usually occasion an error; but the genus of causes without which something is not produced often gives rise to confusion." This is what he said, and he ought then to have presented an example of one or the other or both cases, but instead he gave an example appropriate to neither case. For although he should have presented either a necessary efficient cause or a cause without which something is not produced, he in fact presented an example of the cause that [370/1149] does produce something but not without external aids in the following way: "For although children cannot exist without parents, it is not the case that there is therefore a necessary cause in the parents for begetting children." For a parent, and especially a male parent, is an efficient cause but not without the female parent, that is, not without a sort of matter and that cause without which something cannot come to be, since it itself does not have the power for producing a thing.

Thus, Cicero did not present an example either of a necessary and efficient cause or of a cause without which something cannot come to be; rather he presented an example of a cause that is efficient but not necessary.[78] And in his discussion he seems to have passed over in silence the case for which he then presented this example, for it could have been said more plainly in this way: "The genus of causes which has a necessary power of producing something does not usually occasion an error; but the genus of causes which does not have a necessary power of producing something or the genus of causes without which something is not produced often gives rise to confusion." And we should understand this passage as if Cicero had in fact spoken in this way; for he presented no example of a necessary cause, and what he added is appropriate to both the causes subsequently enumerated, to the cause without which nothing is produced as well as to the cause that is efficient but not necessary. For the female as well as the male is said to be a parent; of these, the male is the cause that produces something but is not necessary, and the female is the cause that does not produce but without which a thing cannot be produced.

Hence we must distinguish causes and discern necessity; not every cause should be taken as a premise in order that an effect might follow, but only the cause that necessarily produces something even when extrinsic aids are lacking.

[16.62]

Cicero makes yet another division of causes in this way.[79] By a certain power of their own and without desire, will, or belief, some causes maintain one and the same order with regard to producing things—for example, all things that are born die. For because a thing is born, it is therefore also necessary that it die; nevertheless, birth itself does not by any desire, will, or belief bring it about that other things die. Rather, from eternity it is the condition of things that whatever is born, in virtue of the fact that it has begun to be, sometime also ceases to be. Other causes, however, consist in will, mental agitation, state, nature, art, or chance. An example of a cause consisting in will is if someone asks why Trebatius is reading a book and we reply, 'Because Trebatius has a will to read it.' A cause consisting in mental agitation is, for example, if someone grows pale with fear, or if someone who is in turmoil because of civil war flees the city.[80] [Causes consisting] in state [are], for example, if Trebatius has ready answers about the nature of law because the knowledge of civil law is a firm state in him as a result of much practice; or if someone is easily enraged because his soul has become savage in virtue of his being in a state of wrathfulness. [Causes consisting] in nature [are], for example, if someone is said to be enraged because he is naturally wrathful and this fault grows in him daily. [Causes consisting] in art [are], for example, if someone paints well because he is (let us suppose) skilled in this art. [Those consisting] in chance [are], for example, those things which are in no way in our power but nonetheless occur,[81] such as a successful voyage, especially during an uncertain time. All of these things have a cause, and there is no thing that some cause has not produced.[82] For all things that come to be have some reason why they are produced, [371/1150] and whoever is able to give this reason will also have given the cause, for a cause is that on account of which a thing comes to be.

All the causes understood to depend on will or mental agitation belong to the cause that is the source of motion, as we said in connection with Aristotle's division of causes, for these causes are the source of motion for the effecting of something. But the cause that has to do with art, state, or nature consists in a formula, for the fashion and formula of a thing to be produced are located in art, state, and nature.[83] Chance, however, is an external cause,[84] and according to Aristotle, it is not numbered among the principal causes; but according to Cicero it is a hidden cause of a thing produced. What kind of thing chance is will be indicated a little later.

[16.63–17.64]

Cicero gives yet another clear and illuminating division of causes: some causes are uniform, and others are not.[85] Uniform causes are those whose effect hardly ever varies. Causes that are not uniform are those which are directed now here, now there, with ready changes.

All causes derived from nature and art are uniform. In fact, nature and art always produce their effects unless there is something mutable in the material subject to them which gets in the way. The fact that one and the same artisan often does not fashion entirely similar statues from the same material is not a result of changeableness in the art but rather of changeableness sometimes in the hand of the artisan, which falls short of the complete art, and sometimes in the material itself, which does not yield uniformly to the efficient cause and the form. The same is true with regard to nature. It maintains its uniformity when it fashions a man from a man; in the same way in other cases, by nature things beget things similar to themselves. When some monstrosity is produced, however, the fault is not in nature but rather in the material, from which nature could not develop what it was trying to produce.

States, too, should have been included among uniform causes, for what arises from the state of anything is usually uniform and not changeable. In fact, something is called a state because it comes to resemble nature in virtue of its stability. But perhaps Cicero saw that nature and art are understood to be uniform not only with respect to their effects but also with respect to their own nature, to such an extent that where art and nature fail, the fault is generally imputed to their material. A state, however, is derived from habitual practice, and it produces something not by its own nature and uniformity but by usage. And perhaps for this reason Cicero separated states from the uniform causes, even though state seems to be more uniform than the other causes, apart from art and nature.

Causes that are not uniform, however, Cicero divided into those which are evident and those which are hidden. Evident causes are those which proceed from some motion or desire of the mind or some reason of the judgment.[86] Hidden causes are those which are subject to fortune. For because the mind always knows what it is inclined toward and never loses its idea of the thing it produces, even if it sometimes loses its judgment of the good, therefore the things that arise from the will or the judgment of the mind must be known, in addition to the things that are entirely grasped by intellect and in which there is no element of will. Fortune and chance, however, are always unknown; their [372/1151] nature and the things that arise from chance are equally uncertain.

Cicero defines chance as an event produced by hidden causes, but this definition does not seem complete. For suppose that the causes that occasioned an eclipse of the sun and the moon were still hidden. Do the things governed by the regular motions of the heavens therefore occur by chance and according to fortune? Would men who could find no reason for the eclipse judge it to be chance, even though considered in its own right it would not in any way be chance? But in his formulation of the definition of chance, Cicero was showing what an event occasioned by fortune is, *not* what might seem to be chance to men who completely fail to perceive its nature. Cicero concludes that chance is an event produced by hidden causes in the following way. Since all things for which a reason is known arise from fixed causes, their outcome demonstrably cannot arise by chance, but things for which reason can find no cause are judged to arise by chance. Hence, an event occasioned by fortune is one that is produced by hidden causes. Here Cicero associates uniformity with things themselves but attributes chance to beliefs rather than to things. Hence, if one man knows the cause of a thing produced, what happens is not an event occasioned by fortune; but the same thing is an event occasioned by fortune if another man does not know its reason. Moreover, although Cicero says that there are causes for all things, he does not determine their nature; therefore he does not show what events fortune causes either.

Stupid, proud men should not censure me because I oppose Cicero's views with what seems to be a presumptuous authority, since if any of Cicero's views seems wrong, I replace it not with our own view but with a view drawn from the ancients. And even if we present our own view also, men should not consider the age of the person presenting the view but rather the reasoning of the views presented. Rather than hate the things said against famous men, they should refute those things with an argument if they can. For if they are well pleased with Cicero's definition of things, why do they begrudge our showing Aristotle's formulation also?

But if they continue to be excessively troublesome, let them hear Cicero in the second book of the *Tusculan Disputations*, where he rather exhorts and urges us to contest views in this way: "all the same we are so far from deprecating criticism that we should welcome it heartily, for . . . Greek philosophy would never have been held in such high honor, if the rivalries and disagreements of its chief exponents had not . . . [made it grow]. For this reason I encourage all, who have the capacity, to wrest from the now failing grasp of Greece the renown won from this field of study and transfer it to this city, just as our ancestors by their indefatigable zeal transferred here all the other really desirable avenues to renown."[87]

In turn, we who pursue what is readily believable and cannot progress beyond what is versimilar are ready to be refuted without obstinacy and to refute without anger. And therefore, blast it!, what sense does it make to overthrow Cicero's will and judgment since they [our critics] rely on his beliefs and authority against us?[88]

But if anyone [373/1152] thinks it not worth his while to examine our commentaries, he should know that we have taken these things from the second book of Aristotle's *Physics*.[89] And even if these things border on reasoning associated with a deeper subject in philosophy, one should nonetheless not begrudge our efforts if we mingle things of a loftier nature into discussions of rhetoric and dialectic. And it would be unreasonable for the reader to become bored or grow weary since the controversial nature of the subject and the inquiry into diverse theories should rather render the reader more attentive and lively, especially since it is the nature of books not to compel the idle but to rivet the studious to their reading. And so let us say what an event occasioned by fortune is and for what things luck is said to be the cause.

All things occur either unchangeably and always (such as that the sun rises) or generally (such as that a horse is born with four feet) or rarely (such as that a horse with five or with three feet is begotten) or indifferently (such as cases where it makes no difference to which one of a number of things to be done we bend our will). What occurs always has no opposite that occurs in some other way. But what happens generally has as an opposite that which happens rarely, for something would not occur generally although not always unless something else different from it happened sometimes, even if rarely. And so what occurs as occasioned by fortune is not among sempiternal things, for who would say that the sun rises by chance? Nor is it among those things which occur frequently, for no one would say that a horse is four footed by chance. Neither is it among the things that in general occur indifferently, for things that are willed do not seem to take place by chance. Therefore, what remains is that an event occasioned by fortune is among those things that occur rarely.

Now some things that occur aim at an end, and some do not. What end can there be, for example, if I stretch out my hand, bend my knees, and, throwing something to the ground, then pick it up but put it to no use? Furthermore, some things that aim at an end are willed, and some are natural. They are willed, for example, when someone leaves his house in order to see a friend. They are natural, as, for example, in the case of animals where all things that occur by nature aim at a definite advantage for the animal, and the motions of all its parts are arranged for the health and preservation of the animal. And so we locate chance and events occasioned by fortune among those things which, although they occur fairly rarely, nonetheless do happen, but by accident, within the group of things that occur for the sake of something else.[90]

Suppose, for example, that someone left his house to see a friend and on the way he was struck by a rock that fell on him. This event should be attributed to a fairly rare cause, and it supervenes on the will, which aimed at a definite end. The cause for his leaving his house was that he might see his friend. Furthermore, since a rock is naturally weighty and weightiness seeks the earth, the rock's falling was produced naturally for the sake of something, for the nature of the rock strove to bring it about that the weight reached its own place and rest. But something that occurs rarely supervened on this natural tendency, namely, the rock smote something. Hence, fortune or chance is an accidental cause of things occurring rarely within the group of things that occur for the sake of something. So, although the Aristotelian definition differs greatly from the Ciceronian definition, [374/1153] this nonetheless is in both: what is subject to fortune is always included among uncertain occurrences. For although fortune often undertakes its acts among things that are willed and directed to some end, nevertheless what pertains to fortune supervenes externally and does not come from the end that the mind in advance had constructed for itself.

Because Cicero divided causes into those which are evident and those which are hidden, and because he said that evident causes are those which extend to the judgment and desire of the mind, it is apparent that he includes art, will, agitation, and state among evident causes. In fact, he includes will and mental agitation under desire, for often we desire something with agitation. Art or state, however, he includes under judgment, for we judge by means of art; but states belong to either desire or judgment, for habitual practice governs acts of the will, and a certain uniformity in judging arises from much use and experience. Chance Cicero included among the nonevident causes.

As for nature, it is not clear whether Cicero included it among evident or among hidden causes. If he included it among hidden causes, he apparently thought that nature itself is chance, which is an unreasonable belief. And if he included it among evident causes, what judgment or desire of the mind is there in nature? Nature does not produce anything either by desiring it or by judging it. Or perhaps Cicero included nature among evident causes because it often gives rise to certain mental and bodily aptitudes, which strengthen the will for a particular thing, for what we want most is what we have an aptitude for. And nature is also connected to judgment (for example, when someone's natural constitution includes a sound judgment) as well as to desire (for example, when the mind by nature strives for something).

To these Cicero adds another division of causes, for he says that some causes are willed and some are unintentional. Those which come from a mental act of judgment are willed; those in which necessity is mistress (that is, those in which we do not will at all or those in which we cannot do otherwise even if we do will, as in nature and chance) are unintentional. For weighty things are borne downward by a certain necessity of nature. Similarly, when someone throws a rock against a wall and unintentionally kills a man who is passing by, we say that it happened by necessity. The necessity in the latter case is of the following sort: it is not the case that it could not have happened otherwise than that the rock smote the man when it was thrown, but rather that the will was lacking and the man did not do what he did because he willed to do it. The necessity in the former case, however, is of this sort: either there is no will in it or what will there is is constrained by a stronger necessity from producing what it wishes. For when a rock is borne downward by its weight, there is no will involved, only a necessity of nature. But if a man falls down, there is a will for not falling; but nature, which is a stronger cause, compels him to be carried where he does not will.

Cicero sundered will from events occasioned by fortune with one and the same very appropriate example: a man throws a weapon and unwillingly strikes a man passing by. The throwing has the will as its source, for he threw the weapon because he wanted to; but his smiting a man was unintentional, for he would not have thrown the weapon if he [375/1154] could have foreseen that he would smite the man, and he did not throw the weapon because he wanted to smite the man. Moreover, if he had not done it unintentionally, then he would have been able not to smite the man. This is the basis for a certain strategem and defense found in the writings of the jurists: "perhaps he did not so much throw the weapon as lose control of it."[91] If no other defense is available in the case of someone accused of murder, the best defense is usually that he did not want to throw the weapon but rather lost control of it, so that the deed might be attributed to unintentionality rather than to the will, which is culpable for crimes.

What we should say about mental agitation is harder to see, for it is unclear whether a transgression committed as a result of agitation comes from the will or from necessity or from unintentionality. For such transgressions seem to be willed because a man who is agitated desires or seeks to avoid something. But his agitation is apparent in the fact that there is no reason to seek to avoid what he shuns or to desire what he clearly longs for. Furthermore, judgments made in agitation are confused, for agitated men would not often desire what they should in fact seek to avoid unless their judgment was blinded and darkened, and often a man who does a deed out of mental confusion is unwilling to have committed that deed. Therefore, mental agitation is among unintentional or necessary causes and not among willed causes. An agitated man, however, does not depart from true discernment so far that he cannot be brought back to it by the right admonition of those who give him good counsel. Hence, mental agitation is rightly separated from voluntary causes and included either among unintentional causes or among necessary causes.

The passage "still, they[92] have such force that things which are willed seem sometimes to be necessary or certainly unintentional" should be understood in the following way. Every mental passion disturbs the judgment; if the passion is very violent, it disorders correct discernment instead of being itself restrained by the bonds of reason. Hence a vehement sort of necessity arises from agitation, so that it is not clear whether a man who does a deed when he is mentally agitated does it unintentionally—that is, whether he commits the crime unintentionally since he does not foresee the outcome—or whether he knows what he is doing but necessity forces him to do it anyway. So Cicero's saying that mental agitation is included under either the necessary or the unintentional and his dividing the unintentional from the necessary are not incompatible with his saying above that things which are unintentional are necessary. For he divides the unintentional to some extent in the following way: Some unintentional things occur as a result of a sort of necessity, either when the will is not involved or when the will that is involved cannot resist the necessity. And other unintentional things occur by chance because what was done was not willed but rather unintentional.[93]

So we should undoubtedly understand Cicero's saying that mental agitation is included under either necessary or unintentional causes to mean that mental agitation is either among unintentional causes in which there is a necessity that the will cannot resist or among causes in which will is not involved but in which blinded judgment results in a crime, as in the case of men who are passionately given to the lust of love. For either such men depart from honorable conduct because of a confused judgment and fall into evil unintentionally while they are desiring an apparent good, and in this case passionate love is included under error and "chance," or such men know that what they desire should be shunned but they are nonetheless impelled by an impulse of lust that is stronger, and this is included under necessary causes in which the will is either not involved or else is so feeble and weak that it does not in any way struggle against the passions that are more powerful.

BOOK VI

[376/1155] I have no doubt, Patricius, most skillful of rhetoricians, that there will be some who will censure in various disparaging ways the introduction of this deeper philosophical discussion[1] among the Topics on the grounds that it inserts natural philosophy into an investigation of logic. These are people who either dislike philosophy as a whole or think that natural causes should not be mixed in with Topics for arguments. Against the first group[2] there is an answer commonly given both by Cicero[3] and also in a way by human reason itself, which, being an operation, always inquires into things and because of its love of knowledge will not bear being deceived or being in the least led away from the nature of truth. But to those who think that the philosophical disciplines are to be isolated from the oratorical art, I think one should give a brief reply. One can obtain a thing by reason, but an artificer will do so better and more easily if he avails himself of art's elegance and ease in the task of construction. The case is clearly the same for arguments, too; for arguments are produced by the power of our natural abilities, but art, which functions like the natural skill, obtains a path and reasoning by means of which it can do so better and more easily.[4]

While we are on this subject, we must censure the error of those who say that rhetorical skill is natural, since a person who is a stranger to the whole art of rhetoric still commonly saddles somebody else with an accusation and exculpates himself and also attempts to prove something by arguments. We should also censure those who say that rhetorical skill consists only in art, for we should call their attention to the fact that every art receives from nature the material for what it produces, although its own character is to provide skill and elegance. Thus, the things that the character of an art produces can also be produced in some way or other by unskilled men, but no one produces anything well and easily unless he is instructed in the character of an art. And so since the purpose of this whole work is to track down by means of an art the arguments that nature supplies in a jumbled and "imprisoned" way, Cicero shows with an example the nature of the thing by means of which an art is able to produce what it promises, for what causes arguments to be found more easily is showing the places (loci) in which arguments are located. For just as someone who is searching for something can hunt for it and find it more easily if we show him the place where what he is seeking is located, so also if [377/1156] we show the place (locus) where an argument is located to a man who is trying to find an argument, he can more easily find the argument he seeks. Thus both Aristotle and Cicero call that in which arguments are located a 'seat', that is, a 'place' (Aristotle calls it a 'Topic').

Since we mentioned the seat of an argument, we should explain in a little more depth what this is, for there is more than one understanding of a Topic. (And we should leave out those places (loci) that Victorinus inserted inappropriately and to no purpose, such as those which enclose corporeal things.)[5] Simply put, we understand those things to be Topics for arguments that contain arguments within themselves. What we say here will become clearer in our subsequent exposition. Here it seems that we should discuss in general the whole nature of Topics, argumentation, questions and propositions, and their terms.

First, since the place (locus) discussed in the Topica is not the place of just any thing but is rather the place only of an argument, we will first explain the concept of an argument and then discuss the nature of a Topic. Cicero defines an argument in this way: an argument is a reason producing belief regarding something that is in doubt. And so he took reason as the genus of arguments, for men who separate rhetorical excellence from the nature of wisdom and who would have it that the art of speaking is one thing and the art of understanding is another are all outrageous. For if in speech we do nothing other than make public our inner thoughts, what reason is there, blast it!, for excluding the importance of thought from the elegance of speech? And how could thought be important without comprehension of the things to be talked about? And what discipline teaches the nature and characteristics of all things or in general promises knowledge of things that can be understood except philosophy alone, that discipline from which we have taken a few points? In philosophical discussions of these matters[6] by wise men, they are generally treated very differently and not so briefly as by us. But if I had undertaken to speak about these matters at more length (as is customary in the books of wise men), who would have been able to bear the heedlessness of haughty men, who are willing to reproach their own progress if they should prefer engaging in learning to lodging complaints? But the ancient period was not free from such quarrels, and we ourselves are not so soft that we are unwilling to bear what very learned men often resisted with hardiness, as long as it is the case both that we can be useful to many and that we are following the judgment of the wise. To this end our labor and the purpose of the whole work strive. But that is enough about this. Now let us follow the order of the exposition we have undertaken.

[17.65–17.66]

Now that the Topic *from causes* has been divided and partitioned in order into its parts, Cicero (as is often his wont) discusses the power of this same Topic and in which cases it has a broader and in which a narrower application. First, he says, there is a great store of arguments from the Topic *from causes* for orators and philosophers, whose discussions contain a generous amount of material. In fact, this Topic *from causes* is observed to be common to orators and philosophers, because causes show philosophers the natures of things, which is proper to philosophy, and they show orators deeds, which belongs to rhetorical [378/1157] skill. For when any thing is investigated, philosophers customarily inquire into its causes; when they have been presented, what is to be concluded follows immediately, as we said above. And orators look for the causes of deeds to excite or remove suspicion. In fact, it is fixed in the minds of men that, apart from the most noble nature of all, neither any deed nor any thing can exist without its appropriate causes. Hence, there is an abundant use of causes in the speeches of rhetoricians and the discussions of philosophers.

In order to appear to address virtually everything to Trebatius in writing this book, Cicero shows that this Topic is also ascribed to jurists; he says, "Even if there are not so many opportunities to use this Topic in the writings of the jurists, it can certainly be dealt with more subtly and keenly according to the nature of this art"; so he substitutes subtlety, which can be present, for abundance, which is lacking. For jurists, too, have their own field of action in which their excellence can shine forth. The province of jurists is questions concerning private cases,[7] and this Topic *from causes* will be considered especially in legal actions where a judgment concerning good faith is involved.[8] For in these legal actions we generally ask about the intention of the men who made the contract, and this can hardly be grasped unless it is understood in terms of the preceding causes. In those judgments, then, in which it is added that judgment be given with regard to good faith (that is, when the judges are appointed to inquire into good faith rather than just into the exact stipulations between the litigants), there is considerable use of causes. The phrase 'that one's dealings with good men should be good' is added; customs are considered; purposes are inquired into; and the causes by means of which something was done are determined. And especially in a judgment concerning a wife's property there is considerable discussion of causes.

There is a judgment concerning a wife's property when there is contention over the dowry after a divorce. For although the dowry is included among the husband's goods while the marriage lasts, nonetheless it is legally the woman's and it can be sued for as the wife's property. For a dowry used, for some time, to be given with the stipulation that if a divorce between the husband and wife occurred, what was more right and equitable would remain with the husband and the rest of the dowry would be restored to the wife.[9] In other words, the part of the dowry that was judged to be better and more equitable to have remain with the husband, the husband would keep for himself, but the part of the dowry that it was not better and more equitable to have remain with the husband, the wife would receive after the divorce. Generally in this judgment not only is the nature of some good considered, but there is also a comparison of goods, so that we should pursue not so much what is good but what is more right and equitable. All these things are generally investigated on the basis of their preceding causes. For if a divorce occurred as a result of the husband's fault, it is more right and equitable if nothing remain with the husband; but if the fault is the wife's, it is more right and equitable that the husband retain a sixth part.

Jurists should be very proficient in all these matters. Hence Cicero stimulates Trebatius to study also, for he says that there are many things that depend on the work of jurists. It is the jurists, Cicero says, who have defined fraud, good faith, equity, what one partner owes to another, [379/1158] what a man who has willingly undertaken to conduct the affairs of another owes to the man whose affairs they are, what a mandator owes the man to whom he has mandated the management of his legal actions,[10] what a husband owes to his wife, and what a wife owes to her husband. All these things are causes for what comes after them, and judgments are made on their basis. For example, the reason a judge should decide whatever he does in the case of a husband and wife is that the husband owes this to his wife. Also, the reason a mandator should be judged to be under an obligation to the man to whom he has given a mandate is that this obligation between a mandator and a man who undertakes his legal actions should be honored. And all the things that one man owes to another are causes in the legal actions to be discussed and judged. Therefore, Cicero rightly concluded that when the Topics for arguments have been carefully understood by orators, philosophers, and jurists, they will have an abundance of arguments.

[18.67]

All things that are related to one another are rightly said to be conjoined, for any relation between things produces a conjoining. And if a cause is a cause of something, it is the cause precisely of its effects. Similarly, if something is an effect, its sources are its causes. And so it is right that we should conjoin the Topic *from effects* to the Topic *from causes*. And since things related to one another are always equal in number, there must be the same abundance of effects as there is of causes. For a cause cannot exist apart from its effect, since a cause is always a cause of effects; therefore if many arguments are obtained from causes, there must also be many arguments from effects and outcomes. For just as from any effect a cause can be drawn, so from any cause one can show what the outcome is. And so Cicero rightly says, "an understanding of causes produces an understanding of outcomes." For as is shown in the *Categories*,[11] one relative cannot be known without knowledge of the other relative.

[18.68–18.71]

Every comparison is twofold, for either equals or unequals are compared to one another. In the case where the things being compared are equal, the equality is observed to be always the same. Unequals, however, are divided into two "parts," namely, the lesser and the greater. For what is lesser is not lesser in itself but in comparison to what is greater; similarly, what is greater is said to be greater in comparison to what is lesser. Hence, Cicero divides and places before our eyes the modes of all comparisons. And, something that he did only rarely in the case of the preceding Topics, he presents the very maximal propositions involved in the comparisons, so that whenever we need to use the Topic from comparison, we have a certain "paradigm" of discovery to which we can direct our searching.

Every comparison has to do with number, form, power, or a relation to something external to it. For whatever we are trying to bring together for comparison, we compare with regard to number, and in accordance with this we discern one thing to be greater and another thing to be lesser; [380/1160] or observing the form and comparing it to something else, we give a judgment about its superiority; or we consider what a thing is and what it can produce and to what extent its nature can grow; or we observe the thing that we want to bring into comparison with something else on the basis of some proximity it has to other things and its relationship with things around it.[12]

If things compared with regard to number are of the same genus, many are preferred to fewer; for example, if all goods are equal, a man rightly prefers more goods to fewer.[13] And the maximal proposition is this: many goods are preferred to fewer. And in other cases as well the same point in the maximal propositions is evident. But if all the things are in the contrary genus,[14] fewer should be preferred to more, as, for example, fewer evils should be preferred to more evils. Evils themselves, however, are not in any way compared to goods, for things that are balanced against one another in some way should be in the same genus and not in contrary ones. For since contraries are opposed to one another and are placed over against one another, they cannot be brought together and compared because they are understood to be discordant with one another. A comparison with regard to number can also be based on the nature of time. Since time is divided into certain definite distances such as hours, days, months, and years, in the case of equal things[15] those which last a longer time are more to be chosen.[16] And everyone knows that this consists in number, for this very duration indicates that there are more days, months, or years during which what is chosen persists. Also, in a comparison with regard to number, widespread goods take precedence over goods that are narrower and confined into one small place; for goods that are spread far and wide are extended to many people and places, and the plurality of anything pertains to number. Moreover, who would not judge that those things from which many goods are generated are better than those whose fruitfulness for good is meager and limited? And who would not think that the good that many people emulate in their actions is superior to other goods that are not such? And who does not know that this consists in number, since plurality consists in number.

Things that have been considered in their own right and that on the merit of some excellence they have are preferred to other things are compared with regard to form. For those things which are sought after for their own sake rather than for the sake of something else are better, such as health, for example, which is sought after for its own sake, unlike medicine, which is sought after for the sake of health, and therefore health is better than medicine. We give our judgment about these things by taking into account not some number of a quantity of any sort but rather the form of health and the consideration of medicine. Also those things which are inborn and natural are judged better than those which are acquired and not native; hence inborn dignity of conduct is far superior to dignity that is pursued by emulation. Also, what is unimpaired is judged better than what is corrupted; for things that are unimpaired preserve their form, but things that are corrupted and damaged in some part lose whatever excellence of form they had. The nature common to all animals judges what is pleasant to be better than what is less pleasant. Wise men prefer what is honorable to what is advantageous. The fact that no one desires to reach his goal by a hard and difficult path when he can arrive there by an easy, ready road shows that what is easy is preferred to what is difficult. [381/1161] In fact, what is difficult is always unpleasant, and what is easy is always pleasant. Also, sometimes necessary things should be preferred to nonnecessary things, and sometimes nonnecessary things should be chosen over necessary things (a point Cicero is silent about[17]). In fact, necessary things are preferred to nonnecessary things that consist in a desire for sensual pleasure rather than in the nature of the good; for example, no wise man would judge sumptuous banquets fit for a king to be better than those which just fulfill nature's needs. But although they are not necessary, things having the form of the good are better than necessary things. It is necessary to live and no animal can subsist without living, but it is not necessary to philosophize. Nevertheless, to live as a philosopher is better and far superior to simply living; to live as a philosopher is granted rarely and to the few who use reason, but simply living we have in common with livestock. Also, things that are really ours are rightly said to be better than things that are not native to us; for example, for men, reason is better than the desire for sensual pleasure, for reason really belongs to man but the desire for sensual pleasure is not native to him. Also things that are rare are better than things that are common. (And this Topic proves what was said above, that life as a philosopher is better than life itself, for things that are rare easily take precedence over what is common.)

The fact that desirable things are desired greatly and that you lead such a straitened life without them shows that desirable things are better than those things you can easily do without. For example, we prefer sight to hair, for it is more difficult to bear the lack of sight than the lack of hair; consequently we judge sight better than hair, because it is easy for us to bear the lack of hair, but the lack of sight is distressing. Also, things that are completely developed are naturally superior to things that are not completely developed, for those that are completely developed have attained their form, but those that are not completely developed have not. Also we think that wholes are in the same way superior to parts, for what is a whole has the form appropriate to its nature, but what is a part and depends on the complete development of the whole has not yet received the form of its excellence (unless it is referred to the completed whole). In addition, no one doubts that things that use reason are better than those devoid of reason. Also, things that are voluntary are rightly preferred to those which are necessary, for things that are voluntary are free, but those which are necessary bind us by the "mastery" of necessity; therefore we consider voluntary things better than necessary ones. (In this regard, we should also grasp the point that, as we said previously, nonnecessary things are often preferred to necessary things, since things that are voluntary are not necessary and voluntary things are better than necessary things; therefore nonnecessary things are often superior to necessary things.) Also, reason convinces us that animate things, judged in light of the quickening of the soul, should be preferred to inanimate things. Also, natural things should be preferred to things that are not natural, and things produced by art to things produced without art; the best ranking is this: you should prefer nature to art and art to the lack of art. In fact, art imitates nature; hence, what excellence it has in itself comes from nature, whose form it desires to imitate. At the very bottom of our ranking are things that lack art and are therefore separated from both the form and the imitation of nature. And these are the things considered with regard to comparisons about form.

We consider power when we consider what a thing can produce, for a thing's power is most correctly said to be what it is capable of. And so an efficient cause has greater power than a cause that produces nothing, as an artisan is better than his material, for the material is inert and immobile and produces nothing unless it receives a form from the artisan, that is, from an efficient cause. [382/1162] Similarly, things that are self-sufficient seem to be better than those which need other things, as for example, God is better than all other things because he needs nothing and all things are in need of him. Similarly, those things that are in our power are more to be chosen than those things which are in the power of others and are easily removed from us. Hence, virtue is better than wealth, for virtue is in our power, but fortune is mistress of wealth. Moreover, who does not understand that, if they are good, things that are permanent and cannot be torn away from us are better than things that are not dependable and can be torn away from us?

With regard to these Topics, each part contains its contrary; in fact, once we have examined things that are better, if we consider their contraries, they are things that are worse.

What remains is the comparison having to do with relation, and this is handled in the following way: a thing that is compared to something else is evaluated not in itself but on the basis of a consideration of some other thing, as, for example, if two things are compared with one another with regard to the extent to which they are joined to some third thing. For suppose there are two things of some sort that are suited to human affairs, and one of these is more suited to the leading citizens and also to the state itself. In this case we will therefore judge that thing to be better which is advantageous for the better (that is, either for the state or for the leading citizens), without considering these things in themselves but only insofar as they are connected to the state or to the leading citizens. And so this thing is compared with regard to a relationship, and what is in the interests of the leading citizens is judged better than what is in the interests of some private persons, since the leading citizens also preserve the condition of the other citizens. Similarly for the things that follow: for example, things that are more pleasant for more people, things that are more renowned among many, and things that are approved by more people are all believed to be better. For, even if they themselves have little of such a nature, nonetheless (as we said) they are reckoned to be better on the basis of their relationship to those things with respect to which they are more pleasant or those people among whom they are more renowned or by whom they are approved. But although Cicero previously included that which is believed to be good by more people in comparison with regard to number, nothing hinders the same Topic from being put under different genera in accordance with different considerations, as, for example, the wing of a bird is a substance, and yet it is understood to be a relative if it is considered with respect to a winged thing.[18] Also, those things which are praised by a man against whom one is arguing with dialectical reason or rhetorical skill seem to be better on the basis of a comparison, for to be able to refute an adversary, it is enough if you show that he has agreed with you and that he at one time praised as very good what you are trying to show is better with regard to the matter at hand.[19]

Now that all the Topics having to do with the better have been discussed, their opposites will contain those having to do with what is worse. There is no separate division for equals, however, for what is equal cannot admit of either superiority or inferiority.[20] But in whatever ways greater things are evaluated among themselves with regard to lesser things, in the same way equals are compared among themselves, for things that are equivalent in number, form, power, or relationship are said to be equal. A common example for all of these is what Cicero gives for equality, which is the same in all equals. But they are equal in number, form, power, or relationship. In a comparison of greater or lesser things, there is one quality, [383/1163] but the amount of that quality which they have varies; for those things will be reckoned to be better which, with regard to the same quality, have a greater amount, a more excellent form, a more efficacious power, or a relationship more conjoined to something that is valued more. But if these things are equal, then they are equal with regard to the same quality.

The example Cicero presented is effective because it catches Trebatius's attention with flattery since it unites Trebatius's skill (that is, oratorical skill) with praise of legal experts, in the following way. "If helping citizens with advice" (this concerns legal experts) "and helping them with assistance"[21] (this concerns orators) "should receive equal praise, then those who give advice" (that is, the legal experts) "should be equal in glory with those who defend" (that is, the orators); "but the first part is the case" (that is, helping citizens with advice and helping citizens with assistance should receive equal praise), "and therefore what follows is the case" (that is, what follows is inferred). And the conclusion is this: "And so those who give advice and those who defend should be equal in glory." Stating this in the following way expresses it concisely in the manner of dialecticians: 'If it is day, it is light; but the first part is the case'—this is like saying 'But it is day', for in the proposition 'If it is day, it is light,' the proposition 'It is day' is first. They conclude 'And therefore what follows is the case,' that is, 'therefore it is light,' for this followed 'If it is day,' which was in the first part of the proposition. And so here too Cicero speaks in this way: "But the first part is the case," that is, helping citizens with advice and helping citizens with assistance should receive equal praise, for this was first in the proposition 'If helping citizens with advice and helping citizens with assistance should receive equal praise, then orators and jurists are equal in glory.' "And therefore what follows is the case," that is, those who give advice and those who defend should be equal in glory, for this was the consequent in the proposition that maintained that if helping citizens with advice and helping citizens with assistance are equal, then those who give advice and those who defend are equals.

[18.71]

Although the things that have been said teach us that no Topic for argument has been passed over, nevertheless to further belief in

Cicero's system I think I should briefly confirm his conclusion in which he says that he has omitted nothing. For if things are discussed with a definite criterion, nothing at all is omitted. But there is no more definite criterion than that provided by a division, for when someone makes a division and derives particulars from general things,[22] if he pursues the right path, he cannot fall into error and be mistaken. And so the first division of all Topics was into those things which inhere in the things themselves and those which are taken from without. No intermediate can be found for this division, for either something is in the thing asked about or it must be taken from without.[23] Let us see here, then, how to produce a treatment of the subject by means of a division that omits nothing.[24]

With regard to the Topics that are in the things at issue, an argument is taken sometimes from a whole, sometimes from parts, sometimes from a word, and sometimes from related things. It is plainly manifest that nothing is left out here. For whatever is conjoined is divided in two ways: one stemming from the thing itself, which is ordered and composed (this is a whole and definitions are also supplied in it), [384/1164] and another consisting in a consideration of its parts, from which the form of the composite thing is conjoined. But since it is the nature of men generally to give utterance to what they understand, a name, which is used to express a concept, must also show some characteristics of the thing it signifies. In fact, it captures a quality of the concept of the thing understood, and therefore a name also designates a quality of a concept. And so it is rightly said that a word signifies certain characteristics of a thing; in this way from a word we can draw an argument, and this is called 'from a sign'. (Cicero gave other divisions of these Topics, and we will briefly classify these a little later.)

Related things (which, as we said above,[25] consist in a relationship) are themselves also duly divided, for those things which are related to something are either substantial or accidents. For example, conjugates are substantial, for justice produces the substance for a just man considered as just. I do not mean that being is constituted of justice for a man but rather for a just man, who ceases to exist when justice is gone. And the same point applies to the adverb 'justly'. Genus, species, differentia, cause, and effect are also substantial.[26] Examples of accidents are a contrary, a similar, an associated thing, equals, greater things, and lesser things. Since, as we said above, consequents and incompatibles consist in a condition,[27] they are sometimes found to be substantial and sometimes are seen in accidents. For example, they are substantial when a genus follows from an antecedent species;[28] they are accidents when *blackness* follows from *raven* which precedes, although there can be some things that are accidents even in causes. And Cicero discussed the characteristics of all of these above.

The whole division of Topics will be summarized with a concise description in this way. Every argument is drawn from those Topics that inhere in the thing asked about or from those Topics that are taken from without. The Topic that is in the things in doubt is divided into the Topic that is from the whole, the Topic that is from parts, the Topic that is from a sign, and the Topic that is from related things. The one that is from the whole is called the Topic *from definition*. Some definitions, however, are definitions strictly speaking, and some are not. Some of those that are not definitions strictly speaking are denoted by individual names, and others are unfolded in a phrase.[29] Some of the definitions that occur as individual names are definitions in which a name is given for a name, and these are called '*kat' antilexin'*.[30] Others substitute a name by way of an example, and these are called '*typoi*'. On the other hand, those definitions expressed in a phrase arise from partition, division, differentiae without a genus (these are called '*ennoematikai*'), from several individual qualities signifying the whole which the entire group of qualities makes manifest (this is called '*poiotes*'), from accidents that produce something when they are taken not individually but as a group,[31] from a differentia,[32] from a metaphor, from the privation of a contrary, from specific names (these are called '*hypotyposeis*'), from the want of the complete thing, from an analogy,[33] from a relation, and from a cause. Again, another division of definition (and this is the chief division according to Cicero[34]) is that some [385/1165] are definitions of corporeal things and some of incorporeal things. And in this way the Topic *from definition* is divided.[35]

The Topic *from parts* is divided into *partition* and *division*, and the Topic *from a sign* is undivided. But the Topic *from related things* is divided into *from conjugates, from a genus, from a kind, from a similar, from a differentia, from contraries, from associated things, from consequents, antecedents, and incompatibles, from a cause, from effects,* and *from a comparison of equals, greater things,* and *lesser things*. Genera are divided into highest genera and genera that can also be species, and species are divided into lowest species and species that can also be genera. Also, some similars are considered with regard to particular things and are called 'examples'; others are considered with regard to many things and are labeled 'induction'; and others are considered with regard to conjoined things and are called 'proportions'. Again, some differentiae are substantial; others are not substantial but are nonetheless inseparable; and others are neither substantial nor inseparable. Some contraries are said to be adverse, others privative, others negating, and others relative. Some associated things exist before the thing with which they are associated, others simultaneously with the thing, and others after the thing. The conditional Topic is divided into *antecedent, consequent,* and *incompatible.*

The Topic *from causes* is manifold.[36] Some causes produce a thing by their own power and others are causes without which something cannot be produced. Some of those which produce something by their own power are necessary and need nothing else in order to produce; others do need something else in order to produce; and others need something else and are not necessary.[37] Some of the causes without which something cannot be produced are variable and others are invariable. Again, some causes are not voluntary, and others arise from the will, from agitation, from habit, from nature, from art, or from chance.[38] Again, some causes are uniform and others are not uniform. Further, some causes are willed, and others are unintentional. Those which are unintentional consist partly in chance and partly in necessity; those which are necessary are included partly under force and partly under ignorance.

Effects can be divided in just as many ways as the causes discussed above to which they are related.

The Topic *from the comparison of lesser things, equals, and greater things* is divided into number, form, power, and relationship to other things.

For these reasons and since nothing has been omitted in this division, Cicero rightly concluded the division by saying that no seat of an argument was passed over. And so there remains the Topic that is taken from without, which Cicero adds not for Trebatius's sake, since it is of no use for jurists, but rather in order that this work might not seem to lack anything needed to complete it.

[19.72]

To keep Trebatius from being indifferent to this Topic which will be of no use to a legal expert, the orator renders Trebatius attentive with the sort of devices used in a proemium. For in the beginning, Cicero says, he made a division of the following sort: he said that some Topics inhere in the things at issue and others are taken from without; since he has discussed the preceding Topics sufficiently, he should not pass over the remaining part which he has not yet dealt with. For, he says, Trebatius is not a man who is content with his own art and indifferent to the study of other things; rather, painstaking and powerfully intelligent, he takes anything in the liberal arts as relevant to himself.

[386/1166] At the same time, since Trebatius will publish this work with Cicero's ready consent, Cicero says he should take pains to make sure that when this work comes into the hands of many others, it can benefit with the whole art those who pursue honorable studies. And he grants Trebatius as an added advantage that the work he composed for many was written to Trebatius and will be published by him.

[19.73]

Cicero calls the Topic for an argument taken from without devoid of art, and he maintains that it consists in testimony. There might be some doubt, however, concerning the way in which this Topic differs from the preceding Topics that Cicero placed in related things.[39] For as related things always consist in a relationship, so too testimonies are related to those things of which they are the testimonies, for every testimony is the testimony of the thing testified to. And so it is open to us to ask why the things previously called related things are not classified as being from without or why the things now called external are not included among related things, especially since the things that we previously said were associated with a legal action are often adduced for the matter at issue as a kind of testimony, since it is customary to consider the deed that was done in light of indications concerning what preceded or followed that deed.

To all of these difficulties there is a common solution. Arguments that arise from related things are found by an orator and are produced by his effort and industry; arguments taken from without, however, offer only testimony concerning the matter at issue, for they are not found by an orator, but the orator uses them already existing and constituted. Arguments from a genus or from a species or from other related things are prepared by the orator himself in some way. But the orator does not produce testimonies for himself; rather he uses them for his case ready-made. Hence, arguments from related things in a case arise from the start and as occasion offers, but arguments consisting in testimony exist before the matter at issue and afterward are useful as confirming evidence for a legal action. And in the case of associated things, the orator draws a conclusion and impresses it on his audience; in the case of testimony, however, the arguments consist not in drawing conclusions or making inferences but in the narration of the action that was done.

Cicero shows cogently what testimony is when he says that what he calls testimony is what is taken from some external matter. Now no related things seem external to the things to which they are related, but the only bond joining testimony to the thing testified to is knowledge, which is no attribute of the action that was done, since if no one knew that action, the deed would nonetheless have been done. This charge can be brought against similarity too though, for a thing would not exist any the less if no similar to it were found. But a similar is conjoined to the thing to which it is similar by one and the same quality, which shapes them both. Knowledge, on the other hand, is not conjoined to the thing of which it is knowledge by any quality, no matter how it produces testimony. The knowledge that the knower has cannot be called a quality of the action done; because if the knowledge could be thought to be a quality of the action, then the action would be destroyed or altered when those who knew the action perished. Neither outcome[40] is necessarily the case, however, because when the knowers are removed, the thing that is then unknown can still remain.

[19.73–20.76]

[387/1168] Since Cicero said that the Topic that is devoid of art consists in testimony, and since in testimony we look for authorization from persons who enhance credibility, we need to explain what sorts of things generally give rise to authority. (And the other points are made very clearly and plainly.)[41] Cicero divided authority into nature and times; among times he included intelligence, wealth, age, fortune, art, experience, necessity, and even occasionally a concurrence of fortuitous events. And so the following questions can arise: Why is intelligence included among times? Why is art? Why is experience? For age and wealth, fortune and the concurrence of fortuitous events are subject to times since each one of them is altered by the various vicissitudes of times. But intelligence should be attributed rather to nature, and art and experience to some third thing, since they are subject neither to times nor to nature, although even virtue, which Cicero put under the classification of nature, seems to be derived not from things that pertain to nature but rather partly from instruction and partly from correct practice in living.

Cicero's division, however, should be understood in the following way. All authority comes either from things that are great and excellent and best by nature or from those things that hold an inferior place and have credibility not because of the quality of their nature but because of the beliefs held by common people. And he subsumed great and excellent things under nature, which always seeks the good, as Cicero himself maintained in many places. But he included lower things under times because all things subject to times do not hold the position of a principal good. Virtue, in other words, cannot be bent into something worse; but intelligence and wealth, fortune,[42] art, and experience are often perverted by the failure to use them correctly, for if any of these is separated from virtue, it loses the honor of true praise.

Cicero postponed saying anything about virtue; but he divided the second part, that is, authority consisting in times, and he clarified it with illuminating examples. For intelligence produces credibility, and a great deal of authority is provided by it. In fact, men believe that people whose intelligence suffices for them to achieve what they planned are people who speak more wisely. Those who are outstandingly wealthy they also think worthy of belief. They bestow the dignity of authority also on those who are especially fortunate and who are in high offices, although perhaps they are not right to do so. But the judgment concerning legal actions and the reputation of a person's life are both thoroughly bound by the opinions of men; because such opinions are very hard to change, an orator is guided by them in everything he undertakes to discuss or manage. Art and experience also count for a great deal, for in both cases knowledge produces credibility.

Necessity, too, is supported with authority because it seems to wrest out something hidden; such necessity is sometimes mental and sometimes physical. It is physical when some hidden truth is revealed by fire, sword, or stripes. It is mental when the mind is muddled as a result of some necessity generated by agitation or ignorance; for in such circumstances the mind does not distinguish between what it should say and what it should keep silent about, and so it betrays and brings to light secret truths. For often wrath and mental agitation [388/1169] fail to hold in what should have been kept secret; these have authority for producing credibility because they are uttered candidly and expressed artlessly and guilelessly. Even childish ignorance, intoxication, and sleep have often disclosed things that would not have been expressed if there had been any judgment in these persons. Also, apart from any mental agitation, men are often unintentionally made liable by their own confessions, when they candidly unburden themselves of everything, thinking they are safe in doing so. This is what Cicero maintained happened to Staienus.[43] While some witnesses were listening concealed behind a wall, [Staienus], unaware[44] that he was being heard by the men who were lying in wait for him, confessed things that caused him to be condemned on a capital charge when they were made public and reported in court. And such ignorance constitutes a sort of necessity, for a man who does not know something cannot avoid what he is ignorant of even if he wants to. Such necessity wrests the truth from a man in such a way that the truth itself seems to be speaking; so since these things are supported with authority, they are given credibility.

A concurrence of fortuitous events also produces credibility; although this sometimes indicates false conclusions, it nevertheless is so forceful that it is hard to disentangle the truth from it. This is the sort of thing told about Palamedes: the dead Phrygian who seemed to have been sent by Priam, the discovery of Priam's letter, the imitation of the Phrygian hand—by their concurrence these things produced credibility in his treachery.[45] What Cicero says is, "And such is the concurrence of fortuitous things."

NOTES TO

THE TRANSLATION

NOTES TO BOOK I

1. Little is known of this Patricius. L. M. de Rijk ("On the Chronology of Boethius's Works on Logic" II, *Vivarium*, 2 [1964], p. 147) and Luca Obertello (*A. M. Severino Boezio, De hypotheticis syllogismis*, pp. 131–135) argue that Boethius's treatise on hypothetical syllogisms is also dedicated to Patricius, but Henry Chadwick (*Boethius: The Consolations of Music, Logic, Theology, and Philosophy* [Oxford: Clarendon Press, 1981], p. 168) thinks this unlikely. According to Cassiodorus (*Variae* x.6–7), Patricius was an advocate in Rome and became quaestor of the Palace in 534.

2. For Boethius's view that things subject to the vicissitudes of fortune are not properly speaking one's own, see *The Consolation of Philosophy*, esp. Book II.

3. Marius Victorinus was a famous rhetorican of the fourth century A.D., who converted to Christianity in his old age. He wrote treatises on rhetoric and dialectic, some of which are still extant, translated work by Plotinus and Porphyry, and wrote commentaries on Cicero's *De inventione* and *Topica*. His commentary on the *Topica* is not extant. For an authoritative study of Victorinus, see Pierre Hadot, *Marius Victorinus* (Paris: Etudes Augustiniennes, 1971).

4. That is, from the beginning of the book to *Topica* I.5.

5. *Topica* II.6–II.8.

6. *Topica* II.8–IV.23.

7. Gaius Trebatius Testa was a Roman jurist and a friend of Cicero's and Horace's. He was a legal adviser to Caesar recommended by Cicero, and himself wrote two treatises on law, *De religionibus* and *De iure civili*. Cicero addressed the letters *ad Familiares* vii.6–22 to him; we also have Cicero's letter recommending him to Caesar, *ad Familiares* vii.5.

8. See, e.g., Cicero, *De inventione* I.xv.20–I.xviii.26.

9. Cicero's *Topica* was probably written in 44 B.C., in the year before his death. The circumstances of the book's composition are explained in the book itself and confirmed by Cicero's letter *ad Familiares* vii.19 which he sent to Trebatius with his *Topica*. Cicero decided to leave Italy in consequence of the political turmoil after Caesar's assassination and Anthony's bid for power. He wrote the *Topica* during the voyage from Italy on his way to Greece to visit his son. He did not complete the voyage; unfavorable winds and favorable politics caused him to return to Italy.

10. Bonitz's *Index* indicates that Aristotle did not use the word *'logikē'* for all of logic. The origin and history of *'logikē'* as a word for logic are not clear.

11. As will quickly become clear, the objects of discovery and judgment are arguments. The division of logic into the discovery and judgment of arguments was apparently traditional by Cicero's time.

12. For a detailed discussion of the history of dialectic, see, e.g., Pierre Michaud-Quantin and J. A. Weisheipl, "Dialectics in the Middle Ages," in the *New Catholic Encyclopedia*.

13. See, e.g., Plato, *Sophist* 218Eff. and 253Dff.; *Philebus* 14E; *Statesman* 262Aff.

14. For Aristotle's use of the term, see note 10, and see Aristotle, *Top.* 105b20ff. and 162b27, and *An. Pos.* 93a15 (and 91b10ff.), 86a22, 88a19ff.

15. See, e.g., Aristotle, *Top.* 100a25ff., 101b11ff., 105a10–34, 163b20–164b7; *An. Pr.* 24b16ff. and 68b9ff.; *An. Pos.* 71a1–72b4, 81b10–84b3, 90a3ff.

16. See *De top. diff.* 1180C–1182A, in Stump 1978: 39–41, and the notes to those pages.

17. See, e.g., Aristotle, *Top.* 100a18–b18.

18. A metaphorical use of the Aristotelian distinction between the matter and form of a thing is common among medieval authors.

19. As the preceding paragraphs make clear, the division in question is the division of a genus into its subordinate species. Such division requires the discovery of the appropriate differentiae by which the genus can be divided into its species. Every definition consists in a genus and a differentia, and therefore defining depends on discovering the appropriate genus and differentia. See the appendix to these notes.

20. As Boethius explains Plato's understanding of collection, it involves gathering things together under a genus; this requires finding the appropriate genus. When Boethius divides collection into parts, however, he seems to understand collecting as a matter of finding arguments. What relation Boethius has in mind between these two notions of collecting is not clear. Collecting as the discovery of arguments is the predominant notion.

21. Discovery is a kind of matter, metaphorically speaking, for definition, partition, and the three parts of collection. These three parts—necessity, ready believability, and sophistry—are then forms, figuratively speaking, that are imposed on discovery. What received these forms, however, seems to be not discovery itself, which is what one would expect, but rather the arguments discovered. The imposition of these three forms produces necessary, readily believable, or sophistical arguments.

22. Boethius made two divisions of logic: first into definition, partition, and collection (itself divided into necessary, readily believable, and sophistical); then, into discovery and judgment. These two divisions are related in a complicated way. Discovery, the first member of the second division, is a metaphorical matter on which the three parts of the first division are imposed as forms, making the discovery (or its objects) definitive or divisive or necessary, readily believable, or sophistical. Then these things, discoveries informed by one or another of the parts of the first division, act as matter for the second member of the second division, namely, judgment. Judgment takes what is discovered as its matter and determines whether the definition, division, or arguments have been made correctly. In making that determination, Boethius apparently thinks, judgment is imposed as a form on the things discovered.

23. Argumentations and syllogisms are at issue here because Boethius is taking collection to consist in the discovery of arguments. For Boethius's definition of syllogism, see *De top. diff.* 1183A–1183D, in Stump 1978: 43–44, and the notes to those pages. For his distinctions between argument and argumentation, see *ICT*, p. 282 (pp. 35–36 below).

24. This is a confusing remark for Boethius to make. He obviously has Aristotle in mind in this discussion; as Boethius knows, Aristotle discusses verisimilar arguments in his *Topics*, which was traditionally placed in the *Organon* after *Posterior Analytics* and before *On Sophistical Refutations*. What Boethius has in mind by saying that verisimilar arguments are not dealt with is something of this sort. In his *Topics* Aristotle is investigating only the discovery of verisimilar arguments, not their nature as verisimilar; nothing in the book explains, for example, how we can tell which arguments are verisimilar as distinct from sophistical or what forms of arguments are distinctively verisimilar. Therefore, the *Topics* belongs to discovery and not to judgment, and there is in Boethius's view no Aristotelian book devoted to judgment of verisimilar arguments.

25. To understand why Boethius puts verisimilar arguments in the middle between necessary and sophistical arguments, it is helpful to be clear about what he means by 'necessary' and 'sophistical'. As he explains in *De. top. diff.* 1181A–1182A (Stump 1978: 40–41), he takes sophistical arguments to be those that are undoubtedly and evidently fallacious.

26. Boethius's point is that discovery is more powerful than judgment in practice in the law courts. Arguments that are discovered and expressed even without the aid of a system for judging arguments are likely to be more advantageous to a litigant than a tacit judgment about someone else's arguments. It seems to me both unreasonable and irrelevant to the issue at hand for Boethius to compare *tacit* judgments with *expressed* arguments.

27. See *De top. diff.* 1180C–1181C, in Stump 1978: 39–41, and the notes to those pages.

28. This view of logic, which is less formal and more practical and psychological than our current understanding of logic, is typical of Boethius. See *De top. diff.* 1181A–1181C, in Stump 1978: 40–41, and the notes to those pages.

29. See *De top. diff.* 1176D–1180B, in Stump 1978: 33–39, and the notes to those pages.

30. See *De top. diff.* 1174D–1176D, in Stump 1978: 30–33, and the notes to those pages.

31. See n. 29. For a discussion of the relative dating of *ICT* and *De top. diff.*, see de Rijk 1964: 151–154.

32. Boethius has now made two general claims about question, first, that every question is a proposition in doubt, and second, that every question consists in contradictories; these two claims are not clearly compatible. The idea behind the first claim is that every question is equivalent to a proposition, such as 'The heaven is spherical,' which is not believed to be true or believed to be false but rather is in doubt for the questioner. The idea behind the second claim is that the proposition underlying a question invariably contains at least implicitly an affirmation and a negation, that every question has the logical form 'Is the heaven spherical or isn't it?' (or in the case of conditionals, 'Is it the case that if something is a man it is an animal, or isn't it?'). According to the second claim, then, the proposition that is comprised in a question is in effect

always a disjunction, such as 'The heaven is spherical or the heaven is not spherical.' But this sort of proposition cannot be *in doubt* for anyone, as the first claim maintains it is. Perhaps what Boethius means is that only one disjunct is the proposition in doubt which constitutes the question, but that that proposition plus the doubt surrounding it is equivalent to the whole disjunction. For example, on this view the question 'Is the heaven spherical?' consists in the proposition 'The heaven is spherical' which is in doubt; but the proposition and the questioner's doubting of it are equivalent to the disjunction 'The heaven is spherical, or the heaven is not spherical.'

33. This may be a reference to Boethius's translation of and commentary on Aristotle's *Topics*. For the dating of these works of Boethius, see de Rijk 1964: 154–156, and Chadwick 1981: 138–139. The translation is edited in *Aristoteles Latinus*, ed. L. Minio-Paluello (Leiden: Desclée de Brouwer, 1969), V: 1–3. The commentary is not extant, as far as we now know.

34. He clearly has Aristotle's *Topics* in mind here, at least, and perhaps also the commentary on that work by Themistius (ca. A.D. 320–390). Themistius's commentary is no longer extant, but fragments of it remain, preserved in quotations and paraphrases in Averroes's middle commentary on the *Topics*. (For a listing and discussion of the Themistian passages in that work of Averroes's, see Eleonore Stump, "Boethius's Works on the Topics" *Vivarium*, 12 [1974], 77–93). There may also have been a commentary on Aristotle's *Topics* by Ammonius Hermiae (435/45–517/26) (see F. E. Peters, *Aristoteles Arabus* [Leiden: E. J. Brill, 1968], p. 20). If there was such a commentary, Boethius might well have known it. On Boethius's acquaintance with Ammonius, see Chadwick, 1981: 20, and Helen Kirkby, "The Scholar and His Public," in Margaret Gibson, ed., *Boethius: His Life, Thought and Influence* (Oxford: Basil Blackwell, 1981), pp. 60–61.

35. Cf. *De top. diff.* 1175B–1176A, in Stump 1978: 31–32, and the notes to those pages. The criterion Boethius apparently has in mind is that if we can truly say 'Every A is B' but *not* 'Every B is A,' then B is the greater and A the lesser term. In the passage cited in *De top. diff.* he also considers cases in which the two terms are equal, such as 'Every risible thing is a man' (all and only risible things are men).

36. Cf. *De top. diff.* 1183A–1183D and 1184B–1185A, in Stump 1978: 43–46, and the notes to those pages.

37. The criterion Boethius seems to be giving here for determining which term is the greater is different from and significantly worse than the criterion he gave earlier (see note 35). As the criterion is expressed here, it seems to amount to deciding which term is greater on the basis of which term occurs later in the sentence. But, of course, we can also truly say 'some substance is an animal'; so this criterion, taken at face value, will not enable us to decide which of the terms is greater than the other. I expect that what Boethius in fact has in mind depends on our recognizing 'A man is a substance' as the conclusion of a syllogism (whose premises Boethius is about to give in this passage). The term expressed second in the conclusion of a syllogism is the greater term.

38. This syllogism is a standard first-figure syllogism in Barbara. The conclusion as Boethius here gives it is a universal affirmative, rather than an indefinite affirmative, as earlier in the passage. Indefinite propositions can be interpreted earlier as universal or as particular propositions. On the whole,

Boethius tends to give almost all his examples for Topics with indefinite propositions (cf. Stump 1978: 185n.18).

39. Boethius's translation of the *Posterior Analytics* is not extant, as far as we now know, but we have two recensions of his translation of the *Prior Analytics*. For a contemporary edition of the latter, see L. Minio-Paluello, *Aristoteles Latinus*, Vol. III: 1–8 (Leiden: Desclée de Brouwer, 1962). Cf. also L. Minio-Paluello, "A Latin Commentary (?translated by Boethius) on the *Prior Analytics* and Its Greek Sources," *Journal of Hellenic Studies*, 77 (1957), 93–102.

40. By 'simple' here Boethius means 'predicative' or 'categorical'. He often uses 'simple' interchangeably with 'categorical', and 'composite' with 'hypothetical' or 'conditional'.

41. See Stump 1978: 180ff.

42. The location of this observation is not clear; perhaps he is referring to his commentary (now lost) on Aristotle's *Topics*.

43. Cf. *De top diff.* 1176C–D and 1185A–1186A, in Stump 1978: 33 and 46–47, and the notes to those pages.

44. For some discussion of the complexities of these examples, see Stump 1978: 113–114 and 183–185.

45. For a discussion of the nature of Aristotle's Topics, see Stump 1978: 159–178 and 180. For a good recent discussion of Aristotle's theory of dialectic, see John D. G. Evans, *Aristotle's Concept of Dialectic* (Cambridge: Cambridge University Press, 1977).

46. For a discussion of constitutive differentiae, see the appendix to these notes. The nature of a differentia, the reasons for thinking it can function as a genus, and philosophical difficulties associated with medieval rules for its use are presented in Stump 1978: 248–261.

47. *Irrational* is a divisive differentia because together with *rational* it divides the genus *animal* into the subaltern species under it. It is a specific differentia for *horse* and *dog* because it specifies the proximate genus, the genus immediately higher on the Porphyrian tree, for these species. For more discussion of all these technical terms, see the appendix.

48. For a discussion of Boethius's understanding of maximal propositions and the sense in which a maximal proposition is *from the whole*, etc., see Stump 1978: 180–193.

49. In fact, the genus is *maximal proposition from the whole* (this is why 'genus' in the preceding and subsequent sentences of the text is in quotation marks); for practical purposes, however, the differentia *from the whole* is sufficient because in this context it picks out the same group of propositions as the genus.

50. I think that Boethius means all other *true* propositions and that by 'are contained in' he means 'are instances of'. For a discussion of the idea that all other true propositions are instances of maximal propositions, see Stump 1978: 191–192.

51. The four possibilities, then, are as follows:

A
thought and meaning ——————— argument
expression and interweaving ⟍
maximal proposition ———————⟋ argumentation

B
thought and meaning
expression and interweaving ⟩————— argument = argumentation
maximal proposition
    C
thought and meaning
expression and interweaving ⟩————— argumentation
maximal proposition ——————————— argument
    D
thought and meaning ———————————argument
expression and interweaving —————————argumentation
maximal proposition ————————————— Topic

Boethius's practice tends to be more like B; when he explains his theory (as in *De top. diff.* 1183A; Stump 1978: 43), he inclines toward D.

52. The point of this passage is that on any sensible reading of 'argument' and 'argumentation', Topics are the differentiae of maximal propositions. The four sentences of the paragraph to this point correspond in order to the cases A–D laid out in the previous note. In the third sentence something seems to be missing; this is the case in which an argumentation is considered both the expression and the thought of the reasoning.

53. For a discussion of the differences among Aristotle's, Cicero's, and Boethius's understanding of Topics, see Stump 1978: 205–214. I do not think Boethius's view of Aristotle's Topics is correct, as I have argued in Stump 1978: 159–178 and 180.

54. For Boethius's understanding of division, see his *Trattato sulla divisione*, tr. Lorenzo Pozzi (Padua: Liviana, 1969); and Stump 1978: 242–247.

55. What Boethius means by 'the thing at issue' will emerge in the course of this discussion.

56. Although Boethius thinks Cicero's division of Topics is exhaustive, he does not think it is the only possible division of Topics. In *De top. diff.* he also presents Themistius's division of Topics, which in his view is a second exhaustive division. See *De top. diff.* 1195B–C and 1203A–1206B, in Stump 1978: 63 and 73–78, and the notes to those pages.

57. Boethius's remark here is peculiar and certainly not validly inferred from his preceding remarks. What we would expect him to say is that there is no intermediate between Topics that inhere in the thing at issue and Topics taken from without. This is, furthermore, what he needs to say in order to make his point, which is that Cicero's division of Topics is exhaustive. If the arguments in question here are dialectical arguments and if all dialectical arguments are based on one or another Topic as Boethius thinks, then what he says here is true, but it is still not clear why he says it.

58. Boethius's remarks in this paragraph appear confusing. They become clearer if the reader keeps in mind the points of this and the preceding sentence. The *thing* at issue is one of the terms of a question. The *doubt* that raises the issue is whether the thing at issue inheres in the other term of the question. Boethius's use of such words as 'term', 'subject', 'predicate', 'definition', etc. seems to be ambiguous; sometimes he appears to mean a linguistic entity and sometimes the thing signified by that linguistic entity. The latter meaning is apparently what he has in mind when he says that a subject or a predicate is the thing at issue.

59. This sentence makes it seem as if the "thing" at issue is the inhering of one of the question's terms in the other term. Boethius, however, is explicit both earlier and later in this paragraph that the thing at issue is a term of the question. (See also *De top. diff.* 1186C–D, in Stump 1978: 47–48, and the notes to those pages.)

60. Verres (ca. 115–ca. 43 B.C.) was governor of various territories, including Sicily (ca. 74 B.C.), which he apparently robbed systematically; he was accused, among other things, of stealing art treasures from temples and shrines in Greece and Asia Minor. Cicero was the prosecutor at his trial, which focused on Verres's misconduct in Sicily, where he went so far as to rob even Roman citizens of their art works. Cicero's speeches against him, which are still extant, were so successful that Verres chose to go into exile before judgment could be pronounced on him. He was killed in the proscriptions of 43 B.C.

61. What Boethius says here pertains just to predicative questions. For his discussion of conditional questions and their relationship to predicative questions, see *De top. diff.* 1178D–1180A, in Stump 1978: 36–38, and the notes to those pages.

62. The point seems to be that things and arguments are separate and distinct types of things, but that nonetheless the things at issue have something within themselves that is the source of arguments. What that something in the term at issue is will become clearer in the ensuing discussion.

63. An example of something inhering in what is at issue is a definition (as the subsequent paragraphs show), because any term in a question has a definition. On Boethius's view, then, a definition is a thing when it is considered in its own right (see note 58 and the appendix for the nature of Boethian definitions). But if an argument is taken from it—because we take as a premise in our argument the definition of one of the terms in the question and use a maximal proposition about definitions to validate the argument—then we are considering definition not as a thing but as a genus for maximal propositions and so as a Topic. The ontological status of definition understood as a Topic is the same as the ontological status of universals for Boethius, because taken as a Topic, *definition* is a kind of genus and a genus is a universal.

64. Every definition consists of a genus (in this case, *rational animal*) and a differentia (*mortal* here). These are the parts of the substance or essence of the thing they define, and therefore Boethius calls them substantial parts.

65. I think Boethius's point is that the word for a thing and the definition for that thing are the same in reference but different in sense. Part of the confusion this paragraph generates stems from Boethius's ambiguity about the ontological status of definitions. In this sentence Boethius gives the impression that a definition is a thing, an impression enhanced by his previous explicit claim to the same effect. But in the preceding sentence a definition seems to be a linguistic entity, on a par with a name.

66. The difference between substantial parts and these other parts (integral parts) can be illustrated quickly with an example. The integral parts of a man are head, chest, abdomen, arms, legs; the substantial parts are *mortality, rationality,* and *animality.*

67. Boethius's language is complicated, but his point is simple. The question he raises is whether there can be a Topic for a Topic, and his answer is 'no'. His reason for thinking so is that a Topic is defined as something from which arguments are drawn. Suppose, then, that we consider the general category of

Topics inhering in the thing at issue as a Topic in its own right. What is drawn from this putative Topic is *from the whole, from the parts, from a sign,* and *from related things.* But these cannot be Topics, on pain of violating the definition of a Topic which tells us that what is drawn from a Topic is an argument; instead, if they really are drawn from our putative Topic, they must be arguments. Boethius might have made this point more simply by claiming that the definition of a Topic rules out Topics of Topics. But, as the next paragraph shows, such a claim raises difficulties for Boethius's previous point that the Topics that are differentiae contain the Topics that are maximal propositions.

68. The point is that maximal propositions themselves are arguments of a sort; they prove the propositions falling within their scope. Therefore, even though maximal propositions are rightly called Topics, there can be Topics for maximal propositions with no violation of the rule that there are no Topics of Topics. Considered as drawn from a Topic, a maximal proposition is an argument. Since no differentia of maximal propositions is an argument in its own right, the same sort of point cannot be made to show that one differentia can be drawn from another. Cases in which it appears that one differentia contains others are really cases in which the first differentia is being divided into the others as into species. Hence the differentiae of maximal propositions are rightly called Topics, but the genus of the Topics *from the whole, from the parts, from a sign,* and *from related things* cannot correctly be considered as a Topic from what inheres in the thing at issue.

69. Given Boethius's views of a definition as a predicable rather than as a proposition, it seems as if the text here should read 'term presented in a question'.

70. Boethius means that these are the subject and predicate of the question this argument is to settle.

71. As it stands, the argument for this conclusion is not valid. If both premises and the conclusion were universal propositions, the argument would be a valid first-figure syllogism in Barbara. As it is, the premises and conclusion are all indefinite propositions. In order for the argument in this form to be validated, a maximal proposition is needed, as Boethius makes clear in the ensuing discussion.

72. The argument is valid with the addition of this maximal proposition provided we make explicit what is clear in the formulation of the argument, namely, that the first premise contains a definition of civil law.

73. The census was a registration of citizens with an evaluation of their property and their assignment to a *centuria,* a social and sometimes military unit of about a hundred people. A slave enrolled in the census with the consent of his master was freed.

74. Manumission of this sort was performed before a magistrate. With the permission of the slave's master, a third person touched the slave with a small rod and claimed that he was free. When the slave's master presented no opposition, the magistrate declared the slave free.

75. A slave could be freed if his master freed him in his will, using a traditional formula such as 'my slave *x* shall be free' or 'I order that my slave *x* be free.' The slave then became free when the heir accepted his inheritance.

76. Here the question raised is predicative, but the argument given to settle the question is hypothetical rather than categorical as in the preceding example. On the face of it, this argument is a somewhat abbreviated but fairly simple instance of *modus tollens,* which seems to leave no room for maximal propositions. The context makes it clear that this is a Topical argument, howev-

er; on p. 45 (Orelli, p. 290) he gives a maximal proposition for this argument. The function of the maximal proposition in such cases is to serve as warrant for the truth of the conditional proposition in the argument. For a detailed discussion of this point, see Stump 1978: 186–187.

77. I am not sure what Boethius has in mind when he says "all these Topics." As far as I can see, there have been two at most in this discussion: the Topic from the enumeration of parts that are species and the Topics from the enumeration of parts that are members of a whole.

78. The parts are actually the parts or species of liberation, being freed; the predicate on Boethius's view is *free*. Boethius's claim that the parts inhere in the predicate seems slightly confused. But perhaps he means us to understand *'liber'*, which I have translated 'free', as narrowed in meaning by its setting in the proposition 'The slave is free.' In that case we might read it as 'freed', and Boethius's claim holds.

79. A guarantor (*vindex*) was someone who guaranteed the appearance of a defendant in court at some specified future date or who intervened to save a condemned defendant either by paying his fine or debt or by contesting the judgment against him. A representative is someone who represents in court the interests either of the plaintiff or of the defendant.

80. The law in question is laid down in the XII Tables, a compilation of ancient Roman law established probably in the fifth century B.C.; only fragments of the XII Tables are now extant. This particular law is found in table 1:4; see *Ancient Roman Statutes*, tr. Allan Chester Johnson, Paul Robinson Coleman-Norton, and Frank Card Bourne (Austin: University of Texas Press, 1961), p. 9. The law of Aelius Sentius is something completely different. It dates from around A.D. 4 and has to do with conditions on manumission, prohibiting, for example, any manumission to the detriment of the creditors of the slave's master. Boethius is misled here, at least in part, because Cicero explains the law about taxpayers by referring to the etymology of 'taxpayer' given by "L. Aelius." This Aelius may be Sextus Aelius Paetus, who was consul in 198 B.C. and wrote a famous book on the XII Tables, which was referred to as *'tripertita'* and which is no longer extant. Or he may be Lucius Aelius Stilo Praeconinus, who was one of Cicero's teachers and a noted rhetorician.

81. The putative etymology of 'taxpayer', which Boethius takes from Cicero, is almost certainly wrong; the point that no one except a wealthy man can pay money is hard to make sense of.

82. The case of this Topic is somewhat more complicated than that of the two preceding Topics. What is said to be in the thing at issue is its name. The argument, however, is not drawn from the name of the thing at issue but from the explanation of the name.

83. Boethius seems to be dividing Cicero's argument into two subsidiary arguments. The first is

(1) A taxpayer is someone who pays money.
(2) Someone who pays money is a wealthy man.
Therefore,
(3) A taxpayer is a wealthy man.

This is not a valid first-figure syllogism in Barbara because the premises are indefinite. The context makes clear that Boethius takes it as a dialectical argument dependent on a maximal proposition. Given the maximal proposition Boethius adduces for this example, I think we can understand his argument in this way.

(1') *Someone who pays money* is the explanation of the name 'taxpayer'.
(2') Someone who pays money is a wealthy man.
(MP) The explanation of a name has the same force as (is equivalent to) the name.
Therefore,
(3') A taxpayer is a wealthy man.

The second subsidiary argument has just one premise:

(4) The law of Aelius Sentius prescribes that a taxpayer be the guarantor for another taxpayer.

Together (4) and (3) entail Boethius's conclusion:

Therefore,
(5) The law of Aelius Sentius prescribes that a wealthy man be the guarantor for another wealthy man.

84. Here it seems that Boethius is taking as the conclusion of this argument not (5), in the preceding note, but rather

(6) If the law of Aelius Sentius prescribes that a taxpayer be the guarantor for another taxpayer, it prescribes that a wealthy man be the guarantor for another wealthy man.

The truth of (6) is confirmed by (3), which is the Topical argument. Why Boethius should think it such a great error to present the argument for a conclusion immediately after presenting the conclusion is not clear to me.

NOTES TO BOOK II

1. For a good account of Boethius's repeated references to hostile critics, see Henry Chadwick, *Boethius: The Consolations of Music, Logic, Theology, and Philosophy* (Oxford: Clarendon Press, 1981), pp. 117–120.
2. See Cicero, *Brutus* L.187, where Cicero alludes to a flutist who advised his pupil whom the audience had heard coldly to make music for his teacher and the Muses. (I am grateful to James O'Donnell for this reference.)
3. A genus and its kind are "congenial in substance" because the substance of any kind includes the substance of its genus. So the substance of the species *man* is mortal rational animality and the substance of its genus is rational animality. As regards cause and effect, however, while perhaps natural efficient causes could be said to be related in substance to their effects, Boethius recognizes many sorts of causes for which the same cannot be said (see the discussion of causes in Book V). And in the exposition of antecedent and consequent in Book V, Boethius is at pains to point out that the connection between antecedent and consequent is one of logical order rather than metaphysical connection.
4. The relationship in question is one in which the related things are related in virtue of sharing a quality. On Boethius's view, two things that are similar have a quality in common. It is not quite so clear how this analysis is supposed to work for conjugates or conjoined things. For the rest of Boethius's discussion of conjugates and conjoined things in this book, see pp. 51 (Orelli, p. 293), 52 (Orelli, p. 294), and 55–56 (Orelli, p. 297).
5. In *De top. diff.* 1199A (Stump 1978: 68) Boethius explains that two things *x*

and z are incompatibles if and only if x and y are contraries and z and y are "associated" (because one of them entails the other). Hence, insofar as contraries are opposed in quality, incompatibles are also. See also pp. 67–68 (Orelli, p. 305) below and note 59 below.

6. See Porphyry, *Isagoge*, in Adolf Busse, ed., *Commentaria in Aristotelem Graeca* (Berlin: Reimer, 1887), vol. IV, pt. 1, pp. 2.15ff.; also Boethius, *In Isagogen*, ed. Samuel Brandt (Leipzig: F. Tempsky, 1906), p. 180.4ff. (PL 91A8ff.). For a discussion of this predicable, see the appendix.

7. Aristotle says that contraries are always in the same genus or in contrary genera or are themselves genera (*Cat*. 14a20–26).

8. I think Boethius's point is that the arguments arising from associated things are only verisimilar or readily believable, and not necessary, because arguments inferring one associated thing from another are only generally and not in every case valid.

9. Cicero was hailed as father of his country for exposing the conspiracy of Catiline and bringing about the execution of the conspirators in 63 B.C. In 58 B.C., P. Clodius, an enemy of Cicero's, carried a bill exiling Cicero. He was recalled in 57 B.C.

10. The point Boethius is at such pains to make here is just that related things, in all their varieties, really are related to one another. This point is important to him because the relationship these things have to one another is the basis for the arguments drawn from these Topics, as the subsequent discussion of examples will make clear.

11. Since conjugates, genus, and the rest are connected to the things they are related to, both the name 'related things' and the definition of related things apply to them and this fact shows that they are species of *related things*.

12. Cf. Cicero, *Top*. III.12 and IX.38; and Aristotle, *Top*. 113a12.

13. Common pasturage is public land set in private holdings which is for the use of neighboring landholders. Agrarian law dating from the second century B.C., based in large part on the preceding Gracchan reforms, stipulates that on common pasture one may pasture free of charge no more than ten large animals and their offspring of up to one-year old. There is some suggestion, for example in the Quinctian Law of 9 B.C., that one could also cut grass or gather hay free of charge on such land.

14. This description of the subject and predicate is puzzling. The question in this example is whether common pasturing is legal in this field, and the conclusion of the immediately following argument is that one may (*licet*) pasture commonly in this field. At the least, then, we might expect Boethius to give the predicate as *legal common pasturing*. Perhaps for Boethius, 'common pasturing' is a term that (sometimes at any rate) carries connotations of legality with it, as the word 'alimony' does for us.

15. That is, common pasturage is the intermediate term that draws the subject and predicate of the question together in the conclusion of the argument by being linked with one of them in the first premise and the other in the second premise.

16. The sense of 'in' according to which common pasturage is in common pasturing is not clear to me. The explanation that constitutes the rest of this sentence seems to suggest that common pasturing and common pasturage are on a par rather than that the former contains the latter.

17. How these maximal propositions are supposed to provide support for the argument in the example is not clear to me. On the face of it, that argument is perfectly valid and does not need to be warranted by any maximal proposi-

tion. The best suggestion, as far as I can see, is to treat this argument as an implicit hypothetical argument of this form:

    (1) This field is common pasturage.
    (2) If anything is common pasturage, one may pasture commonly in it.
Therefore,
    (3) One may pasture commonly in this field.

The maximal proposition in this case then supports the second premise, in this way:

    (MP) The conjugate of a thing can be associated with whatever that thing itself belongs to.
    (i) Common pasturing and common pasturage are conjugates.
Therefore,
    (ii) If *common pasturage* belongs to a thing, *common pasturing* does also.

I think that (ii) is equivalent to (2), especially if 'common pasturing' is understood as in note 14 above.

18. Cf. note 6 above.

19. Cf. Stump 1978: 101–102n.27.

20. If *silver* is the genus of *coin*, then all coins should be silver. The coinage of silver was first undertaken in Rome in the third century B.C., but there were cast bronze coins and bronze currency bars somewhat earlier (perhaps as early as 289 B.C.). Rome first issued gold coins in about 216 B.C. In the second and first century B.C. Rome continued to issue bronze and silver coins, but the issuing of gold coins was interrupted till 82 B.C., when Sulla's return to Italy was commemorated with a gold coin bearing his name, though this has traditionally been regarded as a provincial issue. Up to the time of Augustus, Rome continued to issue coins in bronze, silver, and gold; Augustus reorganized the system of coinage to provide standard issues in all three metals. Issues of coins in all three metals in accordance with varying standards continued through the end of the fifth century. For a detailed discussion of the history of coinage, see R. A. G. Carson, *Principal Coins of the Romans*, vols. I–III (London: British Museum Publications, 1978).

21. The maximal proposition is supposed to support its argument in this way:

    (MP) Any species of a genus belongs to whatever the whole genus belongs to.
    (1) *Silver* is the genus of *coin*.
    (2) *Silver* belongs to the group of things bequeathed.
Therefore,
    (3) *Coin* belongs to the group of things bequeathed.

22. Perhaps the reason for the qualifying clause on the maximal proposition stems in part from the nature of the example. If 'coin', for one reason or another, came to apply also to bronze money, then *coin* would not keep the name *silver*, and this maximal proposition would not apply to it.

23. For a discussion of this view, see, e.g., Harry Wolfson, "The Problem of the Souls of the Spheres, from the Byzantine Commentaries on Aristotle through the Arabs and St. Thomas to Kepler," *Dumbarton Oaks Papers*, 16 (1962), 65–93.

24. A woman who is materfamilias must as a necessary condition be married

with *manus*. Doing so requires leaving her father's family and entering her husband's, thereby becoming subject to her husband's power and holding the position of a daughter to him. At the time of the XII Tables, marriage was ordinarily marriage with *manus*. By the end of the republic, marriage with *manus* was rare. A woman married without *manus* remained in the family and power of her father. If her father was dead, she became *sui iuris* and had a tutor appointed; she was not legally related to her children, who were in the power of her husband.

25. These are three ways in which a woman married with *manus* and came under the authority of her husband. By the end of the republic a marriage without the woman's coming under the authority of her husband could be contracted simply by mutual consent and the bringing of the woman to the man's house. For details about the different types of marriage and the means for contracting them, see Alan Watson, *The Law of Persons in the Later Roman Republic* (Oxford: Clarendon Press, 1967), pp. 19ff.

26. If a woman remained married to a man for an unbroken year, she came under the authority of her husband. She could prevent this change in her status by absenting herself from her husband's home for three nights in each year.

27. This religious ceremony apparently consisted in saying certain solemn words in the presence of ten witnesses and certain priests and sacrificing a cake of coarse wheat to Jupiter. It was probably restricted to patricians.

28. A man can acquire authority over a woman by a symbolic act of sale in which the man claims the woman in the presence of five witnesses, strikes a pair of scales with a piece of bronze, with which he claims to purchase her, and turns the bronze over to her father or guardian as her purchase price.

29. In the republic, 'materfamilias' as a technical term seems to have referred to any sort of marriage in which the wife came under the authority of her husband (marriage *cum manu*). See Watson 1967: 36.

30. Domitius Ulpianus is an important and productive jurist of the third century A.D. His *Institutes* was a book of law for beginners. The passage Boethius is citing is no longer extant.

31. This is a peculiar analysis of the question. We might expect him to say that the subject is *the silver* and the predicate is *bequeathed to the wife Fabia*. Surely some of the peculiarity is a result of Boethius's attempt to impose his analysis on Cicero's argument, given Cicero's characterization of the argument as taken from species.

32. The Latin construction together with the theoretical discussion of species preceding Boethius's explanation of this example strongly suggest that he here means "what is said *specifically* of one species is not appropriately said of another."

33. For discussion of usufruct, see notes 40 and 76 below.

34. This is another peculiar pair of candidates for subject and predicate. In Boethius's own terminology, the predicate either does or does not inhere in the subject. Given Boethius's analysis here, the questioner is apparently asking whether restoration by the heir inheres or does not inhere in the collapse or disrepair of the house.

35. See, e.g., Alan Watson, *The Law of Property in the Later Roman Republic* (Oxford: Clarendon Press, 1968), p. 211.

36. Although the argument has a conditional premise in it, it is not a hypothetical argument in Boethius's sense, and the maximal proposition for this

argument functions as it would in a predicative argument. It does not warrant the conditional proposition; it is necessary for the validity of the argument as a whole.

37. Roman law in general is concerned to protect current possession of both movable and immovable property, so that if *A* has possession of *B*'s property, the legal burden is in general on *B* to recover his property. Something of this attitude may underly this example. Furthermore, the existence of a special sort of legacy, *legatum nominis*, which is a legacy by *A* to *C* of the money *B* owes to *A*, suggests that a bequest of the testator's money was not automatically understood to include a bequest of the money owed him in debts. Finally, some legacies, *legatum per vindecationem*, were restricted to property actually in the possession of the testator; a bequest of money made in this way was restricted to coins in the possession of the testator. See Barry Nicholas, *An Introduction to Roman Law* (Oxford: Clarendon Press, 1962), pp. 264–266.

38. As far as I can see, Boethius has the following scheme in mind.

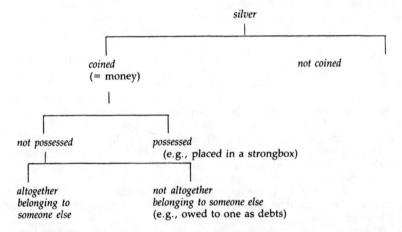

The italicized words are differentiae that specify a species if they are conjoined with the genus *silver* and any preceding differentiae. For Boethius's system for making such divisions, see Stump 1978: 242ff.

39. The question for this example is 'Is the silver owed as debts bequeathed?', and the conclusion sought is a negative answer to the question. Boethius apparently thinks of the argument as taking this form:

(MP) We cannot understand the same thing of things that are very different.
(1) Silver owed as debts is very different from silver placed in a strongbox.
(2) All the silver that was the husband's is bequeathed to the wife.
(3) All the silver that the husband possessed was in his strongbox.
Therefore,
(4) The silver owed as debts was not bequeathed to the wife.

This argument has the following troubles, at least. This maximal proposition, like the preceding one, is very vague and could be interpreted in a variety of ways, not always compatible with one another. The interpretation of 'all the silver that the husband possessed', which I have spelled out in (3), is surely question-begging and perhaps even false; there is clearly some sense of 'possessed' in which the husband possessed money owed him. The argument seems clearly invalid as it stands; at the very least it needs a premise ruling out the possibility that there was a special bequest of the silver owed as debts, though Boethius perhaps takes such a premise to be a tacit assumption in the example. And finally, it is hard to see the sense in which this argument is made from something that is in the thing asked about. The thing asked about is *silver owed as debts*, and the argument is based on its differentia, which is in it. The differentia, however, seems to be just *owed as debts*; it is not clear how this is supposed to be the foundation for this argument. If, however, we take seriously the scheme suggested in note 38, then the differentia is *not possessed although not altogether belonging to someone else*. This differentia does serve as a foundation for the argument and reduces the appearance of question-begging in premise (3).

40. "Usufruct is the right of using and taking the fruits of property belonging to another, *salve rerum substantia,* i.e. without the right of destroying or changing the character of the thing, and lasting only so long as the character remains unchanged. It is usually for the life of the person entitled and cannot be for a longer period." H. F. Jolowicz and Barry Nicholas, *Historical Introduction to the Study of Roman Law* (Cambridge: Cambridge University Press, 1972), p. 269.

41. 'Forfeiture of civil rights' is my translation for the technical term *'capitis deminutio'*. "In connection with *deminutio . . . caput* = the civil status of a Roman citizen, for which three elements were necessary: to be a free man . . . , to have Roman citizenship . . . and to belong to a Roman family. . . . The loss of one of these elements involved the *capitis deminutio,* with all its legal consequences. The gravest effects were connected with the loss of freedom . . . in the case of enslavement. . . . A lesser degree . . . in which a person lost citizenship without losing liberty also resulted in loss of membership in family. . . . Loss of family . . . occurred when a person's agnatic family ties were dissolved either by his entry into another family . . . or by his becoming the head of a new family. . . . The consequences of this lowest degree of *capitis deminutio* were originally perceptible only in economic and social fields (loss of the rights of inheritance in the former family, dissolution of partnership, extinction of personal servitudes, and the like). Some of these consequences were later mitigated . . . under Justinian it [this lowest degree of *capitis deminutio*] is almost without any importance at all." Adolf Berger, *Encyclopedic Dictionary of Roman Law,* Transactions of the American Philosophical Society, n.s., vol. XLIII, pt. 2 (Philadelphia: American Philosophical Society, 1953), p. 381.

42. Coming under the authority of the husband involved a forfeiture of certain civil rights insofar as the woman left her previous family and the rights attendant on belonging to that family and came to hold the legal position of a daughter in her husband's family.

43. In general, a woman was not allowed to engage in business or legal affairs without the consent of her guardian. The alienation of land or slaves, the acceptance of contractual obligations, and the making of a will, in particular, needed the authorization of a guardian. The point of guardianship over women, at least in its origins, was to help ensure that property remain in the agnatic family (the family consisting of relationships traced just through descent from males) and that women did not remove property from the agnatic

family by, for example, marriages undesirable from the point of view of her male relatives.

44. In the days of the republic, praetors were the highest Roman magistrates after consuls. Their chief function was jurisdiction; the edicts or public pronouncements of the praetors were of great importance in the development of Roman law. The praetor could not make law, and his edict did not consist in new legislation but rather in an explanation of what he would do in certain cases, for example, complicated cases of succession or disputed cases of ownership and other cases in which the civil law was unclear or ambiguous. The great powers of the praetors were considerably diminished during the Empire.

45. Like women, children were under the authority of some male, generally their father or a guardian. If they were under the authority of the father or oldest surviving male ascendant, they could not own any property of their own; any property they acquired accrued to their paterfamilias. At best they might have *peculium*, a fund that technically belongs to the paterfamilias but that is the son's to manage. If a child had no paterfamilias, he became independent or *sui iuris* under the authority of a guardian. In this state the child could own property but not alienate it without the consent of the guardian. Slaves could not own property in any circumstances and therefore had no occasion for making a will; they might, however, have *peculium*.

46. Male children who were independent or *sui iuris* but nonetheless had a guardian tended to become fully independent and lose their guardian at the age of fourteen. Female children who were *sui iuris* always had a guardian unless they came under the authority of their husbands.

47. By "narrower" he means more restricted in extension, I think. See Stump 1978: 101–102n.27.

48. According to the XII Tables, if a father sold his child three times, his power over the child was irretrievably lost. One way to remove a person from the authority of his paterfamilias was a fictional or symbolic set of sales. The paterfamilias sold the son twice to the some person, who manumitted him each time; then the paterfamilias sold him to the same person for the third time, and his power over the son was lost. For a clear presentation of the details of this process and its use in the practice of adoption, see Nicholas 1962: 77–78.

49. She might also lose part of her dowry for misconduct as a wife. For a detailed discussion of the complicated rules concerning the disposition of the dowry at the end of a marriage, see W. W. Buckland, *A Text-book of Roman Law from Augustus to Justinian* (Cambridge: Cambridge University Press, 1921), pp. 107–111.

50. Iulius Paulus was a third-century jurist of immense influence and reputation and an important source for the transmission of Roman law to medieval Western nations. He was a voluminous writer; extracts of his work are preserved in Justinian's *Digest*, and one book is preserved in the Code of the Visigoths for Roman law, the *Breviarium Alaricianum*. His *Institutes* is an elementary book of law.

51. A dowry involved a transfer of a substantial portion of property from the wife's family to her husband. If the marriage was without *manus* (and by Cicero's time such marriages were the rule), the wife did not become a member of her husband's agnatic family. If her husband died intestate, her claim on his

estate came only after the claim of his children, his agnatic relations, and his blood relations to the sixth degree. Her children were not in her family but in her husband's family, and the husband or the paterfamilias of the husband's family had far-reaching powers over her children. In case of a divorce between persons who had a valid Roman marriage, the children remained in the husband's family, and a certain portion of the dowry was reserved for them. It was important for the woman, however, that as much of the dowry as possible be returned to her, because her chance at a good second marriage depended on her ability to bring a sizable dowry with her.

52. Boethius gives two hypothetical syllogisms, both simple examples of *modus ponens*, to reach the conclusion he wants for this argument. In general, Boethius's maximal propositions for such arguments warrant the conditional proposition in the hypothetical syllogism. This maximal proposition, however, which is unusual in more than one respect, is a rule for *modus ponens* and warrants the validity of each hypothetical syllogism as a whole.

53. For a union to be legal wedlock, both partners had to be Roman citizens with no obstacles to marriage, or one or both partners had to belong to a group of non-Roman citizens who had the right of legal wedlock. The list of obstacles to marriage even on the part of Roman citizens is long. For example, the XII Tables forbade marriage between a patrician and a plebian; ordinary soldiers were not allowed to marry during service; guardians could not marry their wards; and so on. The children of unions that were not legally recognized wedlock took the status of the mother; they did not enter the father's family, and their claim on his estate at his death was superseded by the claims of the father's agnatic relations. Although these unions were not "legal wedlock," they were recognized as a sort of marriage, and the wife brought a dowry with her into them also.

54. These are particularly odd candidates for subject and predicate. I have no explanation for the oddity of Boethius's choice of subject and predicate here and elsewhere in this book.

55. This maximal proposition is apparently a rule for *modus tollens; mutatis mutandis*, the same things should be said about it as about the preceding maximal proposition for antecedents. See note 52.

56. See below pp. 146–147 (Orelli, p. 362).

57. According to Roman law, a man was allowed to appoint a substitute for his appointed heir within certain limited circumstances. There were two reasons for this provision. First, the appointed heir was permitted on certain conditions to refuse the inheritance. Second, if the heir were a child, he was not legally able to make a will until he reached the age of fourteen. If he should die before that age, the result for the testator would be the same as if he had died intestate; his property would revert to his nearest agnatic relative. To ensure control of his property in the case of either of these eventualities, the testator was allowed under law to designate a substitute for his appointed heir.

58. As far as I understand it, the substitute heir's case is entirely without foundation. Unless the will expressly stipulated otherwise, the substitute took over the entire legal position that the appointed heir had with respect to the will, having exactly the same benefits and duties. The substitute heir is made in effect the heir of the appointed heir, originally only with respect to the provisions of the testator's will but later also with respect to any other property that the son might possess. See Buckland 1921: 298ff.

202 / In Ciceronis Topica

59. Boethius's point here is something of this sort. *A* and *C* are incompatibles just in case *A* and *B* are contraries, and *C* entails *B* or *B* entails *C*. On Boethius's view, receiving legally and not receiving legally are contraries, and receiving legally and losing against one's will are incompatibles. To show the incompatibility, he claims that not receiving legally entails losing against one's will. On the face of it, this is a blatantly false claim; for example, not everyone who receives something illegally loses it against his will. Boethius must be cognizant of this difficulty because he qualifies his claim in the subsequent sentence: if someone receives something illegally, it is just for him to lose it against his will. But in stating the incompatibles he drops the qualification. The incompatibles in fact are receiving legally and *justly* losing against one's will. Stating the incompatibles with this qualification enhances rather than detracts from the soundness of Boethius's argument.

60. I think this premise ought to read "cannot *justly* be taken away etc.," and even then it requires a *ceteris paribus* clause to ensure that no intervening circumstances alter the legality of the possession.

61. The structure of the argument supported by this maximal proposition is something of this sort.

(1) If something is received legally, it cannot be taken away against the will of the one who receives it legally.
(2) Receiving something in a will is receiving something legally.
(3) A woman received the usufruct of maidservants in a will.
Therefore,
(4) The usufruct of the maidservants cannot be taken away from the woman against her will.

The function of the maximal proposition, then, seems to be to warrant the truth of (1).

62. "In some cases the praetor supplements what he considers to be the deficiencies of the civil law by ordering one party to make a promise to the other, such promise being in the form of a stipulation, and giving to the promisee a right, or at least a remedy, which he would not otherwise have. Thus if *A*'s house is in a dangerous condition and likely to fall and damage *B*'s land, *B* can insist on *A*'s promising to pay damages for any harm that may be done. . . . If without such promise having been exacted the house fell and did damage, *B* would have no claim against *A* unless he could show that *A* had been guilty of some willful or negligent act . . . , and this would, of course, not always be the case." Jolowicz and Nicholas 1972: 226–227.

63. A common wall is one that separates two buildings and is held in common by the owners of the two buildings. The demolition of part of a common wall could give rise to a controversy. *Servitus oneris ferendi* is an urban servitude that gave the beneficiary the right to have his edifice supported by his neighbor's wall, which his neighbor was obligated to keep in good condition. Signinian work is a certain style of construction that takes its name from Signia, a town in Southern Latium. Its most characteristic feature was the use of mortar made of sand and potsherds, but it also apparently was used in the construction of vaulted walls. For a description of Signinian architecture, see Vitruvius, *De architectura* 8.7.14–15. See also Columella, *Rei rusticae* 1.6.12, 8.15.3, 8.17.1.

64. In Cicero's example, as I understand it, *A* builds an arched wall at right angles to a common wall in such a way that one of the arches of his wall rests

on the common wall. B, who has some rights over the common wall, promises to make good any damage to A's arched wall which B causes. Then B demolishes part of the common wall, including the part of the wall that supported an arch of A's wall; in consequence, part of A's wall collapses. In spite of his promise B is not liable for the damage to A's wall because the damage resulted from the way A built the wall rather than from anything B did to A's wall. As Boethius understands this example, however, the common wall is arched, and the person who gives a guarantee against future damage is A, not B. On Boethius's reading, A tears down part of the common wall in order to adjoin his own wall—why the demolition is necessary for the new construction is not clear. In consequence, part of the arched common wall is damaged, since the part of it that A destroyed was supporting an arch. In spite of A's promise, he is not liable because the damage resulted from the way the common wall was built and not from anything that A did directly to the part of the wall that collapsed. Cicero's example makes some sense, but Boethius's example is puzzling.

65. Among the many things hard to understand in this discussion is Boethius's claim that the foundation of the argument, which is a cause, is related to and inheres in restitution for damage. His general claim is that a cause is related to and inheres in its effect. But restitution for damage is not an effect of the cause mentioned in the argument; that cause is a cause of damage, not of restitution for damage, as is explicit in the next sentence.

66. As Boethius presents the example, the claim that the man was not the cause of the damage seems blatantly false. If it were true, then by similar reasoning we should be able to argue that A is not the cause of B's death if he slashes B's throat in the course of shaving him but that the cause of death lies in the blood, which flowed out.

67. The argumentation as Boethius gives it is a simple hypothetical syllogism where the conclusion wanted is derived from the initial conditional proposition by *modus ponens*. The maximal proposition seems to be a warrant for the conditional proposition. Restitution of the damage, or making good the damage, is the thing to be judged; according to the maximal proposition, we should judge it on the basis of its causes (more accurately, on the basis of the causes of the damage). If the man is not the cause of the damage, then we should judge that he is not responsible for making good the damage. So if the form of the wall caused the damage, the man is not compelled to make restitution—and this is basically the conditional premise of the hypothetical syllogism.

68. A woman who had come under the authority of her husband held the legal position of a daughter to him. Like a child of his, she could not own property in her own right; what she had as her goods legally belonged entirely to her husband. "When women have passed in manum, all their belongings, corporeal and incorporeal, and everything that is due to them, become acquisitions of the . . . *coemptionator* [the husband]." *The Institutes of Gaius*, tr. James Muirhead (Edinburgh: T. and T. Clark, 1880), p. 205. In the days when marriage with *manus* became rare, the laws regulating the husband's rights to the dowry at the end of a marriage became complicated. See, e.g., Buckland 1921: 109ff. For a discussion of the husband's rights over the property of a woman married with *manus*, see Alan Watson, *Rome of XII Tables, Persons and Property* (Princeton: Princeton University Press, 1975), pp. 38–39.

69. On Boethius's own views, this is not an argument, but just the first

premise of one. The rest of the argument would consist in the assertion of the antecedent and then the assertion of the consequent as conclusion. Boethius goes on to point out some of the oddity of this conditional proposition.

70. This analysis is odd. If an argument is made from effects, the argument is based on an effect of the thing at issue. So in order for this argument to be based on an effect, it needs to be based on something caused by the goods of a woman who came under the authority of her husband. In fact, in this analysis Boethius talks about what is caused by the fact that everything belonging to the woman becomes her husband's under the designation of dowry.

71. This objection seems mistaken. The argument has two premises, one a conditional proposition and one an assertion of the conditional proposition's antecedent. The antecedent is a conjunction of two propositions. The state of affairs described in the first conjunct includes a cause of those described in the second conjunct. But this fact is entirely irrelevant to considerations about the argument as made from causes or effects. All that is relevant to such a consideration is whether anything is a cause or effect of the state of affairs described in the conclusion.

72. This seems to be a second objection. It claims that the argument as a whole is made from a cause because the state of affairs described by the first conjunct in the antecedent of the argument's conditional proposition is a cause of the state of affairs described by the second conjunct, and this is in turn a cause of the state of affairs described by the conclusion. It is perhaps sensible to suppose that these are just two parts of one objection rather than two separate objections. Boethius's rejoinder is given in the following sentence.

73. The objector now suggests that the two conjuncts taken together (see the two preceding notes) describe a state of affairs that is a cause of the state of affairs described by the conclusion. The objector here seems to be right and to represent Boethius's own point of view.

74. It was possible under an old civil law (cf. XII Tables VII.8a) to bring an action "against the owner of a neighboring plot of land for having constructed a work which might change the natural flow of rain-water to the detriment of the plaintiff's property" (Berger 1953: 341). The XII Tables (VII.8b) also prescribes that if a water course through a public place damages a person's property, he has a right to bring an action. For details concerning laws governing rainwater, see Alan Watson, *Roman Private Law* (Edinburgh: Edinburgh University Press, 1971), pp. 77ff.

75. It was possible to bring an action to settle disputes over the boundaries of land. It was possible for a judge to transfer a piece of property from one party to another (see XII Tables VII.2). The law forbade the usucaption of land in a five-foot stretch along the boundaries. For details concerning the rules governing boundaries, see Watson 1975: 157ff.

76. "The Twelve Tables laid down a period of two years for the usucaption of land and one year for movables. . . . The person claiming to usucapt must have had uninterrupted possession for the requisite period; the possession must have acquired both *ex iusta causa* and in good faith; the thing must be capable of being owned (not, for example, a free man believed to be a slave); and it must not at any time have been stolen or taken by force" (Nicholas 1962: 122).

77. The maximal proposition is apparently 'Equity, which wants equal laws for equal cases, should prevail.'

78. Boethius's suggestion is ingenious in some respects, but I see no warrant for anyone's supposing that because there is no specific law about usucaption of houses that they are to be included with movable property.

79. Cf. Aristotle, *Top.* 104a2–38.

80. The ultimate source of this may be Aristotle's claim that the Sophists tried to teach their pupils argumentation by having them memorize set arguments, a method Aristotle says is swift but *atechnos* (*Soph. el.* 184al; cf. also *Soph. el*, 172a34). For mention of an argument from authority, see Aristotle, *Top.* 156b20–23.

81. The site or *ambitus* of a house is an "open space two and a half Roman feet in width . . . between neighboring houses" (Berger 1953: 361). For a detailed discussion of this example of Cicero's, see Watson 1968: 115ff.

82. Publius Mucius Scaevola was consul in 133 B.C. and later *pontifex maximus*. He was called one of the founders of the civil law because he was among the first to write books containing independent discussions of civil law.

83. See note 74 above concerning rainwater.

NOTES TO BOOK III

1. See p. 74 (Orelli, p. 310) above.

2. See p. 31 (Orelli, p. 278) above.

3. Boethius's claim that the name is the same as the thing it designates gains some plausibility when we remember that by 'thing' here he means the subject or predicate of a question. Since Boethius's use of 'subject', 'predicate', and other such terms is ambiguous between linguistic and nonlinguistic entities, this attempt lends only limited plausibility to Boethius's claim.

4. See pp. 36ff. (Orelli, pp. 283ff.) above.

5. At first glance, this is an odd thing for him to say since he has just finished explaining that this Topic *is* a whole under a certain description. Perhaps he is using 'the whole' to refer to a definition considered by itself and 'the Topic' to refer to a definition that has been brought into relation to an argument. In that case there is some sense in his claim that the Topic is from the whole. The same point applies, *mutatis mutandis*, to the similar claims for other Topics in the succeeding cases.

6. See Aristotle, *Cat.* 6b25ff.

7. Why the opposition of related things is supposed to be evidence for their dependence on one another is not clear. The following sentence suggests that what is being emphasized here is not the interdependence of related things but rather their opposition.

8. I think he means something of this sort. Suppose A is half an apple and B is a quarter of an apple. Then A is double B. Considered as A, it takes its form from the conglomerate of essence and accidents that makes it up. But considered as a double, A takes its form from B, because until it is compared to B it does not acquire its nature as a double. Therefore, it needs B for its form and its existence as a double.

9. The point of this labored discussion and others like it in this part of Book III is to provide a justification for the acceptability of Topical arguments. In general, Boethius's point is that the subject or predicate of a question picks out one of a pair of relata, x. In answer to the question, one formulates an argu-

ment based on the other relatum, y, and x recurs in the conclusion of the argument. What makes the argument acceptable is the tie between x and y. In virtue of the relationship between the two—a relationship generally expressed by a maximal proposition—something we know about y warrants our concluding something about x. There is a curious resemblance between this view of Boethius's and the view of the thirteenth-century modists; see Eleonore Stump, "Topics: Their Development and Absorption into Consequences," in Norman Kretzmann et al., eds., *The Cambridge History of Later Medieval Philosophy*, (Cambridge: Cambridge University Press, 1982), pp. 284–286. For a discussion of the example of common pasturing, see pp. 55–56 (Orelli, p. 297) above and Bk. II, nn. 13–17.

10. For Boethius's earlier discussion of this example, see pp. 56–57 (Orelli, p. 298) above and Bk. II, nn. 20–22.

11. This example is discussed above on pp. 58–59 (Orelli, p. 299) and Bk. II, nn. 24–32.

12. For the earlier discussion of this example, see pp. 59–60 (Orelli, p. 300) above and Bk. II, nn. 34–36, 40, and 76.

13. For this example, see pp. 60–61 (Orelli, pp. 300–301) above and Bk. II, nn. 37–39.

14. For this example, see pp. 61–62 (Orelli, p. 301) above and Bk. II, n. 40.

15. For this example, see pp. 62–63 (Orelli, pp. 302–303) above and Bk. II, nn. 42–45.

16. Given the other things Boethius has said about this case (see pp. 64–65 (Orelli, pp. 303–304) above and Bk. II, nn. 48–52), I think he must mean that the man's fault precedes logically rather than temporally. The odd thing about this and the following example, from our point of view, is that straightforwardly logical relations are listed next to the relationship between causes and effects or between sign and *significatum* as just one more kind of relationship that might be taken into consideration in constructing and evaluating arguments.

17. For this example, see pp. 65–67 (Orelli, pp. 304–305) above and Bk. II, nn. 53–55.

18. This sentence (if it is one) is hard to make sense of. The Topic *from an incompatible* in this example consists in receiving legally; that is, it consists in just one of the pair of incompatibles and not in both of them, as this sentence seems to suggest.

19. For this example, see pp. 67–68 (Orelli, pp. 305–306) above and Bk. II, nn. 57–61.

20. For Boethius's more detailed discussion of the examples for the Topics *from effects* and *from efficient causes*, see pp. 68–70 (Orelli, pp. 306–307) above and Bk. II, nn. 62–73.

21. For these examples see pp. 70–72 (Orelli, pp. 307–309) above and Bk. II, nn. 74–78.

22. The reasoning for making species come after genus in the list seems lame. The consideration that "nothing is so near to a genus as a species" is irrelevant, since the point of the ranking is to determine which Topics are closest to the terms at issue and not which are closest to each other. What seems to be motivating the ranking here is a general feeling that species are subordinate to genera. As far as closeness to the term at issue is concerned, species seem on the face of it closer than genera, because a genus shares in

only part of the nature of the term, while a species like a definition shares the whole nature of the term.

23. For the connection between species and substances, see the appendix.

24. A differentia is a quality that a thing has and by which it is distinguished from other things, and a differentia, together with a genus, constitutes the species of anything. So as a part of a species, a differentia is reasonably listed next after species in this ranking based on closeness to the thing at issue. The relationship of differentia and contrary is clarified by remembering Boethius's view that contraries always fall under the same genus and by considering a Porphyrian tree (for discussion of a Porphyrian tree, see the appendix). Let the thing at issue be a man. Then the differentia of the thing at issue is *mortal*, which divides the genus *rational animal* and constitutes the species *man:*

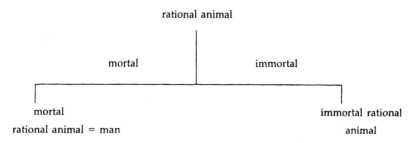

rational animal

mortal   immortal

mortal
rational animal = man

immortal rational
animal

Mortal, then, is part of the species (and so part of the whole) of the thing at issue. A contrary, like a differentia, falls under the same genus as the thing at issue, but it is not part of the thing at issue. Suppose the thing at issue is *being mortal*. Then its contrary, *being immortal*, falls under the same genus as *being mortal*, but it is not itself part of *being mortal*. And so it is appropriate to rank a contrary next after a differentia in the order of closeness to the thing at issue.

25. Associated things are two things that generally but not always occur together. Neither of them shares any part of the nature of the other or any quality with the other, and so they are further removed from one another than one of a pair of contraries is from the other (see the preceding note).

26. Boethius's point is that like associated things, antecedents and consequents do not share a nature or a quality with the thing at issue and yet are joined to it in some way. Why exactly antecedents and consequents should be regarded as more remote than associated things is not clear.

27. Antecedents and consequents do not share a nature or a quality with the thing at issue and yet are joined to it. Incompatibles are at one further remove from the thing at issue. They share neither a nature nor a quality with the thing at issue, and they are joined not to it but to its contrary.

28. I think he means to be claiming that each item in the first ordering is more closely tied to the thing at issue than is its corresponding item in the second ordering. That this is so should be clear from the preceding notes.

29. The way in which Boethius describes the ordering of Topics suggests that he is thinking of their ordering as a division of Topics into a Porphyrian tree, as he also seems to do in *De top. diff.* (see Stump 1978: 237–247). On the basis of what he says here and his views in *De divisione* on how such a division is to be made, I think he has a division of the following sort in mind. What

Boethius has to say about causes, effects, and comparison is so scanty that I have left them off the chart. (This division differs significantly from the division he suggests in *De. top. diff.* for the Themistian ordering of Topics; see Stump 1978: 247.)

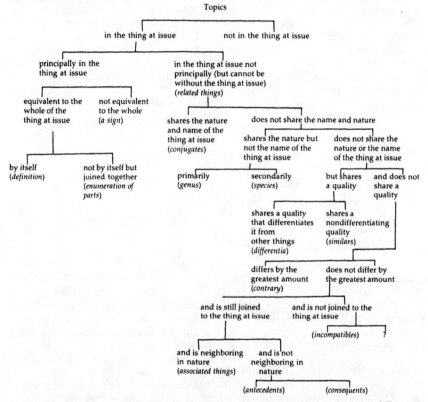

30. Here Boethius is in effect raising an objection to the ordering of Topics which he has just presented, on the grounds that perhaps *definition, enumeration of parts,* and *a sign* are all just kinds of *related things* and should be subsumed under *related things* as under their genus.

31. This pattern of argumentation makes sense only in the context of the relevant Porphyrian tree. The question is whether *animal* entails *living,* that is, whether anything that is in the genus *animal* has the characteristic *living.* The argument given for a negative answer is that the genus *inanimate,* which is the contrary of *animal,* does not entail *being dead.* Now *animal* and *inanimate* are both subaltern genera under *corporeal substance* (see the appendix).

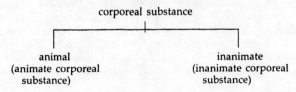

Now every move down the tree is cumulative, carrying with it the preceding genera as the parentheses on the chart indicate; everything on the tree below *corporeal substance* and in its line of descent is itself also a corporeal substance. But each move down the tree also is divisive and splits branches off from one another. So while everything that is animate and everything that is inanimate is a corporeal substance, not every corporeal substance is animate. So what a genus entails is something higher up on the Porphyrian tree. The question whether *animal* entails *living*, then, is a question whether *living* occurs higher on the Porphyrian tree than *animate*. In fact, we can be even more specific. If *living* occurred at or above the level of *corporeal substance* (that is, if *living* were a constitutive differentia for *corporeal substance* or a divisive differentia for any higher genus), then it would be a characteristic of everything below *corporeal substance*. But we know that inanimate things do not live, and therefore if *living* occurs on the Porphyrian tree above *animal*, it must be a differentia that is constitutive of *animal* and that divides *animate corporeal substance* from *inanimate corporeal substance*. But differentiae always come in pairs that are contraries. So if *living* were a constitutive differentia for *animal*, *being dead* would have to be a constitutive differentia for *inanimate*. This is the claim that is the foundation for the argument in Boethius's example here.

32. Among the many things hard to understand about this example is why Boethius picks *substance* as the genus of *animal*. Ordinarily, when *x* is said to be the genus of *y*, *x* is the proximate genus of *y*. But *substance* is not the proximate genus of *animal*; *corporeal substance* is.

33. By "parts" here he almost certainly means species.

34. See p. 38 (Orelli, p. 284) above.

35. See Aristotle, *Top.* 139a24–35 and 141a23–142a16.

36. See pp. 50–56, 57–58, and 60 (Orelli, pp. 293–297, 298, 300).

37. Aristotle, *Top.* 101b38.

38. See Cicero, *Timaeus* 2.

39. A clan (*gens*) is "a major group (clan) of several families really or supposedly descending from a common ancestor. . . . A surviving feature of this ancient organization [or a *gens*] is the right of succession on intestacy of the members of a *gens* (*gentiles*) in default of agnatic relatives. . . . The members of the *gens*, *gentiles*, were also entitled to guardianship if a member had neither a testamentary nor an agnatic tutor." Adolf Berger, *Encyclopedia of Roman Law,* Transactions of the American Philosophical Society, n. s., vol. XLIII, pt. 2 (Philadelphia:American Philosophical Society, 1953), p. 482. Members of a clan also had a common name, common cult ceremonies, and a common burial place.

40. 'Scipio' is the cognomen of one of the most famous families of the clan Cornelius, which was one of the biggest and most important clans in the time of the republic. The Scipio family included P. C. Aemilianus Africanus Numantinus, the soldier and statesman depicted by Cicero in his rhetorical and philosophical writings as the ideal Roman aristocrat. 'Valerius' is the name of a very old and politically influential clan. From the founding of the republic till well into the fourth century A.D., some member or other of the clan held a position of power. L. V. Flaccus was praetor in 92 B.C. and governor in Asia Minor thereafter; he was involved in putting an end to the conspiracy of Catiline. His son, also named L. V. Flaccus, was accused of misgovernment in Asia and brought to trial but was successfully defended by Cicero in a speech that is still extant, *Pro Flacco*. 'Brutus' is a cognomen of the famous Junii, who from 100 B.C. on were held in the highest esteem in Rome. M. Junius Brutus was at-

tached to Cicero and for a number of years was a friend of Caesar's. Cicero's history of Roman oratory, *Brutus*, was written for this Brutus.

41. See Aristotle, *Nic. Eth.* 1179b15, 1171a32, and b14; and *Metaph.* 1073b12.

42. I am reading *'alias'* for *'alius'* here, in accordance with *Vat. lat.* 567 and *Reg. lat.* 1649.

43. See pp. 54–55 (Orelli, p. 296) and pp. 38–40 (Orelli, pp. 285–286) above.

44. A species is a part of a genus in the sense that a genus is always divided into more than one species, and so one species does not exhaust a genus. (And a genus is a part of a species in the sense that a species consists in a genus plus differentiae.) But Boethius's claim is intended as evidence for the general point that a species does not designate the whole substance of the things whose species it is. In connection with that issue, the claim that a species is part of a genus is irrelevant; in light of Boethius's other claims about species (see the appendix), the general point seems false.

45. According to Aristotle, *Cat.* 1a1–6, things are homonymously designaged if they share a name but not a definition.

46. For this same point, see pp. 54–55 (Orelli, p. 296) above.

47. See below pp. 101ff. (Orelli, pp. 331ff.).

48. Technically and primarily, a law is what the people decree, that is, what the popular assembly or plebian gathering enacts; in a broader sense, a law is also a rule from any other source that is binding for the whole people. A decree of the senate is a decision of the senate in response to a request for advice from a magistrate such as a praetor; by the middle of the second century A.D. these decrees acquired the legal force of statutes. Judicial decisions are the conclusions of controversies as a result of the judgment given by a judge; these decisions had the authority of precedents. Jurists were men who held no official position and took no fees but were learned in the law; their legal opinions were not officially binding but owed their authority to the personal reputation of the individual jurist. The jurists were highly influential in shaping Roman law; among the most prominent were Gaius, Julian, Papinian, Paul, and Ulpian. For a detailed account of Roman jurists, see Fritz Schulz, *History of Roman Legal Science* (Oxford: Clarendon Press, 1953). Edicts of the magistrates were edicts issued by consuls, praetors, provincial governors, and other officials at the beginning of their term of office which contained rules by which they would govern. The edicts of praetors and aedils were especially important in shaping Roman law; they interpreted, shaped, and changed existing civil law. Custom gave rise to law in some cases, and in some cases it had the force of law through its influence on judges and jurists even though custom itself was not legally binding. Equity was considered a corrective principle to the positive law, and the principle of equity was an important one for jurists.

49. *"Res mancipi* were land subject to Roman ownership, slaves, beasts of draft and burden, including cattle, and rustic servitudes belonging to land subject to Roman ownership; *res nec mancipi* were all other things. In the developed law the point of the distinction is that full Quiritarian ownership in *res mancipi* can only be transferred by the solemn method of conveyance known as *mancipatio* or the equivalent ceremony of *in iure cessio*, whereas the ownership of *res nec mancipi* can be transferred by mere delivery (*traditio*). Thus if *A* wants to make *B* the gift of a sheep and delivers it to him for that purpose the sheep becomes immediately the full Quiritarian property of *B*, but if he wants to give him an ox and does the same, the ox remains the property *ex iure*

Quiritium of *A*, because an ox is a *res mancipi* whereas a sheep is not." H. F. Jolowicz and Barry Nicholas, *Historical Introduction to the Study of Roman Law* (Cambridge: Cambridge University Press, 1972), p. 137. The phrase *ius Quaritium* denotes absolute rights deriving from Roman citizenship. For the ways of transferring *res mancipi*, see the following notes.

50. The meaning of the term *'nexum'* is somewhat obscure. See Jolowicz and Nicholas 1972: 164ff. In this context the word seems equivalent to *'mancipatio'*. *Mancipatio* is a symbolic sale. If *A* wants to transfer something to *B* by *man-cipatio*, then they must have five adult Roman citizens as witnesses, a pair of scales and an adult Roman citizen to hold them, and a piece of bronze. *B* grasps the thing to be transferred (if it is movable property) and claims it as his own. Then he strikes the scales with the bronze, which he gives to *A* as the "price" of the thing transferred.

51. Cession at law is a fictitious legal action. If *A* wants to transfer property to *B* in this way, both appear before a magistrate. *B* grasps the thing to be transferred and claims it as his. The magistrate asks *A* whether he makes a similar claim. *A* says no, and the magistrate judges the thing to belong to *B*.

52. "The strict theory of Roman law which remained throughout its history was that the *ius civile* was only for citizens, and, as there was originally no other law than the *ius civile*, the foreigner was both rightless and dutiless. . . . whether there was ever a time at which practice was entirely in consonance with this theory may be doubted" (Jolowicz and Nicholas 1972: 102). Boethius's restricting of civil law to the XII Tables is also much too narrow; it is the law of the Roman state arising from statutes and their interpretation and is sometimes contrasted with *ius honorarium*, the law arising from edicts of the magistrates.

53. Gaius was a very important and influential jurist, about whose life we know very little. His *Institutes*, which is still extant, was written in the second half of the second century A.D. and was a traditional textbook for beginning students.

54. Gaius, *Institutes* I.119. Boethius's quotation differs in minor ways from the extant manuscript; see James Muirhead, *The Institutes of Gaius and Rules of Ulpian* (Edinburgh: T. and T. Clark, 1880), p. 45.

55. See Gaius, *Institutes* I.113, which is a discussion of the mancipation that occurs in marriage by purchase.

56. The *mancipium* in this case is a slave.

57. The text may be corrupt here. What we expect Boethius to say is that nothing can be *mancipated* except in this way.

58. Cession at law is a means of transferring ownership both of things that are and of things that are not *mancipium*.

59. Gaius, *Institutes* II.24.

60. Again, the thing being transferred is a slave.

61. "In early times legal proceedings were by what were called actions of the law (*legis actiones*). There were only a limited number of these and they were very inflexible. Gaius believed that if the slightest mistake were made in the form of words used, the case was lost." Alan Watson, *The Law of the Ancient Romans*, (Dallas, Tex. Southern Methodist University Press, 1970), p. 30. "The trial of an action was a matter of solemn formality . . . the procedure took the form of judicial arbitration in which the question to be referred was settled in the presence of a judicial officer, normally the praetor, and was then referred to a single judge (iudex) or arbiter, or to a board of judges (recuperatores) or to a

standing college of judges (centumviri, decemviri). The first stage of the proceedings was said to take place in court (in jure), the second before the judge
(the normal case). . . . The term legis actio, Gaius tells us, was employed either
because the actions were fixed by statutes, or because they were adapted to the
words of statutes and therefore were adhered to as immutable as the statutes
themselves." R. W. Lee, *The Elements of Roman Law* (London: Sweet and Maxwell, 1946), p. 413.

62. If *A* transfers a *mancipium* to *B* but without *nexum* or cession at law, then
provided that the property was not stolen and that *B* bought it in good faith
and so on, the property becomes *B*'s as a result of usucaption, the uninterrupted possession of the property for the requisite period of time, two years for
immovable property and one year for movable property.

63. See pp. 92ff. (Orelli, pp. 324ff.) below.

64. See pp. 93ff. (Orelli, pp. 325ff.) below.

65. For a detailed discussion of the similarity in this respect of genera and
differentiae, see Stump 1978: 251–261.

66. This is the sort of definition Boethius has in mind when he says above
that one kind of definition consists in the parts of the nature of a thing.

67. This sort of definition differs from the first sort (the sort that is a definition in the strict sense of the word), because the first sort gives a proximate
genus plus one differentia that specifies a particular species under that genus,
but this sort of definition gives a proximate genus plus an enumeration of all
the differentiae that divide that genus into its subsidiary species.

68. For the meaning of "greater" here, see Bk. I, nn. 35 and 37.

69. Having done his best to justify Cicero's four species of definitions,
Boethius here adds a qualification to his acceptance of Cicero's claim: the
partition of a whole into the members that constitute it is not always equivalent
to the definition of that whole.

70. Boethius is here referring to Victorinus's book *De definitionibus*. For an
edition of this treatise, see Pierre Hadot, *Marius Victorinus* (Paris: Etudes Augustiniennes, 1971), pp. 329–362. Hadot has reproduced the edition of T.
Stangl (*Tulliana et Mario-Victoriniana* [Munich: Programm München, 1888], pp.
12–48).

71. Aristotle, *Top.* 102a2–5.

72. The Greek here and in the following paragraphs occurs in Victorinus's
De definitionibus. Victorinus's source is as yet unknown. For a detailed discussion of this treatise of Victorinus, with intricate and helpful analysis of the use
of these Greek terms before Victorinus, see Hadot 1971: 163–178. For Victorinus's discussion of *kata lexin*, which he calls '*kat' antilexin*' and gives as the
fifth sort of definition, see Hadot 1971: 350–351. Boethius's examples for this
sort of definition are taken from Victorinus.

73. That is, an example. Victorinus calls this '*hōs typos*' and classifies it as the
tenth sort of definition. Victorinus's example is, "If we ask what an animal is,
the reply is 'for example, a man.'" See Hadot 1971: 356.

74. See p. 93 (Orelli, p. 325) above.

75. See pp. 89–93 (Orelli, pp. 321–324) above.

76. That is, a common concept. It is Victorinus's second sort of definition.
His example is 'A man is what excels all animals by rational comprehension
and action.' See Hadot 1971: 347–348.

77. That is, quality. This is Victorinus's third sort of definition. Boethius's

example reproduces almost exactly the first half of Victorinus's. See Hadot 1971: 348–349.

78. That is, description. This is Victorinus's fourth sort of definition. Boethius gives a somewhat different definition of an extravagant man. See Hadot 1971: 349–350.

79. That is, by means of a differentia. Victorinus presents this as the sixth sort of definition. Only the second of Boethius's examples is in Victorinus's treatise, where it occurs in this form: "what separates a king from a tyrant? . . . a king is self-restrained and moderate, but a tyrant is cruel." (It is perhaps worth noticing that Boethius adds piety as a necessary condition for being a king.) See Hadot 1971: 351–352.

80. This is Victorinus's seventh sort of definition, *kata metaphoran*. Boethius's example is the first half of Victorinus's; see Hadot 1971: 352–353.

81. This is Victorinus's eighth sort of definition, *kat' aphairesin tou enantiou*. Boethius's example reproduces Victorinus's; see Hadot 1971: 353–354.

82. This is Victorinus's ninth sort of definition, and Boethius's example is one of many that Victorinus gives. See Hadot 1971: 355–356.

83. This is Victorinus's eleventh sort of definition, *kat' elleipes tou plērous homoiou genous*. Boethius's example reproduces one of Victorinus's; see Hadot 1971: 356–357.

84. This is Victorinus's twelfth sort of definition, *kat' epainon*. Boethius's example is found in Victorinus, who takes it from Cicero, *Pro Cluentio* 146. See Hadot 1971: 356–357.

85. Victorinus in his discussions of this sort of definition does seem to think that definitions can also arise by censure, but he does not make such definitions into another species of definition.

86. This is Victorinus's thirteenth sort of definition, *kat' analogian*. Boethius's example is found in Victorinus, who attributes it to "the Greeks." See Hadot 1971: 358.

87. This is Victorinus's fourteenth sort of definition, *kata to pros ti*. Boethius's example is the first of several Victorinus gives. See Hadot 1971: 358.

88. This is Victorinus's fifteenth and last sort of definition, *aitologikē*. Boethius's example is the first of two Victorinus gives; see Hadot 1971: 358–359.

89. See p. 93 (Orelli, p. 325) above.

90. I think he means that the number of elements in the definition is increased but that *animal* is in some sense decreased because its application is restricted by the added differentia.

91. See, e.g., Plato *Timaeus* 36E ff. for Plato's doctrine of the soul animating the heavens.

92. Cicero, *Top.* VI.29.

93. An inheritance consists in the goods, rights, and duties of the deceased, all of which become the heir's unless some portion is explicitly and legally transferred to someone other than the heir. A bequest is a portion subtracted from the inheritance and given by the testator's wish to someone other than the heir. It was the heir's responsibility to see that the bequest was made over according to the testator's wish.

94. Cicero, *Top.* VI.29.

95. See note 40 above.

96. For discussion of adoption and forfeiture of civil rights, see Bk. II, n. 41.

97. Q. Mucius Scaevola was *pontifex maximus* and consul in 95 B.C. He was the first jurist who wrote systematic legal treatises that survived to influence later periods, and he was the first jurist to be clearly influenced by Greek philosophy. He had many students, including the famous C. Aquilius Gallus (see note 106).

98. See p. 86 (Orelli, p. 319) above.

99. See pp. 44–45 (Orelli, p. 289) above.

100. See p. 51 (Orelli, p. 293) above.

101. 'Ennoia' is a word that Stoics made much of; cf. Pierre Hadot's (1971:171ff.) discussion of 'ennoēma' in Marius Victorinus's work, and Benedetto Riposati's discussion of *ennoia* in Cicero's work in *Studi sui 'Topica' di Cicerone* (Milan: Società editrice "Vita e pensiero," 1947), pp. 71ff. Cicero discusses *prolepsis* in connection with Epicureanism in, e.g., *De natura deorum* I.16.43 and *De finibus* I.9.31. See Riposati 1947: 70ff.

102. For a discussion of this definition and its sources, see Riposati 1947: 71ff.

103. We would expect Boethius to add in this list that each is corporeal. An animal is a sensitive animate *corporeal* substance. I have no explanation for the omission of *corporeal* from the list.

104. For the notions of differing in number and differing in accident and their relationship, see Boethius, *De trinitate* I.

105. See p. 95 (Orelli, p. 326) above.

106. C. Aquilius Gallus, a pupil of Q. Mucius Scaevola, was an important jurist and contemporary of Cicero's. He was praetor of the *quaestio de ambitu* in 66 B.C. and refrained from seeking the consulship in order to devote himself to the law. He wrote no legal books, but had an important influence on the interpretation of the law in, for example, the *stipulatio Aquiliana* concerning debts and the *actio de dolo* concerning fraud.

NOTES TO BOOK IV

1. The formulary system came to replace the system of *legis actiones*. A formula was "a written document by which in a civil trial authorization was given to a judge (*iudex*) to condemn the defendant if certain factual or legal circumstances appeared proved, or to absolve him if this was not the case. . . . The elasticity of the formula which made it adaptable to any case was its great advantage which explains its existence through centuries" Adolf Berger, *Encyclopedic Dictionary of Roman Law*, Transactions of the American Philosophical Society, n. s., vol. XLIII, pt. 2 (Philadelphia: American Philosophical Society, 1953), p. 474.

2. Greek rhetoricians stressed figures of speech, and Cicero attributes skill at figures of speech even to Cato (*Brutus* 69). Stoic grammarians in the second century B.C. lectured also on style and devoted some attention to figures of speech. The *Rhetorica ad Herennium* discusses sixty-four figures in some detail, including, for example, metaphor, homoioteleuton (words with similar endings), and paronomasia (words with similarity of sound). According to Quintilian (9.1.12), Apollodorus (fl. 64 B.C.) thought that figures were innumerable and practically indefinable, apparently because he used 'figure' to mean any configuration of language. See George Kennedy, *The Art of Rhetoric in the Roman World* (Princeton: Princeton University Press, 1972). The *Ars maior* of Donatus

(fl. A.D. 350) "adds a highly important section on figures of speech (*scema*) and tropes. . . . By the end of the fourth century as many as 200 separate tropes and figures can be distinguished in various books of rhetoric and grammar; the resulting confusions, overlapping, and ambiguities were further complicated by the bilingual nomenclature of the field. Many Greek names for figures were translated into Latin by the Romans." James J. Murphy, *A Synoptic History of Classical Rhetoric* (New York: Random House, 1972), p. 181.

3. For a discussion of how Boethius conceives of division, see Stump 1978: 242ff.

4. The ancients seem to have taken black and white as the primary colors; in *A History of Greek Philosophy* (Cambridge: Cambridge University Press, 1962–1969), II: 445n.1, W. K. C. Guthrie explains that Aristotle (see *De sensu* 440a20) criticizes an explanation of the view that the two primary colors are black and white but that he himself retained such a view.

5. Gaius, *Institutes* I.188, divides guardianship into four sorts on the basis of the appointing authority: (1) *tutela testamentaria:* a father might appoint in his will a guardian for those of his children who would become *sui iuris* at his death; (2) *tutela legitima:* if there was no testamentary tutor, children who were *sui iuris* were in the guardianship of their nearest male agnatic relatives; (3) *tutela fiduciaria:* guardianship arising from a trust; for example, the manumitter of someone else's son became a quasi-patron to him and had fiduciary guardianship; (4) *tutela a magistratu dativa:* if there was no tutor on the basis of the first three provisions, a tutor was appointed by a magistrate, originally perhaps by the praetor and the majority of tribunes but by the time of Marcus Aurelius by a new official, the praetor tutelaris. See W. W. Buckland, *A Text-book of Roman Law from Augustus to Justinian* (Cambridge: Cambridge University Press, 1921), pp. 143ff.

6. This is a surprising thing for Boethius to say in this context, where he is censuring any omissions in the division. Boethius's reservation may have to do with the fact that Gaius's division of guardianship was not the only classification. Ulpian, for example, offers a different classification based on the ultimate authority on which the mode of appointing a tutor rests, e.g., custom, or a decree of the senate.

7. Boethius thinks the example inappropriate as an example for the enumeration of parts, because in this Topic the parts being enumerated are those that compose a whole.

8. This Merobaudes may have been Flavius Merobaudes, a fifth-century Romanized Frank who settled in Spain. He was a poet, scholar, and rhetorician, but nothing of his rhetorical work seems to have survived. For an excellent study of Merobaudes, see Frank M. Clover, *Flavius Merobaudes: A Translation and Historical Commentary*, Transactions of the American Philosophical Society, n.s., vol. LXI, pt. 1 (Philadelphia: American Philosophical Society, 1971).

9. This passage is confusing because Boethius is using 'partition' in an ambiguous way as the following chart of his usage shows:

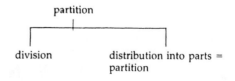

partition

division   distribution into parts = partition

The genus *partition* Boethius divides into two species; one is *division*, by which he means the division of a genus into its species, and the other is *distribution*, by which he means the distribution of a whole into those parts whose conjunction composes the whole. This second species, however, he tends to call by the same name as that of the genus, namely, 'partition'.

10. In *De top. diff.* 1209A Boethius says that 'question' is another name for the point in dispute (*constitutio*) or issue (*status*). In 1209Aff. he gives an elaborate division of such questions. One set of issues, he says, has to do with the nature of the deed done by the man brought to court; these issues can be divided into three groups. The first is the conjectural issues, where the disputed point is whether the defendant did the deed alleged. The second is definitional, because the defendant agrees that the deed occurred but the import of the deed is at issue and needs to be settled by a definition of the deed. And the third is qualitative, where the defendant agrees about the occurrence and import of the deed, but there is controversy about the qualities of the deed. This last sort of issue is elaborately subdivided and includes, for example, cases in which the defendant claims that although he did the deed alleged, he is not guilty of a crime because the victim deserved what he got. The odd thing about Boethius's remark here is that it apparently omits all sort of issues or questions, as Boethius must have known; yet Boethius makes this remark in the process of censuring omissions in a division. Hermagoras of Temnos, a very influential rhetorician of the second century B.C., divided issues into conjecture, definition, and quality, and so there may be some traditional standing for this division of issues. In *De inventione*, Book I, however, Cicero takes issue with Hermagoras's division of issues, and in *De top. diff.* 1210C Boethius cites a passage from *De inv.* in which Cicero is rejecting Hermagoras's views.

11. See p. 106 (Orelli, p. 334) above.

12. This point is dependent on taking 'figure' in a very general sense as any configuration of language. See note 2 above.

13. The worry that begins this paragraph arises because Boethius seems to be making two claims that are not clearly compatible with each other: (1) individual figures are species rather than members of *figure*, and (2) the number of figures is practically unlimited. The appearance of incompatibility depends on Boethius's views that every genus is always divided into just two species, so that unless there are innumerably many steps between a genus and its lowest species, the number of species under that genus is definitely limited. Boethius's attempt to resolve the appearance of incompatibility is based on various ways of undercutting claim (1). This suggestion, that the differences between individual figures are a result of accidental rather than substantial differences, is in fact a repudiation of (1). If figure *A* and figure *B* differ from one another only in accidents and not in substance, then *A* and *B* are not species of *figure* but rather particulars falling under one and the same species.

14. This sentence is ambiguous, but I think Boethius's point is this: although in a crucial respect the case of the division of *figure* resembles the case of the division of a common name into its significations, we cannot assimilate the first case to the second because the fact that the name and definition of *figure* apply to individual figures is sufficient to show that the division of *figure* is a division of a genus into its species.

15. There is perhaps a play on words here. The Latin for 'sign' is *'nota'* and for 'known' is *'notam'*.

16. See Aristotle, *De int.* 16a3–8.

17. "A Roman citizen who had been caught by an enemy as a prisoner of war became a slave of the enemy, but he regained freedom and 'all his former rights through *postliminium* (*iure postliminii*),' when he returned to Roman territory. His marriage, however, which was dissolved through his captivity, did not revive; the same applied to possession, which was a factual situation . . . ; hence his things had to be taken into possession anew." Berger 1953: 639.

18. Things that return with postliminium are things that, when they have been returned after having been captured by the enemy, are restored to their original owner.

19. Servius Sulpicius Rufus, a famous jurist, was consul in 51 B.C. and proconsul of Achaia in 46–45 B.C. He was a friend of Cicero and a student of C. Aquilius Gallus (see Bk. III, n. 106). Very little of his writing survives. See Wolfgang Kunkel, *An Introduction to Roman Legal and Constitutional History* (Oxford: Clarendon Press, 1973), pp. 104ff.

20. This is Quintus Mucius Scaevola. See Bk. III, n. 97.

21. Gaius Hostilius Mancinus was praetor in 140 B.C. and consul in 137. He was defeated by Numantia in 136 and concluded a treaty. The senate refused to ratify his treaty and delivered him over to Numantia, but Numantia refused to accept him. He returned to Rome and eventually regained his place in the senate. Cf. Cicero, *De oratore* I.181.

22. For exclusion of rainwater, see note 39 below.

23. This Mucius is probably Q. Mucius Scaevola, pontifex; see Book. III, n. 97. For detailed discussion of Scaevola and his contribution to Roman law, see Fritz Schulz, *History of Roman Legal Science* (Oxford: Clarendon Press, 1953), pp. 47, 64ff, and 94ff.

24. This is a somewhat peculiar description of the ascent from Cicero to substance. It leaves out the genus *rational animal,* man's proximate genus, and it fails to give the usual differentiae for the ascent to substance (*corporeal, sensitive,* and *mortal* are missing). The absence of the differentiae may be a consequence of Boethius's desire to make the ascent "by means of species and genera," so that he uses species names rather than a phrase consisting of genus plus differentia to pick out species.

25. Elsewhere Boethius indicates that the proximate genus for man is *rational animal.* See Stump 1978: 256ff.

26. Boethius's point is that a genus must have species under it. By saying that the water to be excluded has many, similar waters subsumed under it, then, he must mean that the subsumed waters are different in species from one another.

27. Boethius, *In Isagogen,* ed. Samuel Brandt, Corpus scriptorum ecclesiasticorum latinorum, 48 (Leipzig: G. Freytag, 1906).

28. "Originally, . . . there was no redress for mere deceit any more than for threats. If a man had been cheated e.g. into making a conveyance of his property he had made it none the less, and perhaps in very early times the deceit was not even regarded as morally reprehensible. No remedy was found until Aquillius Gallus, in Cicero's words [*Off.* 3.60], 'produced the *formulae de dolo'.* . . . it gave only simple damages for the loss which had been inflicted by the fraud, and was available only if the plaintiff had no other remedy open to him." H. F. Jolowicz and Barry Nicholas, *Historical Introduction to the Study of Roman Law* (Cambridge: Cambridge University Press, 1972), pp. 278–279.

29. It is peculiar to find the phrase "and is intended for habitation" here, because it does not refer to a part of the house and so, it seems, should not be included in the enumeration.

30. To see that this argument is not blatantly invalid, we must remember its context: this is supposed to be an example of the division of a genus and the subsuming of the thing at issue under one of the species of that genus. The first premise, then, is 'The genus *animal* is divided into *rational* and *irrational*'. The second premise tells us that Cicero is included within the species constituted by *rational*. And these two premises entitle us to the conclusion that Cicero is included within the genus *animal*.

31. It seems to me clear that this argument is made from species, rather than from genus. The peculiarity of the example is enhanced by the rule Boethius gives for it in the succeeding pages: whatever things are predicated of a genus are also predicated in all modes of the species. The rule seems not to apply to this example, where the species are mentioned in the premises and the genus occurs in the conclusion.

32. The argument is this:

(1) Man is rational.
(2) Socrates is a man.
Therefore,
(3) Socrates is rational.

The question, then, has to be 'Is Socrates rational?', and its two terms are *Socrates* and *rational*. The argument is thus made from *man*, in Boethius's terminology. Since *man* is the species of Socrates, it seems reasonable to conclude that the argument is drawn from a species. The reason for thinking that the argument is not drawn from a genus is that the argument is drawn from *man*, which is a lowest species, and no species that is lowest can also be a genus (see appendix for lowest species and subaltern genera). The reason given for thinking that the argument is not drawn from a species, however, seems simply confused. It amounts to no more than that Socrates cannot be a species. But the fact that Socrates cannot be a species is entirely irrelevant to the questions of whether *man* is a species (which has been answered in the affirmative when it was designated a lowest species) and whether the argument is drawn from a species.

33. See Boethius's discussion of induction in *De top. diff.* 1183Dff., in Stump 1978: 44ff.

34. A partner or *socius* is someone engaged in a contractual business arrangement with one or more other persons; controversies among the partners were settled by a legal action brought by one of them.

35. A mandator is one who commissions another man, the mandatary, to do something for him when the performance of the act mandated carries no compensation. The contract between mandator and mandatary was based on friendship and personal confidence. An example of a mandate is this. A mandator *A* commissions a mandatary *B* to lend money at interest to a third party *C*. *A* cannot pay *B* for his services or in any other way officially compensate him (though he can pay *B*'s expenses), and yet *B* is legally obligated to lend money at interest to *C* in virtue of *B*'s having accepted *A*'s mandate.

36. A trustee *A* assumes certain responsibilities with regard to certain property that a transferor *B* has transferred to *A* with mancipation, or *A* receives the

property on the condition that he later retransfer it to *B*. The agreement was based simply on personal trust between *A* and *B* but was actionable.

37. An agent was a general manager of the property of another man. His powers were virtually unlimited with respect to managing the property, except that he could not alienate it.

38. A dispute over boundaries was a dispute between neighbors over the five-foot border strip between their rural properties, which was to be left unploughed and which could not be acquired by usucaption, or over the two-and-one-half foot *ambitus* that was supposed to be left around a building. This rule was originally meant to apply to both city and country but was later restricted to the country.

39. A man *A* had the right to exclude from his land rainwater or other water mixed with rainwater which ran onto his land in consequence of something his neighbor *B* had done and which was injurious to *A*. By Cicero's time this right was engendering considerable controversy. On one interpretation of this right, the interpretation Cicero is arguing for, the right applies only to the country and not to the town. For a thorough discussion of the right, the controversy, and contemporary interpretations of both, see Alan Rodger, *Owners and Neighbours in Roman Law* (Oxford: Clarendon Press, 1972), pp. 141–166; and Alan Watson, *The Law of Property in the Later Roman Empire* (Oxford: Clarendon Press, 1968), pp. 155–175.

40. L. Licinius Crassus (140–91 b.c.) was one of the most important orators of his time. He was consul in 95 with Q. Mucius Scaevola. He was especially famous for his defense in the case of Curius (see note 41 below).

41. Curius is known because of a suit over inheritance in which he was engaged with Coponius around 91 b.c. "A testator who did not have a son but apparently had hopes named as heir his son if he had one, and then appointed a *secundus heres*. . . . No son was born to the testator, and a dispute arose between the *secundus heres* and the *agnati*. The *agnati*, for whom Quintus Mucius Scaevola appeared, argued that the *secundus heres* could not be heir since no son had been born to the testator and under the will the *secundus heres* was substituted only for the situation where a son had been born who died an *impubes*. L. Crassus appeared for the *substitutus* and argued that the intention of the testator was that the *substitutus* should succeed where no son of the testator reached puberty, whether a son was born but died before puberty or no son was born at all." Alan Watson, *The Law of Succession in the Later Roman Republic* (Oxford: Clarendon Press, 1971), pp. 53–54. Cicero discusses the case in *De oratore* I.xxxix.180, *De inv.* II.xlii.122, and *Brutus* 52.194–53.198. Crassus won, and Curius inherited.

42. The appointment of a substitute for a minor is the appointment by the father of a substitute heir for his son in case the son died before reaching puberty, that is, before he could make a will of his own. This appointment is to be distinguished from *substitutio vulgaris*, which is the appointment by the testator of another heir in case the heir first appointed could not or would not take the inheritance. For a detailed and helpful discussion of these institutions, see Buckland 1921: 298ff.

43. A contract in Roman law is basically an enforceable agreement. "But we shall misread the history of Roman law if we imagine that the idea of contract as an agreement was always present. . . . The presence or absence of agreement was not a significant factor. . . . [Roman law] had a formal act which

embodied the bare essentials of agreement. This was the *stipulatio*, an exchange of a question and answer in formal words. . . . the validity of a *stipulatio* . . . came from its form and not from the agreement which the form no doubt embodied. . . . if the form had been defective (e.g. because the debtor said '*promitto*' instead of '*spondeo*'), the creditor could not plead that there had nevertheless been an agreement in substance." Barry Nicholas, *An Introduction to Roman Law* (Oxford: Clarendon Press, 1962), pp. 159–160. Nonetheless, the consent of the contracting parties was essential to a contract, and not all contracts are equally dependent on the precise form of the solemn words employed in making the contract. In consensual contracts, those involving sale, for example, "the parties could be bound by a mere formless agreement" (ibid., p. 162).

44. See Bk. III, note 49, for property that can be transferred by mancipation.

45. Cicero, *Pro Caelio* XIV.33ff. This part of Cicero's speech was famous in antiquity for the rhetorical figure known as *prosopopoiia*, a speech in character, in which he speaks in the person of someone long dead.

46. That is, for necessary and dialectical argumentation (and perhaps also for sophistical argumentation). See *De top. diff.* 1181C–D, Stump 1978: 41.

47. I think Boethius's point here is that everything shares a substance or a quality or a quantity, etc., with something else.

48. This classification is Porphyry's. See Boethius, *In Isagogen*, ed. Brandt, pp. 239ff.

49. *Black* is an accident that inheres inseparably in *raven* and helps to differentiate ravens from other things.

50. Cf. Aristotle, *Top.* 102b20–26, where Aristotle is discussing property and accident.

51. See the appendix for an explanation of divisive and constitutive differentiae.

52. For an explanation of this claim, which turns out to be both complicated and controversial, see Stump 1978: 251–261.

53. This is another way of stating what Boethius elsewhere expresses by saying that contraries always belong to the same genus, which they divide into the two species under that genus. The general point is that an argument drawn from a differentia is always, strictly speaking, drawn from divisive differentiae. Arguments drawn from constitutive differentiae are assimilable to arguments drawn from a genus.

54. When the ward was a child, the guardian administered his ward's property entirely as he saw fit, though he had an obligation to try to do so profitably. The child did not have a legal position on the basis of which he could conduct business. So, for example, if a debtor payed a child directly what he owed the child, the debt was not thereby discharged, and the guardian might sue the debtor for the money. The debtor might pay the ward and discharge his debt if he first obtained the guardian's consent to do so and the guardian's consent was declared when the act of payment was performed. When the ward was a woman, the guardian had no power over her property, and his only important function was to give his assent to or withhold it from certain legal acts that the woman wanted to engage in. Even that power of the guardian was limited. A woman could give a loan or alienate property (without mancipation) without her guardian's consent, and a debtor who payed her what he owed her was discharged from his debt even without the guardian's consent to the

payment. See Fritz Schulz, *Classical Roman Law* (Oxford: Clarendon Press, 1951), pp. 162ff.

55. For an interesting discussion of the Roman attitude toward the ability of women to conduct business, see Schulz 1951: 180–184.

56. Cf. Aristotle, *Cat.* 11b17–14a25.

57. I am reading 'sursum' for 'rursum' in accordance with *Vat. lat.* 567 and *Reg. lat.* 1649.

58. The point about both sorts of contraries and about privation and possession is to be understood with a qualification. One or another exclusive contrary must always be in a subject, for those subjects to which such contraries can belong; and similarly, in the case of other contraries, both contraries can fail to be in a subject when the intermediate is in that subject, for those subjects to which such contraries can belong. The point about privation and possession is that with regard to the subjects to which they can belong, they do not admit of an intermediate, and yet it is not the case that one or the other of them must always be in a subject.

59. These examples seem not to make Boethius's point. In the first example, it is not clear that a baby not yet born *is* a subject to which the privation and possession can belong. And the second example seems to demonstrate that the privation and possession do admit of an intermediate. Between *seeing*, which is the possession, and *blindness*, which is the state of having lost the possession (on Boethius's view as he explains them here), there is *sighted but not yet seeing*, the state of newborn animals that are not able to see as soon as they are born.

60. The point about the first two groups of pairs of opposites is that both members of a pair cannot exist together at the same time and place in the same thing. If he were then going to show that relatives do *not* share this characteristic, he would have to show that in general both members of a pair of relatives can exist in the same thing at the same time and place. Instead he shows that there can never be one member of a pair of relatives without the other. (By this he cannot mean that both members of a pair must exist simultaneously—some live on after their fathers die—but only that one member of the pair is what it is just in virtue of its relation to the other member of the pair. A is a son only insofar as he stands in the appropriate relationship to B, who is his father.)

61. See Boethius, *In Categorias Aristotelis, PL* 64, 264Bff.

62. What Boethius says here seems just false. The affirmation 'The sun was over the earth' destroys *not* the negation 'It was not night' but rather the corresponding affirmation 'It was night.' (What appears to be a modality in the negation in the text is just the *necessitas consequentiae* that Boethius thinks attaches to all true conditionals.)

63. This sentence seems to be raising a worry about the status of such propositions as 'The sun was over the earth' and 'It was not night.' These are in fact not negating contraries because they are not opposed and they can exist simultaneously.

64. See pp. 62–63 (Orelli, pp. 302–303) above.

65. See note 10 above.

66. In this and the preceding paragraphs there is some indication that Boethius is following a source that he does not find entirely satisfactory. Even though Victorinus's commentary on Cicero's *Topica* breaks off well before this point, it is reasonable to wonder whether the objection and response Boethius

222 / *In Ciceronis Topica*

is considering here might have come from Victorinus's commentary. Our available evidence about Victorinus's commentary does not suggest that he raises or replies to such an objection, but we do not have enough evidence to be sure. See Pierre Hadot, *Marius Victorinus* (Paris: Etudes Augustiniennes, 1971), pp. 115ff.

67. Boethius here seems to suggest that antecedents, consequents, and incompatibles are unlike associated things in virtue of the fact that the former "bring about or complete the nature of one another" as the latter do not. This suggestion is not entirely accurate, however, because although on Boethius's understanding of antecedents and consequents it is perhaps reasonable to say that they bring about or complete one another, it is clearly not true to say the same of incompatibles. On the contrary, as Boethius repeatedly explains, incompatibles cannot exist together, because their natures are opposed to one another; therefore *a fortiori* they do not bring about or complete the nature of one another. But perhaps Boethius makes this suggestion not to indicate a criterion for distinguishing associated things from antecedents, consequents, and incompatibles, but rather only as a preliminary consideration for accepting the criterion he proposes a little later in this paragraph: unlike associated things, antecedents, consequents, and incompatibles are always found together.

68. This sentence suggests that Boethius understands conditionals as somehow causal, that the state of affairs in the antecedent somehow causes or produces the state of affairs in the consequent. If he did hold such a view, it clearly would not apply to incompatibles since no incompatible causes its complementary incompatible. But the subsequent examples in this paragraph show that Boethius cannot be holding this view even for antecedents and consequents. With regard to the conditional 'If it is a man, it is an animal,' for example, Boethius cannot suppose that something's being a man *causes* it to be an animal. So I think in this sentence Boethius should be read just as rejecting the one reason that might be given for supporting the view that associated things were always found together.

69. See, for example, *De top. diff.* 1178Dff., in Stump 1978: 37ff.

70. There is some unclarity about the case of 'species' in this sentence, and so some ambiguity in how this sentence is to be read. Boethius could mean either

(a) a genus always follows from a species, and a species always precedes a genus,

or

(b) a species always follows from a genus, and a genus always precedes a species.

What Boethius is considering in this context is the issue whether the Topic *from antecedents and consequents* is identical to the Topics *from a genus* and *from a species*. So in this context, (a) and (b) may be understood as claims of this sort:

(a') if something is a member of species x, it is a member of genus y;
(b') if something is a member of genus y, it is a member of species x.

According to Boethius's own metaphysical and logical views, conditional inferences of the form (a') are acceptable but those of form (b') are not. If something is a member of the species *man*, we may legitimately infer that it is a member of the genus *animal*. But if something is a member of the genus *animal*, we may not make any legitimate inferences about its species. Since Boethius's views on this point are both clear and explicit and since the text is ambiguous, I have read the text as (*a*). *Vat. lat.* 567 and *Reg. lat.* 1649 also support (*a*); both read, "*Nam genus semper speciem sequitur, species genus praecedit.*" The Orelli text, however, takes this sentence as (*b*). The subsequent paragraph appears to contain a confusion. One sentence clearly supports my reading, and another supports the Orelli reading (see the notes to the next paragraph).

71. This sentence supports my reading of the last sentence in the preceding paragraph. If the Orelli reading of that sentence were correct, this sentence would have to read, 'not every consequent is a species, nor is every antecedent a genus.'

72. See p. 67 (Orelli, p. 305) above.

73. This sentence and the preceding one apparently clash with my reading of the last sentence of the preceding paragraph and also with the claim Boethius makes at the start of this paragraph. To be consistent with both the text at the start of this paragraph and my suggested reading of the preceding paragraph, the text here should read, 'But when we are trying to show something on the basis of antecedents and consequents, we use what preceded in the conditional proposition as a premise in our argument even if it was not a *species*. Similarly, if an argument arises from a consequent, the argument is drawn from the consequent part of the conditional proposition even if it is not a *genus*.' There is, however, an alternate interpretation of these sentences which is suggested by the subsequent paragraph. It makes this sentence as it stands consistent with what has gone before, including my reading of the text, but it is a somewhat tenuous interpretation and needs to be offered diffidently. There are legitimate arguments that employ a genus in the minor premise and conclude something about a species. These are *not* arguments based on the claim that the genus precedes and the species follows. Rather they are arguments based on the fact that the genus *contains* the species and that some information about the species can be derived from that fact. It is such arguments from a genus which Boethius is thinking of when he talks in the subsequent paragraph about taking the genus in the minor premise not as preceding but as containing. Perhaps he has such arguments in mind here also. If so, these sentences as they now read in the text would be consistent with my reading at the end of the preceding paragraph and with Boethius's claims at the start of this paragraph.

74. On Boethius's views, lightness is almost certainly inseparably tied to fire, either as a differentia or as an inseparable accident, but it is not the genus or species of fire because it is not in the same category as fire. Fire must be in the category of substance, and lightness is a quality. Therefore, the two are in different predicamental lines, and consequently neither is a genus or species of the other.

75. Such arguments are not ones in which a species is understood to follow from a genus, but rather ones based on the idea that a genus contains its species and that therefore what is true of all members of that genus will be true of members of the species as well.

76. See the fuller discussion of this example, pp. 58–59 (Orelli, p. 299) above.

77. Boethius is here addressing a question of considerable importance for the history of logic. How are we to understand conditional inferences? Are they

simply inferences based on necessary metaphysical connections? Or are they something other than and divorced from metaphysics? The history of logic in the first part of the scholastic period is to some extent an attempt to answer these questions and to work out the appropriate relations between formal logic and metaphysics. In raising this issue and in the answer he gives to it in the following pages, Boethius is considerably more sophisticated than the early scholastic logicians such as Garlandus Compotista and the authors of the anonymous logic texts from the first decades of the twelfth century.

78. The claims in the first three sentences of this paragraph do not seem clearly compatible with the claims in the preceding paragraph in which Boethius says that every predicative proposition can be turned into a conditional but not vice versa. Perhaps the two paragraphs are intended to work together to show that although we can easily construct conditional propositions corresponding to predicative ones, the two forms do not express exactly equivalent ideas. There is some confirmation for this suggestion in the fact that the example Boethius uses to show that a predicative proposition can be turned into a conditional is the very example he uses in the next sentence to show that when a predicative is turned into a conditional, it becomes a different proposition.

79. That is, although a definition (or parts, or conjugates, etc.) enters into the argument, the validity of the argument does not depend on the nature and logical relations of definitions but rather on something associated with the nature of the condition. In this sense, then, the definition is not a Topic for that argument, since the argument is not based on it.

80. The first conditional is dependent on a property (being risible is a property of a man), and the second rests on an inseparable accident (being black is an inseparable accident of ravens).

NOTES TO BOOK V

1. Boethius, *De hypotheticis syllogismis*, ed. and tr. Luca Obertello (Brescia: Paideia, 1969).

2. Chrysippus (280–207 B.C.), who succeeded Cleanthes as head of the Stoic school, apparently recognized five valid inference schemata as basic and indemonstrable. They are these:

(1) If the first, then the second; but the first; therefore the second.
(2) If the first, then the second; but not the second; therefore not the first.
(3) Not both the first and the second; but the first; therefore not the second.
(4) Either the first or the second; but the first; therefore not the second.
(5) Either the first or the second; but not the first; therefore the second.

By Cicero's time it had evidently become customary to add a sixth and a seventh to this list; Cicero gives them in this form (*Top.* XIV.57):

(6) Not both this and that; but this; therefore not that.
(7) Not both this and that; but not this; therefore that.

In *The Development of Logic* (Oxford: Clarendon Press, 1962), William Kneale and Martha Kneale conjecture that in the original list of seven, (3) and (7) have a form of this sort (p. 180):

(3') Not both the first and not the second; but the first; therefore the second.

(7') Not both not the first and not the second; but not the first; therefore the second.

Michael Frede rejects the Kneales's conjecture and mounts an impressive array of evidence that neither Cicero nor his copyists presented (7) mistakenly; see *Die stoische Logik* (Goettingen: Vandenhoeck und Ruprecht, 1974), pp. 161ff. The problem in assessing the full list of seven as Cicero gives it is that (6) seems just a repetition of (3), and (7) seems clearly invalid. Frede suggests (pp. 164ff.) reading (6) and (7) as subdisjunctive syllogisms where the subdisjunctive major premise is true in case both disjuncts can be false together, cannot be true together, and one disjunct is true. For a full and detailed discussion of the criteria for inclusive disjunction, see Frede, pp. 98ff.

3. For a discussion of the kind of relationship supposed to hold between antecedent and consequent in a conditional according to various Stoic logicians, see Kneale and Kneale 1962: 128–138; and Benson Mates, *Stoic Logic* (Berkeley: University of California Press, 1953), pp. 42–51.

4. As explained in Book II, note 5, Boethius understands incompatibles in this way. If x and y are contraries and if z entails y or y entails z, then x and z are incompatibles. In the earlier discussion the incompatibles used in the examples are properties or terms. Here it is propositions that are said to be incompatible, and the general criteria for such incompatibles seem to be this: if p entails q and if we negate q, then 'p entails $\sim q$' is an incompatible. (Boethius does at one point suggest that negating the antecedent will also produce an incompatible, but negating the consequent seems his fundamental method for producing an incompatible.) It seems reasonable to suppose that there is some way of assimilating the criteria for incompatible propositions to the criteria for incompatible properties or terms. If we may take 'contraries' loosely to mean either 'contraries strictly speaking or contradictories', then we might reason in this way. Loosely understood, q and $\sim q$ are contraries; because p entails q, p and $\sim q$ are incompatibles. Therefore, by roughly the same criteria as those we are to use for incompatible properties or terms, p and $\sim q$ are incompatibles.

5. There can be no doubt that Boethius was competent in the logic of categorical syllogisms, but here it seems to be just hypothetical syllogisms he has in mind.

6. This reference is probably to *De inventione*, whose original title was *Rhetorici libri*; see *De inv.* XXXIV.57–59. Cicero opts for the view that a syllogism need not have only three parts (*De inv.* XXXV.61–XXXVI.65).

7. The Stoics held that a disjunction (sometimes called an exclusive disjunction) was a proposition in which the disjuncts were completely opposed to one another, so that one and only one of the disjuncts is true, or, alternatively, a proposition in which the disjuncts could not both be true or both be false (for discussion of these alternatives, see Mates 1953: 51ff.). But they came to recognize also a weaker form of disjunction, what is called a quasi-disjunction, subdisjunction, or inclusive disjunction (see note 2 above). Boethius is here taking disjunction as the modal version of exclusive disjunction.

8. Cicero understands the third mode as this:

(3) Not both the first and the second; but the first; therefore not the second.

Here Boethius suggests a formulation for the first premise of the third mode reminiscent of the sort the Kneales conjecture may have been its original sort:

(3') Not both the first and not the second.

See notes 2 and 9 to this book for further discussion of this issue. This is not his favored formulation for the initial premise of the third mode, as the text subsequently makes clear.

9. On the face of it, the first premise of Cicero's third mode is identical to the first premise in both the sixth and the seventh modes. Here, however, Boethius seems to be saying that the first premise of the third mode is a connected proposition and the first premise of the sixth and seventh modes is a disjunction incorporating a negation. As the text subsequently makes clear, Boethius thinks the first premise of both the sixth and seventh modes is a conjunction, but one that is based on the truth of a disjunction of a particular sort. Furthermore, he later presents examples for the third mode in which the first premise is not the negation of a conjunction, but the negation of a conditional. Michael Frede (1974: 152) maintains that Boethius takes the first premise of mode three to be a negated conjunction with one negated conjunct, and he cites ICT 1142C for his view. Boethius does there explain Cicero's view in those terms; but in presenting and explaining examples, he even there uses a conditional premise rather than a conjunction for the third mode. See, e.g., pp. 149–152 (Orelli, pp. 364–365) below.

10. There was a famous debate between Diodorus Cronus and his disciple Philo over the nature of a conditional, to which later Stoic logicians added suggestions of their own. Put very roughly, their views are as follows. According to Philo, a sound conventional is one that does not have a true antecendent and a false consequent. Diodorus held that a conditional was sound just in case it neither can nor could have a true antecedent and a false consequent. We have evidence for two further Stoic views about conditionals. One maintains that a sound conditional is one in which the contradictory of the consequent is logically incompatible with the antecedent, and the other maintains that in a sound conditional the consequent is contained potentially in the antecedent. We are not certain about the proponents of these last two views, though scholars now tend to associate the third with Chrysippus. For some basic discussion of these views, see Kneale and Kneale 1962: 128ff.; Josiah Gould, The Philosophy of Chrysippus (Albany: State University of New York Press, 1970), pp. 72ff.; and Mates 1953: 42ff. Boethius here is apparently allying himself with Chrysippus's view.

11. In the case of inferences in the first mode, the inferences are valid regardless of the meanings of the terms used in them; the form of the inference itself guarantees the soundness of the inference. In the case of the inferences involving man and risible thing mentioned here, the inferences are valid not in virtue of their form but in virtue of the meaning of the terms. In raising these latter inferences in the context of inferences of the first mode, Boethius gives the impression that he has not clearly distinguished these two different ways of warranting inferences.

12. Boethius does not raise the case of man and risible in connection with the second mode, but what he says about that case in connection with the first mode applies mutatis mutandis here. Using man and risible, we can make an acceptable inference of the form Boethius has been at pains to rule out here:

(1) If it is a man, it is risible.
(2) But it is not a man.
Therefore,
(3) it is not risible.

This inference is warranted in virtue of the fact that all and only those things that are men are risible.

13. Mates (1953: 31) explains *hyperapophatikon* as the negation of a negation and gives the following example taken from Diogenes Laertius (*Vitae* VII.69): it is not the case that it is not day. This is the same example Boethius gives shortly below.

14. Given what Boethius says at the start of this book, we can safely conclude that he understands 'If it is day, it is not light' as an incompatible. See note 4 to this book.

15. Boethius here is not maintaining that if we negate the incompatible we have a conditional in which the antecedent entails that it is not possible for the consequent to be false. Instead the modal operator attaches to the whole conditional: it is not possible that if it is day, it is not light. This reading, and what Boethius says earlier in this book about the nature of a conditional (see note 10), suggests that, on Boethius's view, by negating an incompatible we get a true conditional. The example Boethius gives in the next paragraph supports this reading since the minor premise and conclusion are the same as for the first mode. And Boethius's subsequent discussion of the third mode makes evident that he adopts this interpretation. Furthermore, it is clear here that Boethius's interpretation of the third mode differs from Cicero's text, as we currently have it, and also from the Kneales' conjecture as to how the third mode might have been originally formulated by Stoic logicians (see note 2 to this book), because unlike either Cicero or the Kneales, Boethius takes the first premise of the third mode as a conditional and not as a conjunction, although he subsequently explains that he takes his first premise to be equivalent to the one offered by the Kneales in their conjectured version of the third mode. Why Boethius takes this to be another indemonstrable mode of inference and not just a version of the first mode is not clear; see note 17 to this Book.

16. This example is in fact an incomplete sentence that is taken from a line of Virgil's *Georgics* (II.385). The point of this part of the sentence is to identify the Ausonians as Trojan colonists. I am grateful to my friend J. A. Arieti for this reference.

17. Boethius here seems to anticipate the objection that the third mode is only a version of the first and not an indemonstrable form in its own right, and he answers the objection by pointing to the form of the inference. In the first mode the minor premise is the antecedent and the conclusion is the consequent of the conditional in the first premise. In the second mode the minor premise is the negation of the consequent and the conclusion is the negation of the antecedent of the conditional in the first premise. According to Boethius, what makes the third mode distinct from the first two is that its minor premise takes the antecedent and its conclusion takes the denial of the consequent of the conditional in the first premise. On this view of the third mode, it is a cross between the first two. The problem is that this interpretation of the third mode ignores the fact that it begins not with a conditional but with the negation of a conditional. If we consider just the conditional within the scope of the negation and ignore the negation, then Boethius's analysis of the third mode seems reasonable. But we need to remember that the conditional in the third mode is negated. On Boethius's own views the negated conditional is equivalent to the conditional of the first mode, and the minor premise and conclusion of the third mode are identical in form to those of the first mode. And so Boethius's explanation of the third mode's difference from the previous two seems inadequate or even inapplicable. See note 30 below for further elucidation of this point.

18. In other words Boethius takes

    (1) It is not the case that if p, then $\sim q$

to be equivalent to

    (2) If p, then q.

This equivalence does not hold on truth-functional interpretations of conditionals. Nor does it hold on a Chrysippean analysis of conditionals on which we apparently get the following version of (1):

    (1') It is not the case that necessarily if p, then $\sim q$.

(1') is also clearly not equivalent to its corresponding version of (2):

    (2') Necessarily, if p, then q.

Why, then, does Boethius equate (1) and (2)? One possible explanation is simply that he thinks the two negations in (1) cancel each other out. Another more complicated and perhaps more satisfactory answer depends on considering the nature of the propositions that can be substituted for p and q. The third mode is the mode for incompatibles. So any substitution for p and $\sim q$ in a legitimate version of (1) must be incompatibles, and Boethius seems to understand (1) as expressing the negation of that incompatibility. If that is indeed how he reads (1), then on his reading (1) says that p and $\sim q$ cannot be true together, or that no p-world is a $\sim q$-world. If we understand (2) on Boethius's reading to express a necessary connection between p and q, such that every p-world is also a q-world, (1) and (2) on these readings do seem equivalent.

19. See pp. 133–134 (Orelli, p. 354) above.

20. It is worth noting that only in the case of a conditional in which an affirmation follows from a negation does Boethius suggest producing an incompatible by negating the antecedent rather than the consequent. His examples of conditionals include these:

    (1) if it is day, it is light;
    (2) if it is not light, it is not day;
    (3) if it is not day, it is night;
    (4) if he is awake, he is not snoring.

If we introduce a negation into the antecedents of these examples, we get these conditionals:

    (1') if it is not day, it is light;
    (2') if it is light, it is not day;
    (3') if it is day, it is night;
    (4') if he is not awake, he is not snoring.

If Boethius understands incompatibles in this context as propositions that cannot be true together, then (1'), (2'), and (4') are not incompatibles because in each case the antecedent and consequent could both be true together. Therefore, it is apparently not an accident that Boethius produces an incompatible by negating the antecedent only in cases like (3) where an affirmation follows from a negation.

21. The closest thing to a rule that Cicero gives in connection with the third mode is this: "When you deny that certain things are conjoined and take as your minor premise one or more of them, so that what remains is to be taken away, this is called the third mode of conclusion" (*Top.* XIII.55). This certainly does not fit Boethius's description of a rule for a conclusion produced in the third mode by a conditional consisting of two affirmatives, although it does fit the version of the third mode in the Chrysippean list (see note 2 to this book). It is tempting to account for this discrepancy by supposing that Boethius's text of Cicero was different from ours. On the other hand, in his discussion of Boethius's views regarding this sort of inference, Ivo Thomas argues that Boethius confuses conjunctions and conditionals. *Methodos*, 1(1949), 303–307; see also R. van den Driessche, "Sur le 'De syllogismo hypothetico' de Boèce," *Methodos*, 1(1949), 293–302. Thomas goes astray in reaching this implausible conclusion because he tends to dismiss any indication of modality in Boethius's understanding of conditionals as "irrelevant" (p. 306). For Boethius's own explanation of how his formulation is related to Cicero's, see p. 147 (Orelli, pp. 362–363) below.

22. The example Cicero gives is very abbreviated and consists just in a sentence: "You condemn a woman whom you accuse of nothing." As is clear later (p. 151; Orelli, p. 365), Boethius is taking the implied argument to have something like this logical form:

(1) It is not the case that if you do not accuse a woman of anything, you condemn her.
(2) But you do not accuse her of anything.
Therefore,
(3) You do not condemn her.

On the interpretation of the third mode Cicero himself seems to be adopting, the implied argument would presumably take this form:

(1') No one both accuses a woman of nothing and condemns her.
(2') But you accuse her of nothing.
Therefore,
(3') You do not condemn her.

Cicero's other example that seems to fit this subset of inferences in mode three is the following line: "What you know is of no use; is what you do not know a hindrance?" But as Boethius explains later, he takes the implied argument here to be this:

(4) It is not the case that what you know is useful and what you do not know is not a hindrance.

The conclusion drawn here, then, is that what you do not know is a hindrance. When he presents this argument later in this book, he also identifies it as based on a proposition made up of two affirmations, and so it does not fit in the subgroup of mode three at issue here.

23. Cicero's example is "Fear this and do not be afraid of the other." Put in Boethius's form, the implied argument (apart from the imperatives) is this:

(1) It is not the case that if you fear this, you are afraid of that.
(2) But you fear this.

Therefore,
> (3) You are not afraid of that.

Boethius himself gives a different reading of this example and its argument later in this book; see p. 150 (Orelli, pp. 364–365) below. Cicero's other example is "You claim that the woman whom you believe deserves reward merits punishment." Boethius proposes the following argument for this example (see p. 151 (Orelli, p. 365) below:

> (1) It is not the case that you believe that she deserves reward and that she deserves punishment.
> (2) But you believe that she deserves reward.
> Therefore,
> (3) She does not deserve punishment.

24. The first five modes were traditionally said to be indemonstrable. (See Frede 1974: 127ff. for a discussion of what is meant by 'indemonstrable' here.) Boethius here makes clear that he does not consider the sixth and seventh modes indemonstrable in the sense that they cannot be demonstrated by anything else: they are derived from the fourth and fifth modes.

25. The point about deriving the conjunction of the sixth and seventh modes from a disjunction seems to be that for the negation of the conjunction to be true in this case, it must be the case that the two conjuncts *cannot* be true together but at least one of them must be true, as on Boethius's understanding of a true disjunction, one and only one disjunct can and must be true.

26. See Boethius, *De hyp. syll.*, ed. and tr. Obertello.

27. It is not clear in what sense an affirmation overturns a negation in this example. Perhaps Boethius is thinking of the production of an affirmative consequent 'It is day' by negating the negative 'It is not day.' Or perhaps he is simply thinking of the opposition of 'It is day' or 'It is not day,' which he might understand as a negation's being overturned by an affirmation.

28. Here it looks as if the fact that 'it is not night' is negated by 'it is night' is the example of an affirmation overturning a negation.

29. As in the first example, so too in the third and fourth examples, it is hard to see what is supposed to count as an affirmation overturning a negation. In the third example, the antecedent of the conditional is a negation 'it is not day' which is negated with the affirmation 'it is day.' And in the fourth example, the negative consequent 'he is not snoring' is negated with the affirmation 'he is snoring.' Perhaps these negations of negations are the features of these examples to which Boethius wants to call attention.

30. That the antecedent is affirmed in order to deny the consequent makes this mode different at least in external form from the first two modes, in which if the antecedent is affirmed, the consequent is also, and if the consequent is denied, the antecedent is not affirmed but denied. And this point is worth calling attention to, because on Boethius's understanding of the conditional premise for the third mode it is equivalent to the conditional of the first mode, so that we might wonder why he considers the third mode a distinct mode in its own right. The explanation lies at least partially in the different external forms of the first and third modes.

31. The Orelli edition lists as a variant for line 5 what must in fact be a variant for line 7 and which affects the reading of this sentence. As this sentence

stands, it is false. If we adopt the alternate reading listed by the Orelli edition, the sentence becomes true and makes sense. So I propose to read this sentence as 'The minor premise *presents* the former part of the conditional proposition . . .' The point is that the minor premise in the third mode always has the same quality as the antecedent of the conditional in this mode; either both are affirmative or both are negative. This reading of this sentence is corroborated by what Boethius says about the third mode earlier: "the former part of the connected proposition is taken as the minor premise in the way in which it is stated in that proposition" (p. 141; Orelli, p. 358).

32. This rule of thumb does not hold even for all the examples Boethius himself has just given in this section of Book V. Why he maintains it here as a general rule is not clear.

33. That the propositions making up the first premise of this mode "can enter into a disjunction" shows that one of them must be true; that they are contraries lacking an intermediate or are incompatibles shows that only one of them can be true.

34. This sentence may appear to make some special point about metaphysical relations between *man* and *animal*; but as the Latin makes clear, the point of the sentence is just that the antecedent concerns *man* and the consequent concerns *animal*.

35. This sentence appears out of place here if we understand Boethius's aim in the paragraph to be just the presentation of an example for the second mode. But in fact Boethius's purpose in giving these examples for the first three modes is to make good on Cicero's position in XIII.53 that we can use any of the first three modes as means to get to the same conclusion. Unlike the first and third modes, however, the second mode by itself does not give us the conclusion that Cicero is an animal. Boethius therefore adds this sentence to reach that conclusion on the basis of the second mode. The problem, of course, is that the added example seems to be just a use of the first mode, so that Boethius has not here accomplished what he subsequently claims to have done, namely, to have shown how we can conclude "in three different ways" that Cicero is an animal. In fact, his examples here give us only *two* different ways of reaching that conclusion.

36. Strictly speaking, this claim is not true. If we begin with 'if *p*, then *q*' (adjusting it to 'It is not the case that if *p*, then ~*q*' for the third mode), then we get *q* as the conclusion for the first and third modes, but ~*q* as the conclusion for the second mode. As Boethius's subsequent examples make clear, however, he has in mind as the conditional premise for the second mode *not* 'If *p*, then *q*' but 'If ~*q*, then ~*p*'; with *p* as the minor premise, the second mode will then yield *q*.

37. For the earlier discussion of this example, see pp. 56ff. (Orelli, pp. 298ff.).

38. Because the form of this argument is supposed to be in the second mode and because the conclusion wanted is 'the coin was bequeathed to the wife,' Boethius takes as the conditional for this argument the contrapositive of the conditional he gives for the preceding version in the first mode.

39. The added phrase is obviously not significant or clarifying for the validity of the argument. Rather it is necessary for the truth of the conditional. On Boethius's understanding of conditionals, 'If the coin was not bequeathed to the wife, it is not silver' is not true because it is possible that the antecedent is

true and the consequent false. The added phrase 'when all the silver was bequeathed to the wife' rules out that possibility.

40. See pp. 65ff. (Orelli, pp. 304ff.) above. Cicero, in fact, gives not an argument but a complicated conditional. Boethius assumes that the issue in this case is 'Should any of the dowry remain with the husband?'; but the conditional itself provides no evidence about what the issue was or what Cicero takes the conclusion of the argument to be.

41. In fact, the antecedent is *not*

(1)   the woman was united with a man with whom there was no wedlock,

but rather

(1')   a woman who was united with a man with whom there was no wedlock sent him a letter of divorce.

Perhaps Boethius is formulating the antecedent in a way that, in his view, captures its main thought even if it is not true to the external form of the antecedent. In other words, the importance of the antecedent on Boethius's understanding of this argument is that it identifies the relationship between the man and the woman as a union that is not legal wedlock, and the claim that it was the woman rather than the man who sent the letter of divorce is ancillary.

42. Of course, we could make an argument contrary to Boethius's. We could assume that the intended argument here really is from consequents. In that case, the minor premise would be 'something of the dowry should remain with the husband for the children'; if we understand the antecedent as Boethius does, the conclusion would be 'therefore, the woman was united with a man with whom legal wedlock was permitted.' In this case we would be drawing a conclusion about the legal status of the union between the pair on the basis of the man's retention of part of the dowry. Why Boethius seems so sure that this is not what Cicero intended for this argument is not clear. Perhaps the phrase 'since they do not follow their father' which is attached to the consequent is some evidence for Boethius's reading, indicating that the issue is the retention of the dowry, not the legal status of the union, which is implied by the added phrase. That this is the right explanation for Boethius's position is to some extent confirmed by his explanation (given shortly below) about reformulating this argument as a genuine argument from consequents.

43. In other words, in his attempt to reformulate Cicero's example as a true argument from consequents, Boethius holds the issue, the minor premise, and the conclusion the same as Cicero's (on Boethius's understanding of Cicero) and alters the initial conditional premise.

44. As Boethius gives this argument, it has the following form:

(1)   If any of the dowry should remain for the children because they follow their father, the woman was united with a man with whom there was no legal wedlock.
(2)   But the woman was not united with a man with whom there was no legal wedlock, and for that reason the children who were begotten do not follow their father.

Therefore,

(3)   Nothing should remain for the children.

There are several things worthy of notice about this argument. In the first place, Cicero's phrase indicating that the woman sent the letter of divorce has dropped out; furthermore, Boethius's reformulation of the conditional shows us that he thinks we can draw a conclusion about the legal status of the union from the retention or nonretention of the dowry. It is, in other words, possible on Boethius's own views to make a legitimate argument from consequents on the basis of the initial conditional Cicero gives if we understand the issue as concerning the legal status of the union. Second, this argument has an odd form. The minor premise consists not just in the negation of the consequent of (1) but also in a conclusion drawn from that negation. And the conclusion is a further inference from that conclusion and not a negation of the antecedent of (2). As Boethius seems to be thinking of this argument, then, its logical form is this:

(1') If any of the dowry should remain for the children because they follow their father, the woman was united with a man with whom there was legal wedlock.
(2') But the woman was not united with a man with whom there was legal wedlock.
Therefore,
(3') The children who were begotten do not follow their father. (from 2')
Therefore,
(4') None of the dowry should remain for the children. (from 3')

The inferences to (3') and (4') are invalid as the argument stands; their validity depends on certain points of Roman law (see the note to the earlier discussion of this example, Book II, note 53). And the argument itself is not in the second mode.

45. The point here seems to be that Boethius has formulated the initial premise of the third mode as a conditional rather than as a conjunction in order to make manifest the sort of proposition from which an incompatible arises. An incompatible, on Boethius's view, is produced in general by negating the consequent of a true conditional, not by denying the second conjunct of a conjunction.

46. We have seen earlier (see note 18 to this book) that Boethius equates

(1) It is not the case that if p, then $\sim q$

with

(2) if p, then q.

Here he is apparently saying that (1) is also equivalent to

(3) It is not the case that p and $\sim q$.

I suggested above (note 18) that to understand why Boethius thinks (1) and (2) equivalent we read (1) as 'No p-world is a $\sim q$-world' and (2) as 'Every p-world is a q-world.' If we suppose that for Boethius (3) is also modalized in this way:

(3') Necessarily, it is not the case that p and $\sim q$, then on Boethius's view (3) says that there is no possible world that is both a *p*-world and a ~*q*-world; this does seem equivalent to my suggested Boethian readings of (1) and (2). The justification for reading (3) as modalized is that this mode is understood to be the mode for incompatibles, and incompatibles are generated from true conditionals, which are modal conditionals on Boethius's view. So *p* and ~*q* can be used in the third mode only if they are incompatibles; they are incompatibles just in case 'if *p*, then *q*' is a necessarily true conditional. On these readings the logical form of the third mode as Boethius generally presents it is roughly of this sort: 'No *p*-world is a ~*q*-world; but this is a *p*-world; therefore, this is a *q*-world.'

47. See pp. 143ff. (Orelli, pp. 360ff.).

48. Boethius elaborates this claim at the end of Bk. IV, pp. 127ff. (Orelli, pp. 350ff.) above.

49. See pp. 129–130 (Orelli, p. 351) above for a discussion of this issue with a different example. Perhaps here Boethius means just that his frequently used example involving *day* and *light* is a counterexample to the objection that this Topic is the same as the Topic *from genus*.

50. Cicero does not add the offending clause 'if a connected proposition is made up of affirmative parts', but Boethius apparently thinks this clause must be implied by Cicero's use of 'negate' rather than some more neutral term, such as 'destroy'.

51. The basic meaning of the Greek verb cognate with the noun we render 'enthymeme' is 'to think', 'to ponder'.

52. Publius Cornelius Lentulus Sura was expelled from the senate in 71 B.C. but was elected to a second praetorship in 63 B.C. He was part of the Catiline conspiracy and was in fact the ringleader in the city. His part in the conspiracy was discovered; he was compelled to lay down his office and was condemned to death in the very year in which he had been elected to office. Gaius Cornelius Cethegus was a Roman senator who also conspired with Catiline; he too was put to death in 63 B.C.

53. This example is an allusion to Cicero's role in the execution of the conspirators in Catiline's conspiracy. The responsibility for authorizing the executions was largely Cicero's. The justification for the executions was that without such a severe measure the conspiracy would eventually have been renewed and would endanger the republic. In the immediate aftermath of the executions Cicero was acclaimed savior and father of his country. Later, however, he was attacked by his enemies for ordering the executions without allowing an appeal to the people.

54. In other words, Boethius takes (*a*) 'You fear this; do you not fear that?' to be somehow equivalent to (*b*) 'It is not the case that if you fear this, you do not fear that.' Perhaps the conversational force of the question in (*a*) is to produce the same effect as the initial negation in (*b*). Something similar can be said with regard to the other enthymemes Boethius goes on to discuss.

55. Suppose we take as our paradigm examples of contraries *sleeping* and *waking*, and *snoring* and *waking* as our paradigm incompatibles. Ascriptions of these two pairs are not truth-functionally distinct; for each pair of ascriptions, both members of the pair can be false but only one member can be true at a time. Something besides a truth-functional analysis is thus needed to distinguish contraries from incompatibles. What Boethius has in mind as a distinction, I think, is something of this sort. Contraries are opposed differentiae within a genus; within the genus, one contrary is the negation of the other. So

rational and *irrational* are the opposed differentiae dividing the genus *animal;* but they are contraries (rather than contradictories) because *irrational* in this sense applies only to animals and not, for example, to inanimate objects, so that it is possible for something to be neither rational nor irrational. On this scheme, *risible* and *irrational* are incompatibles: they meet the truth-conditions for contraries, but they are not directly opposed to each other; one is a differentia under *animal,* and the other is just a property associated with the species specified by the other differentia under *animal.* So (a) *to fear* and (b) *not to fear* are contraries, on Boethius's view, while (c) *do not be fearful* and (d) *fear* are incompatibles because (a) and (b) are directly opposed but (c) and (d) are not.

56. Boethius gives the initial premise for this argument as a conjunction in the full statement of the argument just above and as a conditional in this explanation of the argument. In the subsequent example the initial premise is also given as a conjunction. Why Boethius does not stick consistently to his practice of formulating these premises as conditionals is not clear. For a discussion of his treatment of the conditional and conjunctive forms of these premises as equivalent, see note 46 to this book. The particular conditional used in this example is peculiar, especially on Boethius's views, because it seems to derive a claim about a woman's merits from a claim about someone's belief concerning those merits. The context of dialogue makes a difference here, I think. The oddity of the conditional is somewhat reduced because the premise contains a reference to the person accepting the premise. In other words,

(1) If Jones believes she deserves reward, she does not deserve punishment

is plainly false, particularly on Boethius's views about the conditional, but

(2) If you believe that she deserves reward, she does not deserve punishment

has more plausibility because there is some sort of obvious incompatibility about your asserting both

(a) I believe she deserves reward
and
(b) she deserves punishment.

57. What Cicero says here (*Top.* XIV.56) is actually just that in a disjunction, more than one disjunct cannot be true. Boethius turns this point about the nature of a disjunction into a point about the nature of the things that can enter into a true disjunction. Furthermore, Cicero's point rules out the possibility that both disjuncts could be true; Boethius's point rules out also the possibility that both disjuncts could be false.

58. In other words, on Boethius's view of disjunction, a true disjunction '*p* or *q*' is such that it is not possible for both *p* and *q* to be false or for both to be true. On our views of disjunction, if the referent of the pronoun 'it' is white (or is black), the disjunction 'either it is white or it is black' is true. But on Boethius's view, this disjunction is false because its disjuncts do not exhaust the possibilities and both of them could be false. This view is similar to Stoic views on disjunction; see Mates 1953: 51ff.

59. On our views of conjunction this inference is obviously invalid. We take the negation of a conjunction to be true if one or the other or both of the conjuncts are false. Therefore, from a negated conjunction and the falsity of

one of the conjuncts, nothing can be legitimately inferred about the truth or falsity of the remaining conjunct. Boethius's subsequent example and analysis show that at least in connection with the sixth and seventh modes he has a different view of a negated conjunction, closely associated with his view of disjunction.

60. Here, too, Boethius takes as a constraint on the initial premise that the predicative propositions it contains cannot both be false. With that constraint, arguments of the seventh mode are valid; if one of the predicative propositions in the initial premise is false, the other must be true. For Stoic understanding of a negated conjunction, see Frede 1974: 97ff.

61. As contemporary historians of philosophy have understood Cicero's list of Stoic inference-schemes, three sources of perplexity have emerged. First, the third and sixth modes seem equivalent, so that one of them is redundant. Second, the modes based on some form of conjunction are not grouped together. And, third, the seventh mode seems obviously invalid. Frede (1974: 165ff.) suggests that the sixth and seventh modes are subdisjunctive (for subdisjunction see note 2 above). The weakness he sees in his own suggestion is that there is no direct evidence for it. Boethius's presentation and analysis of the list of Stoic inference schemes, on the other hand, does provide evidence for a different but consistent solution to the problems listed above. On Boethius's presentation the grouping of the modes is orderly; the first three are conditional, the next two are disjunctive, and the last two are conjunctive. The third mode is

(1) It is not the case that if p, then $\sim q$;
(2) but p;
Therefore,
(3) q;

the sixth mode is

(4) Not both p and q;
(5) but p;
Therefore,
(6) $\sim q$.

Clearly, then, on Boethius's presentation the sixth mode is not a redundant re-expression of the third mode. And the constraint Boethius places on the sixth and seventh modes explains why on his views the seventh mode is not obviously invalid. On his constraint, the particular propositions substituted for p and q in modes six and seven must be mutually exclusive; with that constraint added, the seventh mode—

(7) Not both p and q;
(8) but $\sim p$;
Therefore,
(9) q

—is valid. And the added constraint is not an ad hoc attempt to validate this mode but rather a consequence of the recognition of the conjunction in these modes as derived from disjunctions and a view of disjunction as exclusive. If we take

(10) p or q

as a true exclusive disjunction, then either p or q but not both must be true. From the truth of this disjunction we can derive

(11) Not both p and q,

where p and q are mutually exclusive. On this interpretation of (11), with the addition of the premise '$\sim p$', we can legitimately conclude 'q', as the seventh mode requires.

62. This point is further evidence that Boethius holds the third mode to be conditional. The third mode, as he explains here, is the mode for incompatibles. On his view, however, incompatibles form one Topic with antecedents and consequents, and that Topic, as Boethius is at pains to make clear, is conditional in nature.

63. Cf. Aristotle, *Physics* 194b16ff.

64. For the division of causes which Cicero goes on to make, the reader might find the attached figure helpful.

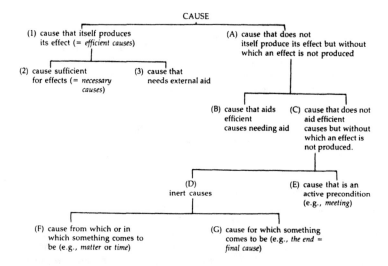

65. In other words, matter is not identical with the cause without which an effect cannot be produced but just with one of its species.

66. This is a peculiar thing for Boethius to say since he in many different places acknowledges the existence of incorporeal entities, such as angels, that clearly come to be and yet need not occupy a place.

67. It is worth noticing that Fate, on Boethius's interpretation (taken over from Cicero) of the Stoic doctrine, is not equivalent to what we call 'determinism'. The causes in question are not efficient causes, and they are also not sufficient by themselves to produce their effect. Stoic Fate does not determine or make inevitable its results; it is more like a snare of coincidences than like an external compulsion.

68. See Aristotle, *Nic. Eth.* 1099a31–b8 and 1178b32–1179a2.

69. Boethius here seems to be suggesting one more division of causes, name-

ly, the division of (G), the cause for which something comes to be, into (G1), the end of a thing effected, and (G2), the cause provided for the sake of the end. But there is something counterintuitive about regarding implements themselves as any kind of cause.

70. In short, the fictitious objector wonders why meeting and other causes like it are not reckoned as efficient causes and included in the species of *efficient cause*, which is not by itself sufficient to produce its effect.

71. For Merobaudes, see Bk. IV, n. 8.

72. This partition, then, overlaps the more complicated division that Boethius has been painstakingly developing, but the overlapping seems very simple. The species of causes that are efficient causes sufficient by themselves to produce their effects constitutes the group of necessary causes, and all the other causes are not necessary causes. By 'necessary' in this case, Boethius seems to mean that there is a necessary connection between the postulation of such a cause and the postulation of its effect; that is, necessarily, if there is such a cause, there is its effect.

73. These are the efficient causes that need external aid to produce their effects.

74. See p. 156 (Orelli, p. 368) above.

75. In other words, Boethius, following Cicero, puts parents (or, more accurately perhaps, couples who might be parents) in the group of causes that are efficient but do not by themselves produce their effect. This is a peculiar classification and an infelicitous example for his purposes. That Boethius himself is troubled by this example is made clear a little below.

76. The quotation is from the opening lines of Euripides's *Medea* translated by Ennius (239–170 B.C.), known for his hellenized style of poetry and famous for his *Annales*, a chronological narrative of Roman history in verse, of which only a few fragments remain. He translated several Greek tragedies and wrote some dramas of his own, modeled especially on the plays of Euripides. Even after the fall of the republic, Ennius continued to be honored as the father of Latin poetry.

77. The line of Cicero to which this line alludes can be found in Otto Ribbeck, *Tragicorum Romanorum fragmenta*, Scaenicae Romanorum Poesis Fragmenta vol. 1: (Leipzig: Teubner, 1897–1898).

78. Strictly speaking, this claim of Boethius's, on his own view, is not entirely accurate. Boethius understands the *male* parent as an efficient cause not sufficient to produce its effect; but the *female* parent he assigns to the group of causes without which an effect does not come to be, and he likens her to the cause that is the matter of its effect. So, even in Boethius's eyes, Cicero's example is appropriate with regard to the female parent.

79. This division of causes does not map in any neat way onto the preceding divisions of causes. Boethius goes on to associate will and agitation with one species of efficient cause and judgment with one group of formal causes (art and state), but the nonvoluntary group of causes in this division is scattered through the species of the preceding divisions.

80. This sentence is stated somewhat misleadingly. Growing pale and fleeing are not examples of causes associated with mental agitation, but are rather examples of effects produced by mental agitation.

81. This is clearly an inadequate definition of chance; as Boethius himself

subsequently points out, on this definition eclipses occur by chance. In what follows, Boethius is at pains to develop a more satisfactory account of chance.

82. In making this point Boethius is just following Cicero, but it is an odd thing for Boethius to say since he surely holds that God is not caused. The Latin here says literally, "Nor is there anything among things (res) that some cause does not produce"; just possibly Boethius means to emphasize the phrase 'among things' to suggest that this point refers to creatures only, and not to the Creator also. This interpretation is strengthened by the following sentence, which begins, "For all things that come to be."

83. In the preceding major division of causes, three of the Aristotelian causes—the efficient, material, and final cause—are mentioned and assigned a place in the division. The formal cause alone is omitted, and it is not clear where in the hierarchy it should go. Material and final causes are identified as species of causes without which an effect is not prdouced. Perhaps then the formal cause should be classified in the same way. If so, then art, state, and nature might be included among that species of causes which is an active precondition for an effect.

84. By "external" here Boethius may mean to suggest that chance does not belong at all in the major division of causes sketched above; it is external in the sense of being outside the predicamental division of the genus *cause.*

85. As is clear from what follows, uniform causes are either identical to or a subset of formal causes; all other causes are nonuniform.

86. There is a confusing interweaving of classifications here. Uniform causes are or are included among formal causes. Nonuniform causes, which comprise all other causes, are divided into two groups, the evident and the hidden. The evident have to do with the mind, but causes of this sort were apparently assigned just above to a species of efficient causes. Since hidden causes are assigned here to fortune, it looks as if this division roughly sketched has the following form:

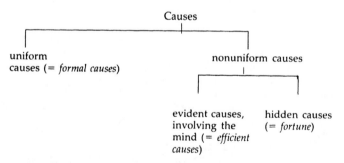

Clearly, this division leaves out a great many of the causes enumerated so far, unless we assign all causes that are not efficient or formal to fortune. But material and final causes are clearly not assimilable to fortune.

87. Cicero, *Tusculan Disputations* II.ii.4–5. I have quoted from J. E. King's translation in the Loeb volume of *Tusculan Disputations* (Cambridge, Mass: Harvard University Press, 1966), p. 151, with two small changes to account for the slight difference between the Loeb text of Cicero and Boethius's text.

88. In other words, in criticizing Boethius for opposing Cicero's beliefs and authority, Boethius's detractors will be overturning the desire and judgment Cicero expressed in *Tusculan Disputations*.

89. Aristotle's discussion of chance in the second book of the *Physics* occurs in Chapters 4–6.

90. On this understanding of chance, then, it is not an external cause (as Boethius maintained earlier when he was expounding Cicero's text) in the sense of being outside the major division of causes made earlier. Instead it is a species of cause subsumed under final causes. It might still, however, be said to be external in the sense of being outside the end aimed at by nature or mind.

91. If this is to be an appropriate juristic example for the case under discussion, the sense of the quoted line must be that the defendant did not throw the weapon *at the victim*, and that he lost control of the weapon in the sense that the weapon hit a target (namely, the victim) not intended or desired by the defendant.

92. That is, states of mental agitation.

93. Cicero's language suggests that within the same paragraph he maintains both that (*a*) the unintentional is necessary and that (*b*) there is a dichotomy between the unintentional and the necessary. Boethius's solution to this apparent embarrassment is to postulate two species of the unintentional, one tied to the necessary and the other entirely separate from it. Then he associates Cicero's claim (*a*) with the first species of the unintentional and his claim (*b*) with the fact that there are two sorts of unintentional acts, only one of which is connected to necessity.

NOTES TO BOOK VI

1. The deeper discussion is the examination of the causes and the arguments over the nature of chance with which the preceding book ended.

2. By "the first group" he means those people who dislike philosophy as a whole.

3. See, e.g., p. 162 (Orelli, p. 372) above, where Boethius cites Cicero's approval of philosophical discussion and disagreement.

4. It is not clear how this "brief reply," which provides reasons for valuing art, constitutes a reply to those objectors who want to keep separate rhetorical art and philosophical issues. As Boethius goes on to discuss rhetoric, however, he returns to this issue and provides a more detailed reply to the objectors.

5. This part of Victorinus's commentary on Cicero is no longer extant, as far as we now know.

6. That is, of causation and chance.

7. Private law in the Republic covered (among other things) marriage, guardianship, succession, property rights, contracts, and obligations. The jurists of the republic were very influential in molding and systematizing Roman law, especially private law. See, for example, Cicero, *De oratore* 1.212, where Cicero says that the ideal jurist must be skilled in giving opinions and conducting cases in all matters of private law.

8. A judgment concerning good faith was a contractual action in which the insertion of the clause 'in good faith' into the contract gave the judge of the action the discretionary power to determine what the defendant should pay

the plaintiff. For a more detailed discussion of Roman law on this issue, see F. de Zulueta, *The Roman Law of Sale* (Oxford: Clarendon Press, 1945), pp. 8–9, 49–50.

9. The husband's ownership of the dowry was formal and hedged with constraints. He could not, for example, alienate land or manumit slaves included in the dowry without the wife's consent, and he was liable for the value of any slaves manumitted without her consent. An action against the husband for the recovery of the dowry may have been an action "in good faith"; at any rate, the judge had to determine "what was right and equitable." Originally an action concerning what is right and equitable differed in significant ways from actions concerning good faith, although in both the judge had broad discretionary power; but the differences were gradually minimized and eventually by Justinian's time disappeared.

10. For the notion of mandating in Roman law, see Bk. IV, n. 35.

11. See Aristotle, *Cat.* 8b35–37.

12. The point is that two things can be compared with regard to quantity (number), quality (form), capacities and dispositions (power), or on the basis of some nonintrinsic characteristics, such as their relation to some third thing.

13. This point makes sense only if the things being compared are good; the requirement that they be of the same genus is neither necessary nor sufficient for the conclusion that many are preferred to fewer. In Cicero's *Topica*, it is made explicit that the things being compared are good.

14. What is meant by "the contrary genus" here is not clear. If the preceding reference was to the genus of the good, then this phrase might make sense as referring to the genus of the bad. But it is very unlikely that Boethius thought the good and the bad were genera; in any event the preceding reference is just to the same genus, not to a genus of the good. Perhaps, however, 'genus' is being used nontechnically here to mean simply 'sort'. The following sentence lends some credibility to this interpretation since there *good* and *bad* do seem sorted into different 'genera'.

15. The sense of 'equal' here is not apparent, and the entire claim seems obviously false—it is not true that in the case of two tortures equal in pain the one that lasts longer is to be preferred. No doubt we are to understand that it is things equal in goodness which are at issue here, and the context of the rest of the paragraph strengthens such an interpretation. Perhaps the fact that Cicero's text is explicit that only good things are at issue here is responsible for Boethius's failure to be explicit.

16. Although Boethius does not say so, it seems probable that he intends this claim, that (in the case of equal things) the longer lasting are preferable (and all the subsequent claims about what is preferable), to be maximal propositions.

17. The sense of 'necessary' here seems to be just 'necessary to sustain life'. Cicero maintains that the necessary is preferable to the nonnecessary, but says nothing directly about cases in which the nonnecessary is preferable to the necessary. He does claim that voluntary acts are preferable to those that are necessary, and when Boethius later discusses Cicero's claim about the voluntary, he takes it as evidence for his general point that the nonnecessary is sometimes preferable.

18. See Aristotle, *Cat.* 6b38–7a5.

19. The point is that in the context of a dialectical dispute or rhetorical

speech, supporting one's point by showing that it has been praised by one's opponent is preferable to supporting it with other authorities.

20. Boethius seems here to be accounting for the fact that although there is one set of Topics for what is better and another set for what is worse, there is no set of Topics for what is equal. His explanation is, apparently, that we cannot give a set of claims about what is preferable in the case of equals. The most that can be claimed, as Boethius says just below, is that "things that are equivalent in number, form, power, or relationship are said to be equal."

21. The jurists or legal experts aid citizens in the sense that they help mold the law, and their opinion concerning the interpretation of the law carries weight with judges. Orators help citizens in the sense that they speak for them in courts of law.

22. Boethius is here thinking of a Porphyrian division of genera into species by means of differentiae.

23. In the Themistian division of Topics considered in De top. diff., there is a third category of intermediate Topics that are partly intrinsic and partly not; they include the Topics from case, conjugates, and division.

24. In the subsequent discussion, Boethius constructs this Porphyrian tree for Cicero's division of Topics.

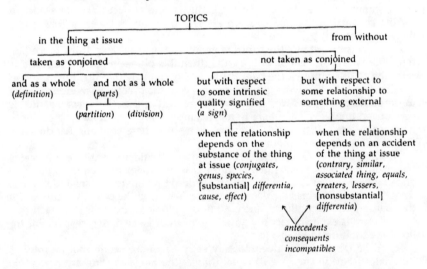

25. See, e.g., p. 171 (Orelli, p. 379) above.

26. For the reasons why genus, species, and differentia are considered substantial, see the discussion of these predicables in the appendix. Why cause and effect are also considered substantial rather than accidental is not clear.

27. It looks as if 'antecedents' should be part of this list and has been inadvertently omitted.

28. For Boethius's discussion of the way in which the Topic from antecedents, consequents, and incompatibles is related to the other Topics, see pp. 127ff. (Orelli, pp. 349ff.) above.

29. For the various sorts of definitions enumerated here and in the rest of this paragraph, see pp. 93ff. (Orelli, pp. 324ff.) and the notes on that part of the text.

30. See p. 94 (Orelli, p. 325) above; there Boethius refers to this sort of definition as *kata lexin*.

31. In the earlier discussion on pp. 95 (Orelli, p. 326), this sort of definition is called '*hypographikē*'.

32. This is called '*kata diaphoran*' in the earlier discussion on p. 95 (Orelli, p. 326).

33. Before *analogy* in the earlier list is the group of definitions Victorinus said were made by means of praise; see pp. 95–96 (Orelli, p. 326) above. In the earlier discussion Boethius says that this is an unreasonable grouping of definitions; perhaps his opposition to this sort of definition is the explanation for its omission from its original place in the list.

34. See, e.g., pp. 86ff. (Orelli, pp. 319ff.) above.

35. I have not attempted to include these subdivisions of definition on the chart in note 24 because Boethius gives no indication of the way in which these subdivisions should be hierarchically ordered.

36. For the complicated division of causes, see pp. 154ff. (Orelli, pp. 367ff.) above and the notes to that part of the text. Bk. V, note 64, contains a chart of this division.

37. The description of this division is somewhat misleading. The first group is the species of efficient causes which is sufficient by itself to produce its effect and is necessary in the sense that if we postulate the cause, the effect necessarily follows. The second group of causes, which "do need something else in order to produce," is the species of efficient causes that produce their effects but only with the help of some external aid; in Boethius's terminology, they are not necessary. The last group of causes mentioned in this sentence of the text is the genus of causes that do not themselves produce their effects but without which the effects are not produced. This genus has many species under it; none of its causes is necessary in Boethius's sense of 'necessary cause'.

38. For the way in which nature, art, and chance are associated with the voluntary, see pp. 159ff. (Orelli, pp. 370ff.) above.

39. For the preceding list of those Topics, see p. 178 (Orelli, p. 385) above.

40. That is, neither the destruction nor the alteration of the action.

41. In this sentence Boethius is just excusing himself (and Cicero) from examining anything in Cicero's main claim about this last Topic except for the nature of authority.

42. I am reading '*fortuna*' for '*forma*', as the context demands; *Vat. lat.* 567 and *Reg. lat.* 1649 also have '*fortuna*'.

43. Gaius Staienus is mentioned in Cicero's *Brutus* (LXVIII.241) as an orator whose peculiar style of speaking was gaining popularity when he was convicted of crimes; in *Pro Cluentio* Cicero maintains that he bribed juries.

44. The variant '*ignorans*', which the Orelli text rejects in favor of '*imprudens*', seems to me to make better sense here; *Vat. lat.* 567 and *Reg. lat.* 1649, however, both have '*imprudens*'.

45. Palamedes is mentioned in Virgil's *Aeneid* ii.81–85. According to the story, he was a member of the Greek army who was unjustly convicted of treason on the basis of circumstantial evidence fabricated by Odysseus.

APPENDIX

CATEGORIES AND PREDICABLES

In this appendix, my purpose is simply to make the reader acquainted with the technical ancient and scholastic notions of the categories, predicables, and the Porphyrian Tree, which pervade scholastic philosophy.[1] I base my account principally on three sources: Aristotle's *Categories*, Porphyry's *Isagoge*, and various works of Boethius, including his commentaries on Porphyry, his *De divisione*, and his discussion of the predicables in *De topicis differentiis*. For my purposes here it is the medievals' understanding of these ancient concepts which is important, and their understanding was shaped primarily by Boethius. So I rely heavily on Boethius in what I present here, leaving to one side any direct consideration of Aristotle's or Porphyry's theory. Finally, I give the categories fairly short shrift and concentrate on the predicables because they are far more significant than the categories for scholastic logic (as distinct from scholastic metaphysics or theology). In any event, the predicables are taken up before the categories in the traditional order (for reasons that will become clear), and I follow that order in my presentation.

As the name suggests, the predicables are whatever can be predicated of something. In the *Topics* Aristotle discusses four predicables: definition, property, genus, and accident.[2] The ontological status of these predicables is not clear; whether or not they are linguistic entities was a moot point throughout the Middle Ages. In Boethius's work,

---

1. For a more detailed discussion of scholastic views of the predicables, see my *Boethius's De topicis differentiis* (Cornell University Press: Ithaca: 1978), pp. 237–247 and 248–261. For some study of the history of the predicables, see Eike-Henner Kluge, "William of Ockham's Commentary on Porphyry," *Franciscan Studies*, 33 (1973), 171–254, and 34 (1974), 306–382. A detailed study of the philosophical role of categories and predicables in the work of a typical scholastic can be found in Daniel Dahlstrom, "Signification and Logic: Scotus on Universals from a Logical Point of View," *Vivarium*, 18 (1980), 81–111.

2. See, for example, *Top.* 101b37ff.

although 'subject', 'predicate', 'is predicated of', and other words relating to the predicables are used ambiguously, generally the subject of 'Socrates is wise' is the man rather than the proper name 'Socrates', and the predicate is wisdom rather than the adjective 'wise'. In this tendency to focus on what is signified rather than on the signs themselves, Boethius seems to be following Porphyry. For example, Boethius and Porphyry both say that if a differentia is destroyed or ceases to be, then its corresponding species is also destroyed, but not vice versa; if a species is destroyed, the corresponding differentia remains—not the sort of thing one would say about such linguistic entities as 'rational' and 'man'.[3] Just what Porphyry and Boethius think the ontological status of the predicables is, if they are not linguistic entities, is not clear. Porphyry says explicitly in the *Isagoge* that he means to avoid committing himself to one side or another on the question,[4] and Boethius seems to take a conceptualist view of the predicables, intermediate between realism and nominalism.[5]

According to Aristotle, a definition consists in a genus and differentiae, which together constitute the essence of what is being defined.[6] A property is what belongs to one particular species and to no other and is predicated convertibly (interchangeably) of the species, without being part of the essence of the species. One property of man, for example, is *capable of learning grammar;* if something is a man, it is capable of learning grammar, and if something is capable of learning grammar, it is a man.[7] Genus is what is predicated of many things differing in species in respect of what they are (i.e., in respect of their essence); the genus of *man,* for example, as well as of *horse* and *bat,* is *animal.*[8] An accident is what can belong or not belong to a thing; sitting, for example, or whiteness can belong or not belong to something.[9]

In the *Isagoge,* Porphyry discusses five predicables, omitting one of Aristotle's (definition) and adding two that Aristotle mentions but does not examine in detail (species and differentia), so that for Porphyry the predicables are genus, species, property, accident, and differentia. Genus and property he defines as Aristotle does. His definition of species is analogous to the definition of genus: a species is that which is

---

3. See Boethius, *In Isagogen,* ed. Samuel Brandt (Leipzig, 1906), pp. 328.21–329.3 (the corresponding passage in the *Patrologia* is *PL* 64.151B6–12); and Porphyry, *Isagoge,* in *Commentaria in Aristotelem Graeca (CAG)* IV, pt. 1, p. 18.21–23.
4. Porphyry, *Isagoge, CAG,* p. 1.8ff.
5. See Boethius, *In Isag.,* ed. Brandt, p. 159.10ff. (*PL* 64,82B3ff.).
6. Aristotle, *Top.* 139a28–29.
7. Ibid., 102a18ff.
8. Ibid., 102a31ff.
9. Ibid., 102b4ff.

predicated of many things differing *in number* (rather than *in kind* or
species) and in respect of what they are.[10] He offers two definitions of
accident, Aristotle's and this one: an accident is what is present to or
absent from a thing without the destruction of that thing.[11] A differentia is what is predicated of many things differing in species in respect
of what kind of thing they are, and all differentiae have to do with the
essence or substance of what they are predicated of.[12]

Differentiae can be thought of in two different ways: either as dividing a genus, in which case they are called divisive differentiae; or as
constituting a species, in which case they are called constitutive differentiae. The same differentia can be both divisive and constitutive, but
it is divisive of one thing and constitutive of another. For example, the
differentia *rational* is divisive of the genus *animal* and constitutive of the
species *man*. A genus that cannot itself be subsumed as a species under
some higher genus is called a highest genus—Aristotle's ten categories
are the ten highest genera of everything—and a species that can have
no species subsumed under it for which it serves as a genus is called a
lowest species. Except for highest genera, all genera are subaltern genera—that is, they can all be described also as species; all species except
lowest species are subaltern species—that is, they can all be described
also as genera. Every subaltern genus or species is associated with two
different sets of differentiae, those that divide it (its divisive differentiae) and that which constitutes it (its constitutive differentia). The
subaltern genus *animal*, for example, is divided by the differentiae
rational and *irrational* and constituted by the differentia *capable of perceiving*. Almost all species fall under more than one genus; the species
man, for example, falls under the genera *rational animal*, *animal*, *animate
corporeal substance*, *corporeal substance*, and *substance.*But the genus immediately above a given species is the proximate genus of that species.
For example, *rational animal* is the proximate genus of *man*, because *man*
is defined as a *mortal* rational animal, where *mortal* is the constitutive
differentia for *man*. Definitions define species and are composed of the
proximate genus and constitutive differentia of the species they define.

Porphyry and Aristotle both describe each of the predicables in various ways in an attempt to make clear what each one is, but there are
four sets of characteristics which I think basically distinguish the predicables among themselves. Boethius gives two of these when he is
explaining the Aristotelian predicables in *De top. diff*.[13] First, subjects
have essences, and all predicates are either part of their subject's es-

10. Porphyry, *Isagoge*, CAG, p. 4.11–12.
11. Ibid., p. 12.24–25.
12. Ibid., p. 9.4ff.
13. 1177D12ff.

sence or not. (I am restricting the discussion here to cases of true predication, and the distinction between predicate and predicable is just that the former is what is predicated and the latter is the sort of thing that can be predicated.) Second, all predicates and so all predicables must be either greater than or equal to the subjects they are said of; no predicate can be less than its subject.[14] A predicate is equal to its subject if it is predicated convertibly of the subject.[15] For example, *risible* is a predicate equal to its subject *man*, because it is predicated convertibly; man is risible, and, conversely, what is risible is man. The point seems to be that an equal predicate is said of nothing other than the subject to which it is equal. A predicate that is greater than its subject, then, must be said of other things beside the subject in question; hence such a predicate is not predicated convertibly. A predicable, then, is either greater than or equal to its subject and either belongs or does not belong to its subject's essence.

Boethius uses these two sets of characteristics to distinguish and describe the four Aristotelian predicables. A genus is greater than its subject and is part of the subject's essence. A definition is equal to its subject and part of the subject's essence. A property is equal to its subject but not part of the subject's essence. And an accident is greater than its subject but not part of the subject's essence. So we can chart the Aristotelian predicables this way:

Genus	Greater	Part of essence
Definition	Equal	Part of essence
Property	Equal	Not part of essence
Accident	Greater	Not part of essence

If we look at this chart for Aristotelian predicables, then, we can see certain patterns emerging. A definition and a property are alike in being equal to their subjects and thus convertible with them, but they differ because a definition is part of the subject's essence, while property is not. A genus and an accident resemble one another in that both are greater than and thus not convertible with their subjects, but they differ in the same way a definition differed from a property: a genus is part of the subject's essence, and an accident is not.

14. *De top. diff.* 1175C14–D3. For a discussion of this claim, see Stump 1978: 101–102n.27.
15. See *De top. diff.* 1175C9ff.

In order to distinguish the remaining two predicables, species and differentia, from the Aristotelian four, two more pairs of characteristics need to be added. First, a predicate can be predicated either of what is singular and individual or else of what is common and general; that is, something can be said of Socrates, for example, or of *man*. According to Boethius, who is following Porphyry here, genus, differentia, property, and definition are said primarily of what is common and general and secondarily of what is individual. On this view, in a proposition such as 'Man is animal,' the predicate is being used in a way conceptually prior to its secondary, derived use in 'Socrates is animal'; that is, *animal* attaches to Socrates insofar as he is a man, but it attaches to *man* without any "insofar as" rider. Species, on the other hand, is said only of individuals and not at all of what is common. Accidents fall into two groups; one resembles genus and the other resembles species in this respect. Accidents belong to their subjects either separably (i.e., the subject may sometimes have the accident and sometimes not) or inseparably. Inseparable accidents are like genus: they belong primarily to what is common and only secondarily to individuals. Separable accidents, however, are said primarily of individuals and secondarily of what is common; being pale, for example, belongs primarily to Socrates and secondarily to *man*.[16]

One more pair of attributes is required to separate genus and differentia, which are so far the same, since both are greater than their subjects, part of the essence of their subjects, and said primarily of what is common.[17] To distinguish the two, a distinction needs to be made between predicating a thing in respect of what the subject is (*in eo quod quid est*) or in respect of what characteristics the subject has (*in eo quod quale est*).

These two sorts of predication are often said to be answers to questions that might be expressed in colloquial English, such as "What is it?" and "What's it like?" If we ask what man is, the answer is animal; if we ask what man is like, the answer is rational or two legged or bilateral, and so on. This second answer, the response to the question "What's it like?", can consist of characteristics that belong to the essence of the subject or of characteristics that are only accidental to the subject. A differentia is distinguished from a genus, because a genus is predicated in respect of what its subject is and a differentia is predicated in respect of the characteristics its subject has. An accident, too, is predicated in respect of what its subject is like; but, unlike differ-

---

16. See Porphyry, *Isagoge, CAG*, p. 13.10-21; and Boethius, *In Isag.* ed. Brandt, pp. 286-291 (*PL* 64,134C9-136C).
17. See, e.g., Porphyry, *Isagoge, CAG*, pp. 19.11-14, 9.7-16, and 13.10-21.12.

entia, it picks out characteristics that are not part of the subject's essence.

With this last pair of characteristics, we have enough to specify all the predicables and distinguish them from one another.

	In respect of what characteristic	In respect of what it is	Of what is common	Of what is individual	Of the essence	Not of the essence	Greater than	Equal to
Differentia	X		X		X		X	
Property	X		X			X		X
Accident	X		X*	X**		X	X	
Genus		X	X		X		X	
Species		X		X	X			X
Definition		X	X		X			X

*Inseparable accident.
**Separable accident.

As the table shows, of the six predicables, then, differentia, property, and accident are alike in being predicated in respect of what the subject is like (*in eo quod quale*) and so are distinguished from genus, species, and definition, which are all predicated *in eo quod quid*, in respect of what the subject is. But differentia is allied with genus, species, and definition in being part of the subject's essence. In this single respect, differentia is distinguished from accident: both are alike in being predicated in respect of what the subject is like, in being predicated of what is common rather than what is individual, and in being greater than the subject; but differentia is part of the subject's essence, and accident is not. Accidents are distinguished from properties, too, in only a single respect: accidents, whether separable or inseparable, are greater than their subject, while properties are equal to their subject. On the very same grounds, genus is distinguished from definition; though they are the same in other respects, a definition is equal to its subject, and a genus is not. And there are other patterns as well.

Finally, it may be useful to say something about the connection between the predicables and the medieval controversy over universals. Theoretically, the debate concerning the ontological status of universals could have arisen with respect to any of the Porphyrian predicables, as Boethius and Porphyry both acknowledge. But in fact it tended to center on the status of genera and species. Now if we look at Porphyry's definitions of genus and species, we can see the origin of the difficulty in those definitions. If we assess Porphyry's definitions of genus and species by the criteria of a true definition, it becomes apparent at once that Porphyry's definitions are faulty: they lack a genus. Where the genus ought to appear in a definition, they have instead only the place-keeping phrase "what" or "that which." The medieval debate over universals can be understood as a controversy over how to fill in that gap in the definitions of genus and species and how to specify a genus for these two predicables themselves.

With that background material on the predicables I turn now to the categories, and then I will conclude by saying something about the interaction between categories and predicables.

There has been a lot of controversy over the nature of Aristotle's work in the *Categories*. Scholars have argued for a variety of positions: that Aristotle's purpose in this work is to categorize certain linguistic entities, that Aristotle is presenting an ontological classification, or that he is doing both in one or another complicated way. I think, however, that the second view, that Aristotle is classifying nonlinguistic entities in the *Categories*, is the most common scholastic view, at least in the early scholastic period; for that reason (as well as for the sake of simplicity), it is the view of the categories which I will rely on here.

On this view, in his work *Categories* Aristotle divides everything in the world into ten categories: substance, quantity, relation, quality, action, passion, position, place, time, and possession. None of these categories is reducible to or subsumed under any of the others. None of them together fall under any other, more general category. But everything is subsumed under one or another of them; each of these ten is a genus to many other things but is not itself a species of anything.

Substances Aristotle divides into two sorts: primary and secondary substances. Primary substances are individual things such as Socrates or this chair or this tree. Secondary substances are the species and genera of such individual things: animal, furniture, plant, and so on.

The categories of quantity and quality should be reasonably self-explanatory for present purposes, though I will return to the category of quality shortly. Under the category of relation falls whatever is what it is just in virtue of being *of* or *than* something else, or in some other way *in relation to* something else. *Larger*, for example, is what it is in virtue of being *than* something else (it is larger than something); *double* is what it is in virtue of being *of* something else (it is double of something); and so on. And so relatives always come in pairs or reciprocate, Aristotle says: what is larger is larger than something smaller; what is double is double of something that is half of it, and so on.

Action is the category of *doing:* heating, cooling, burning, and stabbing all fall in this category. The category of passion is its mirror image: being heated, being cooled, being burned, and being stabbed fall within this category.

Position includes characteristics such as lying, sitting, and standing; it seems to be the category for characteristics that are ways of being in a place. The categories place and time are relatively self-explanatory. The last category, *possession*, is somewhat obscure; Aristotle gives as examples of what falls within this category the characteristics having shoes on and having armor on.

In his initial presentation of the categories, Aristotle relies on two phrases, 'being said of a subject' and 'being in a subject'. First, some things, Aristotle says, are said of a subject but are not *in* that subject. By being in a subject, Aristotle means being unable to exist independent of a subject but not being a part—a discernible, separable member—of that subject.[18] *Animal* is an example of something said of a subject but not in that subject. We say *animal* of a cat, for example, because a cat is an animal but *animal* is not *in* a cat. On the whole, when he talks about what is said of a subject but is not *in* a subject, Aristotle seems to be thinking of the species and genera of individual things, that is, secondary substances. Second, there are also things that are in a subject without being said of that subject. An individual quality such as Socrates's whiteness is an example. Socrates's whiteness is *in* Socrates but it is not *said of* Socrates; we do not say that Socrates is whiteness. Third, some things *both* are said of something and are in something. Knowledge, for example, is *in* the soul, Aristotle says, and it is *said of* knowledge-of-grammar. That is, knowledge is a genus of knowledge-of-grammar; it is also in a soul, as whiteness is in a body. Finally, there are things that neither are said of anything nor are in anything. Examples of such things, he says, are an individual man or an individual horse—primary substances, in other words. Aristotle, then, seems to have had a fourfold distinction in mind with regard to the categories. First, there are primary substances, individual entities, which neither are said of a subject nor are in a subject. Unlike things in any of the other categories, then, they are not logically or conceptually dependent on anything else for their being, and hence they are *substances*—independently existing things—in the strictest and most fundamental sense of the word.[19] Second, there are the things said of a subject but not in a subject; these are the genera and species of primary substances, that is, the secondary substances. Next are the things that

18. Aristotle, *Cat.* 1a20ff.
19. Ibid., 2a11ff.

are in but not said of a subject. This group consists in individual instances from all the nine categories other than substance. And it is distinguished from the last group because included in that group are things that are both in a subject and said of a subject. This last group, then, consists of genera and species, but genera and species *in categories other than that of substance*.

This fourfold grouping, together with Aristotle's account of the predicables, suggests another, philosophically and historically significant grouping among the categories. The fundamental ontological entities in Aristotle's view are primary substances. Secondary substances are the genera and species of primary substances and are part of the essence of their subjects, the primary substances. Now a species is that which a definition defines, and a definition consists in genus plus differentiae. So all the predicables that can be part of their subject's essence are included in genus and species, and hence secondary substances constitute the whole essence of primary substances. Consequently, things in the other nine categories, which are all attributes of one sort or another, are *accidents* or *properties* of primary substances. For our purposes here, the distinction between properties and accidents is insignificant; we can simplify the discussion by saying that for all practical purposes the nine categories other than substances all consist in *accidents* of primary substances.

It is important to recognize, however, that, on Aristotle's view, everything insofar as it *is* has an essence, so that *accidents* themselves also have essences—that is, a certain group of individual accidents will fall under a species of accident, and that species of accident will be defined by a definition that consists in the genus and differentiae for that accident. Consequently, there are species, genera, definitions, and differentiae to be found in all the categories, not just in the category of substance. That this is so may make it seem as if the whole delicate, complicated edifice of distinctions is collapsing, but a closer look at the nature of a differentia should do something to dispel such an impression. A differentia, such as *rational*, which falls within the category of substance, is distinguished from an attribute in the category of quality, such as *black*, because the differentia *rational* is part of the essence of a primary substance; the quality *black*, which is an accident, is not part of the essence of a primary substance. Now suppose that we define the quality *black*, and suppose that one of the differentiae of the quality *black* is *light-absorbing*. This differentia *light-absorbing*, then, like any other differentia, is part of the essence of its subject (which in this case is the quality *black*); yet (we might worry) it falls within the category of quality, which is supposed to consist in accidents, rather than within the category of substance, which contains differentiae that are part of the essence of their subjects. But what distinguishes the differentia *light-absorbing* in the category of quality from the differentia *rational* in the category of substance is this: the differentia *rational* is part of the essence of *a primary substance;* the differentia *light-absorbing* is part of the essence of *an accident* of a primary substance. The two sorts of differentiae, then, are not incoherently identified in Aristotle's scheme but rather differ from one another in an important respect.

The result, then, of this first attempt at combining the categories and the predicables gives us a richer understanding of both. It shows us that the first category *substance* consists in primary substances and their essences, while the other nine categories comprise the accidents of primary substances. But these accidents, too, have essences; so, like primary substances, the accidents are also ordered and constituted by those predicables which are part of the essence of their subject, though there is this difference between a differentia (for example) in the category of substance and a differentia in any of the other nine categories: a substantial differentia is part of the essence of a primary substance, and an accidental differentia is part of the essence of an accident of a primary substance.

We can conclude our examination of this material by looking at one last result of combining categories and predicables, namely, the diagram that is traditionally called the Porphyrian Tree.

Substance, quantity, relation, quality, and the rest of the ten categories are each of them the head of a Porphyrian Tree (more accurately, the root of it; Porphyrian Trees grow upside down). Beginning with one or another of these categories, a Porphyrian Tree is generated by means of the predicables. By far the most common example of a Porphyrian Tree in medieval authors is that which begins with substance as the highest genus, and I will take it as my example here, too.

A highest genus is divided by a pair of opposite characteristics, its divisive differentiae, into two species, each of which is picked out and constituted by one of that pair of differentiae. Thus, *substance* is divided by the divisive differentiae *corporeal* and *incorporeal* into two species, which do not have their own names but are referred to by the genus plus the appropriate differentia—in this case *corporeal substance* and *incorporeal substance.* Though these two are species of *substance,* they are also genera for other things; they can be divided by divisive differentiae just as *substance* was. *Corporeal substance* is divided by the differentiae *animate* and *inanimate* into the two species *animate corporeal substance* and *inanimate corporeal substance. Incorporeal substance* is presumably also divided, but I follow common medieval practice and

Porphyrian Tree of Substance

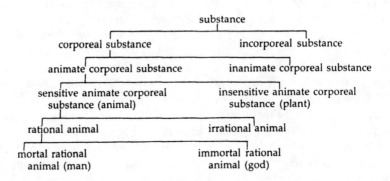

complete only one branch or "predicamental line" of this Porphyrian tree (see figure). Like *corporeal substance, animate corporeal substance* and *inanimate corporeal substance* are subaltern genera, being species of the genus immediately above them in the tree and genera for what is below them. *Animate corporeal substance* is divided by differentiae into *sensitive* (i.e., capable of perceiving) *animate corporeal substance* and *insensitive animate corporeal substance*. For these two subaltern genera there are names and not just descriptions; the first is the genus *animal*, and the second, the genus *plant*. *Animal* is divided into *rational animal* and *irrational animal*, or *rational sensitive animate corporeal substance* and *irrational sensitive animate corporeal substance*. And the subaltern genus *rational animal* is in turn divided into *mortal rational animal* (*mortal rational sensitive animate corporeal substance*) and *immortal rational animal*; these two also have their own names—'*man*' and '*god*'. (By '*god*' in this context the medievals tended to understand something like the intelligent movers of the heavenly spheres; they did *not* understand it to refer to the supreme being and creator of the universe.)

These last two species, *man* and *god*, are mirror images of *substance*: *substance* is a genus that is not a species of anything and hence is a highest genus, and these two are species that are not genera for anything and hence are lowest species. There is just one highest genus for a Porphyrian Tree, but *man* and *god* are two of many lowest species for this particular tree. By working out the other branches of this tree, one would end with a large number of lowest species, all subsumed under the highest genus, *substance*. As there are ten different categories or highest genera, so there are ten Porphyrian Trees that can be worked out in this way; on the theory of the categories and predicables, if they were worked out fully, they would contain among themselves all the species of things there are in the world, each fully defined with its entire essence revealed. Though there are many philosophical difficulties with these notions, they constitute a breathtakingly bold and rich philosophical theory, which forms the centerpiece of the *logica vetus* and the cornerstone of all medieval philosophy.

SELECTED BIBLIOGRAPHY

This bibliography is a list of those books and articles I found most helpful in annotating this treatise. Because of the technical nature of *ICT*, with its examples drawn from Roman law, a good part of the bibliography is devoted to ancient law. The reader interested in a more complete general bibliography on ancient dialectic or Boethius should consult the bibliographies in my earlier book and in Chadwick's *Boethius* (listed below).

Abelard. *Dialectica.* Ed. L. M. de Rijk. 2d ed. Assen: Van Gorcum, 1970.

Adamo, Luigi. "Boezio e Mario Vittorino traduttori e interpreti dell' 'Isagoge' di Porfirio." *Rivista critica di Storia della Filosofia*, 22 (1967), 141–164.

Albert of Saxony. *Perutilis logica.* Venice, 1522.

Alexander of Aphrodisias. *In Aristotelis Topicorum libros octo commentaria.* Ed. Maximilian Wallies. *Commentaria in Aristotelem Graeca*, sup. vol. II, pt. 2. Berlin: G. Reimer, 1891.

Alfonsi, Luigi. "Studi Boeziani." *Aevum*, 19 (1945), 142–157.

——. "Studi Boeziani (continua)." *Aevum*, 25 (1951), 132–146, 210–229.

Angelleli, Ignacio. "The Techniques of Disputation in the History of Logic." *Journal of Philosophy*, 67 (1970), 800–815.

Anonymous. *Rhetorica ad Herennium.* Tr. H. Caplan. Cambridge, Mass.: Harvard University Press, 1954.

Arnold, E. Vernon. *Roman Stoicism.* Cambridge: Cambridge University Press, 1911.

Baldwin, Charles Sears. *Medieval Rhetoric and Poetic to 1400.* Gloucester, Mass.: Peter Smith, 1959.

Barrett, Helen Marjorie. *Boethius: Some Aspects of His Times and Work.* Cambridge: Cambridge University Press, 1940.

Berger, Adolf. *Encyclopedic Dictionary of Roman Law.* Transactions of the American Philosophical Society, new series, vol. XLIII, pt. 2. Philadelphia: American Philosophical Society, 1953.

Bidez, J. "Boèce et Porphyre." *Revue Belge de Philologie et d'Histoire*, 2 (1923), 189–201.

Biraghi, Luigi. *Boezio filosofo.* Milan: Boniardi-Pogliani de E. Besozzi, 1865.

Bird, Otto. "The Logical Interest of the Topics as Seen in Abelard." *Modern Schoolman*, 37 (1959), 53–57.

Bloos, Lutz. *Probleme der stoischen Physik.* Hamburg: Helmut Buske Verlag, 1973.

Bochenski, Innocentius M. *Ancient Formal Logic*. Amsterdam: North-Holland, 1951.

Boethius. "A Critical Edition of Boethius' Commentary on Cicero's Topica Bk. I." Ed. A. Perdamo. Ph.D. dissertation, St. Louis University, 1963.

——. *De hypotheticis syllogismis*. Ed. and tr. Luca Obertello. Brescia: Paideia, 1969.

——. *In Ciceronis Topica*. In *Ciceronis Opera*, ed. J. C. Orelli and G. Baiterus, vol. V, pt. 1. Zurich: Fuesslini, 1833.

——. *In Isagogen*. Ed. Samuel Brandt. Corpus scriptorum ecclesiasticorum latinorum, 48. Leipzig: G. Freytag, 1906.

——. *In Perihermeneias*. Ed. Carolus Meiser. Leipzig: Teubner, 1880.

——. *Manlii Severini Boetii Opera omnia: Opera philosophica et Opera theologica*. Ed. J.-P. Migne. *Patrologiae latinae*. Vol. LXIV. Turnholt: Brepols, n.d.

——. *Trattato sulla divisione*. Tr. Lorenzo Pozzi. Padua: Liviana, 1969.

Bonnaud, R. "L'education scientifique de Boèce." *Speculum*, 4 (1929), 198–206.

Brandt, Samuel. "Entstehungszeit und zeitliche Folge der Werke von Boethius." *Philologus*, 62 (1903), 141–154, 234–275.

Bruns, C. G., ed. *Fontes Iuris Romani Antiqui*. 7th ed. Tübingen: Libraria I. C. B. Mohrii (P. Siebeck), 1909.

Bryant, Donald C. *Ancient Greek and Roman Rhetoricians: A Biographical Dictionary*. Columbia, Mo.: Artcraft Press, 1968.

Buckland, W. W. *Elementary Principles of the Roman Private Law*. Cambridge: Cambridge University Press, 1912.

——. *Equity in Roman Law*. London: University of London Press, 1911.

——. *A Textbook of Roman Law from Augustus to Justinian*. Cambridge: Cambridge University Press, 1921.

Buckland, W. W., and Arnold D. McNair. *Roman Law and Common Law: A Comparison in Outline*. Cambridge: Cambridge University Press, 1936.

Buckler, W. H. *The Origin and History of Contract in Roman Law down to the End of the Republican Period*. London: C. J. Clay, 1895.

Burnyeat, Myles, ed. *The Skeptical Tradition*. Berkeley: University of California Press, 1983.

Carson, R. A. G. *Principal Coins of the Romans*. Vols. I–III. London: British Museum Publications, 1978.

Cassiodorus. *Institutiones*. Ed. R. A. B. Mynors. Oxford: Clarendon Press, 1937.

Chadwick, Henry. *Boethius: The Consolations of Music, Logic, Theology, and Philosophy*. Oxford: Clarendon Press, 1981.

Cicero. *The Letters to His Friends*. Vol. II. Tr. W. G. Williams. Loeb Classical Library. London: Heinemann, 1928.

——. *Topica*. Tr. H. M. Hubbell. Loeb Classical Library. London: Heinemann, 1960.

——. *Tusculan Disputations*. Tr. J. E. King. Loeb Classical Library. Cambridge, Mass.: Harvard University Press, 1966.

Clover, Frank M. *Flavius Merobaudes: A Translation and Historical Commentary*. Transactions of the American Philosophical Society, new series, Vol. LXI, pt 1. Philadelphia: American Philosophical Society, 1971.

Collins, James. "Progress and Problems in the Reassessment of Boethius." *Modern Schoolman*, 23 (1945–1946), 1–23.

Costa, Emilio. *Cicerone giureconsulto.* Rome: "L'Erma" di Bretschneider, 1964.

Courcelle, Pierre-Paul. "Boèce et l'école d'Alexandrie." *Mélanges d'Archéologie et d'Histoire*, 52 (1935), 185–223.

———. "*La consolation de philosophie*" dans la tradition littéraire, antecedents et posterité de Boèce. Paris: Etudes Augustiniennes, 1967.

———. "Etudes critiques sur les commentaires de la 'Consolation' de Boèce (ix–xv siècles)." *Archives d'Histoire Doctrinale et Littéraire du Moyen-Age*, 14 (1939), 5–140.

———. *Les lettres grecques en occident de Macrobe à Cassiodore.* Paris: E. de Boccard, 1943. Tr. H. Wedeck as *Late Latin Writers and Their Greek Sources*. Cambridge, Mass.: Harvard University Press, 1969; 1st ed., 1948.

Crifo, G. "*L'Argumentum ex contrario* in Cicerone e Boezio con particolare riferimento a Cicerone Top. 3.17." In *Hommages à Marcel Renard*, vol. I, pp. 280–292. Brussels: Latomus, 1969.

Crocco, Antonio. *Introduzione a Boezio.* Naples: Empireo, 1970.

Crook, John. *Law and Life of Rome.* Ithaca: Cornell University Press, 1967.

Dahlstrom, Daniel. "Signification and Logic: Scotus on Universals from a Logical Point of View." *Vivarium*, 18 (1980), 81–111.

Davis, Charles, and H. Stanley. *Greek and Roman Stoicism and Some of Its Disciples.* Boston: Herbert B. Turner, 1903.

De Pater, Walter. "La fonction du lieu et de l'instrument dans les *Topiques*." In G. E. L. Owen, ed., *Aristotle on Dialectic: Proceedings of the Third Symposim Aristotelicum*, pp. 164–188. Oxford: Clarendon Press, 1968.

———. *Les Topiques d'Aristote et la dialectique platonicienne: La méthodologie de la définition.* Etudes thomistiques, 10. Fribourg: Editions St. Paul, 1956.

de Rijk, Lambertus Marie. "On the Chronology of Boethius' Works on Logic." I and II. *Vivarium*, 2 (1964), 1–49, 125–162.

De Vogel, Cornelia J. "Boethiana." I and II. *Vivarium*, 9 (1971), 49–66, and 10 (1972), 1–40.

DeWitt, Norman W. "The Gods of Epicurus and the Canon." *Transactions of the Royal Society of Canada.* Section II, 3 ser., vol. 36, (1942), 33–49.

Driessche, R. van den. "Sur le 'De syllogismo hypothetico' de Boèce." *Methodos*, 1 (1949), 293–302.

Duff, J. Wright. *A Literary History of Rome: From the Origins to the Close of the Golden Age.* New York: Charles Scribner's, 1927.

———. *A Literary History of Rome in the Silver Age: From Tiberius to Hadrian.* New York: Barnes and Noble, 1927. 3d ed., 1964.

Durr, Karl. *The Propositional Logic of Boethius.* Tr. Norman Martin. Studies in Logic and the Foundations of Mathematics. Amsterdam: North-Holland, 1951.

Eisenhut, Werner. *Einführung in die antike Rhetorik und ihre Geschichte.* Darmstadt: Wissenschaftliche Buchgesellschaft, 1974.

Enders, Heinz Werner. *Sprachlogische Konzeptionen der Scholastik und die Frage einer Wissenschaftlichen Grundlegung der Semantik.* Inaugural dissertation, Ludwig-Maximilians Universität, Munich, 1973.

———. *Sprachlogische Traktate des Mittelalters und der Semantikbegriff.* Munich: Verlag Ferdinand Schöningh, 1975.

Erickson, Keith V. *Aristotle: The Classical Heritage of Rhetoric.* Metuchen, N.J.: Scarecrow Press, 1974.

Evans, John D. G. *Aristotle's Concept of Dialectic.* Cambridge: Cambridge University Press, 1977.

Frede, Michael. *Die stoische Logik.* Göttingen: Vandenhoeck and Ruprecht, 1974.

Garlandus Compotista. *Dialectica.* Ed. L. M. de Rijk. Assen: Van Gorcum, 1959.

Gelzer, Matthias. *Cicero: Ein biographischer Versuch.* Wiesbaden: Franz Steiner Verlag, 1969.

Gibson, Margaret, ed. *Boethius: His Life, Thought and Influence.* Oxford: Basil Blackwell, 1981.

Gigon, Olof. "Cicero und Aristoteles." *Hermes,* 87 (1959), 143–162.

Giomini, Remo. *Richerche sul testo del Timeo Ciceroniano.* Rome: Angelo Signorelli Editore, 1967.

Goldschmidt, Victor. "Logique et rhétorique chez les Stoiciens." In *La théorie de l'argumentation,* pp. 450–456. Louvain: Nauwelaerts, 1963.

Gould, Josiah B. *The Philosophy of Chrysippus.* Albany, N.Y.: State University of New York Press, 1970.

Green-Pedersen, Niels J. "The Doctrine of 'Maxima Propositio' and 'Locus Differentia' in Commentaries from the 12th Century on Boethius' 'Topics.' " *Studia Mediewistyczne,* 18 (1977), 125–163.

——. "The Summulae of John Buridan: Tractatus VI de locis." In Jan Pinborg, ed., *The Logic of John Buridan,* pp. 121–138. Acts of the Third European Symposium on Medieval Logic and Semantics. Copenhagen: Museum Tusculanum, 1976.

——. *The Tradition of the Topics in the Middle Ages.* Munich: Philosophia Verlag, 1984.

Guthrie, W. K. C. *A History of Greek Philosophy II.* Cambridge: Cambridge University Press, 1962–1969.

Hadot, Pierre. *Marius Victorinus.* Paris: Etudes Augustiniennes, 1971.

——. "Marius Victorinus et Alcuin." *Archives d'Histoire Doctrinale et Littéraire du Moyen-Age,* 29 (1954), 5–19.

——. "Un vocabulaire raissoné de Marius Victorinus Afer." *Studia Patristica I,* 5th ser., 8 (1957), 194–208.

Halm, Charles, ed. *M. Fabii Quintiliani Institutionis Oratoriae libri duodecem.* Leipzig: Teubner, 1868.

——. *Rhetores latini minores.* Leipzig: Teubner, 1863.

Hammer, Caspar. *Commentatio de Ciceronis Topicis.* Landavi: Formis Kaussleri, 1879.

Honoré, A. M. *Gaius.* Oxford: Clarendon Press, 1962.

Horne, Winifred. *Historical Rhetoric: An Annotated Bibliography of Selected Sources in English.* Boston: G. K. Hall, 1980.

Johnson, Allan Chester, Paul Robinson Coleman-Norton, and Frank Card Bourne, trs. *Ancient Roman Statues.* Austin: University of Texas Press, 1961.

Jolowicz, H. F. *Roman Foundations of Modern Law.* Oxford: Clarendon Press, 1957.

Jolowicz, H. F., and Barry Nicholas. *Historical Introduction to the Study of Roman Law.* 3d ed. Cambridge: Cambridge University Press, 1972.

Jones, A. H. M. *The Criminal Courts of the Roman Republic and Principate.* Totowa, N.J.: Rowan and Littlefield, 1972.

Kaimio, Jorma. *Cicero's "Topica": The Preface and Sources*. Turku: Turun Yliopisto, 1976.

Kennedy, George. *The Art of Rhetoric in the Roman World, 300 B.C.–A.D. 300*. Princeton: Princeton University Press, 1972.

Kirkby, Helen. "The Scholar and His Public." In Gibson 1981: 44–69.

Klein, Johann Joseph. *Dissertatio de fontibus Topicorum Ciceronis*. Bonn: C. et F. Kruegor, 1844.

Kluge, Eike-Henner. "William of Ockham's Commentary on Porphyry." *Franciscan Studies*. 33 (1973), 171–254, and 34 (1974), 306–382.

Kneale, William, and Martha Kneale. *The Development of Logic*. Oxford: Clarendon Press, 1962.

Kunkel, Wolfgang. *An Introduction to Roman Legal and Constitutional History*. Tr. J. M. Kelly. Oxford: Clarendon Press, 1973.

Lawson, F. H. *Negligence in the Civil Law*. Oxford: Clarendon Press, 1950.

Leage, R. W. *Roman Private Law*. London: Macmillan, 1906.

Lee, R. W. *The Elements of Roman Law with a Translation of the Institutes of Justinian*. London: Sweet and Maxwell, 1946.

Leeman, A. D. *Orationis Ratio: The Stylistic Theories and Practices of the Roman Orators, Historians, and Philosophers*. Amsterdam: A. M. Hakkert, 1963.

Leff, Michael. "Boethius and the History of Medieval Rhetoric." *Central States Speech Journal*, 25 (1974), 135–141.

———. "Boethius's *De top. diff.*, Book IV." In James J. Murphy, ed., *Medieval Eloquence: Studies in the Theory and Practice of Medieval Rhetoric*, pp. 3–24. Berkeley and Los Angeles: University of California Press, 1978.

Levy, Ernest. *West Roman Vulgar Law: The Law of Property*. Philadelphia: American Philosophical Society, 1951.

McKeon, Richard. "The Methods of Rhetoric and Philosophy: Invention and Judgment." In Luitpold Wallach, ed., *The Classical Tradition: Literary and Historical Studies in Honor of Harry Caplan*, pp. 365–373. Ithaca: Cornell University Press, 1966.

McKinlay, Arthur Patch. "Stylistic Tests and the Chronology of the Works of Boethius." *Harvard Studies in Classical Philology*, 18 (1907), 123–156.

Marenbon, John. *Early Medieval Philosophy (480–1150): An Introduction*. London: Routledge and Kegan Paul, 1983.

Masi, Michael, ed. *Boethius and the Liberal Arts*. Barne: Peter Lang, 1981.

Mates, Benson. *Stoic Logic*. Berkeley: University of California Press, 1953.

Mathiesen, Thomas J., tr. *Aristides Quintilianus: On Music in Three Books*. New Haven: Yale University Press, 1983.

Merguet, H. *Lexikon zu den Schriften Ciceros*. Jena: G. Fischer, 1887–1894.

Merlan, Philip. "Ammonius Hermiae, Zacharias Scholasticus, and Boethius." *Greek, Roman, and Byzantine Studies*, 9 (1968), 193–203.

Michaud-Quantin, Pierre. *Etudes sur le vocabulaire philosophique du moyen âge*. Rome: Edizioni dell' Ateneo, 1970.

Michaud-Quantin, Pierre, and James Weisheipl. "Dialectics in the Middle Ages." In William J. MacDonald, ed., *The New Catholic Encyclopedia*. New York: McGraw-Hill, 1967.

Michel, Alain. *Le "Dialogue des orateurs" de Tacite et la philosophie de Cicéron*. Paris: Librairie C. Klincksieck, 1962.

———. *Les rapports de la rhétorique et de la philosophie dans l'oeuvre de Cicéron*. Paris: Presses universitaires de France, 1960.

———. *Rhétorique et philosophie chez Cicéron: Essai sur les fondements philosophiques de l'art de persuader*. Paris: Presses universitaires de France, 1961.

Michel, Alain, and Raoul Verdière. *Ciceroniana: Hommages à Kazimierz Kumaniecki*. Leiden: E. J. Brill, 1975.

Minio-Paluello, Lorenzo. "A Latin Commentary (?Translated by Boethius) on the *Prior Analytics* and Its Greek Sources." *Journal of Hellenic Studies*, 77 (1957): 93–102.

———. "Les traductions et les commentaires aristotéliciens de Boèce." *Studia Patristica II*, 5th ser., 9, (1957), 358–365.

Mommsen, Theodore, ed. *Cassiodori Senatoris Variae*. Berlin: Weidmann, 1894.

Muirhead, James, tr. *The Institutes of Gaius and Rules of Ulpian*. Edinburgh: T. and T. Clark, 1880.

Murphy, James J. *Rhetoric in the Middle Ages: A History of Rhetorical Theory from St. Augustine to the Renaissance*. Berkeley: University of California Press, 1974.

———. *A Synoptic History of Classical Rhetoric*. New York: Random House, 1972.

Nicholas, Barry. *An Introduction to Roman Law*. Oxford: Clarendon Press, 1962.

Nitzsch, Friedrich. *Das System des Boethius*. Berlin: Wiegandt und Grieben, 1860.

Nuchelmans, Gabriel. *Theories of the Proposition: Ancient and Medieval Conceptions of the Bearers of Truth and Falsity*. Amsterdam: North-Holland, 1973.

Obertello, Luca. *Severino Boezio*. 2 vols. Genoa: Accademia Ligure di scienze e lettere, 1972.

———, ed. *Atti congresso internazionale di studi Boeziani*. Rome: Editrice Herder, 1981.

O'Donnell, James J. *Cassiodorus*. Berkeley: University of California Press, 1979.

Orth, E. "De Ciceronis 'Topicis.'" *Helmantica*, 9 (1958), 393–413.

Pagallo, G. "Per una edizione critica del 'De hypotheticis syllogismis' di Boezio." *Italia medievale e umanistica*, 1 (1958), 69–101.

Patch, Howard Rollin. "Necessity in Boethius and the Neoplatonists." *Speculum*, 10 (1935), 393–404.

———. *The Tradition of Boethius*. New York: Oxford University Press, 1935.

Peters, F. E. *Aristoteles Arabus*. Leiden: E. J. Brill, 1968.

Petersson, Torsten. *Cicero: A Biography*. Berkeley: University of California Press, 1920.

Pfligersdorffer, Georg. "Andronikos von Rhodos und die Postprädikamente bei Boethius." *Vigiliae Christianae*, 7 (1953), 98–115.

———. "Zu Boethius De Interpr. Ed. Sec. I, p. 4, 4 sqq. Meiser nebst Beobachtungen zur Geschichte der Dialektik bei den Römern." *Wiener Studien*, 66 (1953): 131–154.

Pinborg, Jan. *Logik und Semantik im Mittelalter*. Stuttgart-Bad Cannstatt: Frommann-Holzborg, 1972.

———. "Topik und Syllogistik im Mittelalter." In F. Hoffman, L. Scheffczyk, and K. Feiereis, eds., *Sapienter Ordinare: Festgabe für Erich Kleineidam*, pp. 157–178. Erfurter Theologische Studien, 24. Leipzig: St.-Benno Verlag, 1969.

Plebe, Armando. "Retorica aristotelica e logica stoica." *Filosofia*, 10 (1959), 391–424.

Polheim, Karl. *Die Lateinische Reimprosa*. Berlin: Weidmannsche Buchhandlung, 1925.

Porphyry. *Isagoge*. In Adolf Busse, ed., *Commentaria in Aristotelem Graeca*. IV, pt.i. Berlin: Reimer, 1887.

Pozzi, Lorenzo. *Le Consequentiae nella logica medievale.* Padua: Liviana editrice, 1978.
——. *Studi di logica antica e medioevale.* Padua: Liviana editrice, 1974.
Prior, Arthur Norman. "The Logic of Negative Terms in Boethius." *Franciscan Studies,* 13 (1953), 1–6.
Pseudo-Scotus. *Super librum I Priorum.* In John Duns Scotus, *Opera omnia.* Editio nova juxta editionem Waddingi XII tomos continentem a patribus Franciscanis de observantia accurante recognita. Vol. II. Vivès, 1891.
Quintilian. *The Institutio oratoria of Quintilian.* Tr. H. E. Butler. London: Heinemann, 1920–1922.
Rabe, Hugo, ed. *Syriani in Hermogenem Commentaria.* Vol. I. Leipzig: Teubner, 1892.
Reber, Franz, tr. *Des Vitruvius zehn Bücher über Architektur.* Stuttgart: Krais and Hoffman, 1865.
Reiley, Katherine Campbell. *Studies in the Philosophical Terminology of Lucretius and Cicero.* New York: Columbia University Press, 1949.
Riposati, Benedetto. "Quid Cicero de thesi et hypothesi in 'Topicis' senserit." *Aevum,* 18 (1944), 61–71.
——. "Quo modo partitiones oratoriae cum topicis cohaereant." In *Atti I congr. stud. Cic.,* pp. 253–263. Rome, 1961.
——. *Studi sui "Topica" di Cicerone.* Milan: Società editrice "Vita e pensiero," 1947.
Rist, John M., ed. *The Stoics.* Berkeley: University of California Press, 1978.
Rodger, Alan. *Owners and Neighbours in Roman Law.* Oxford: Clarendon Press, 1972.
Rose, H. J. *A Handbook of Latin Literature: From the Earliest Times to the Death of St. Augustine.* London: Methuen, 1936. 3d ed., 1954.
Rose, Valentinus, and Herman Müller-Strübing, eds. *Vitruvii de Architectura libri decem.* Leipzig: Teubner, 1867.
Schofield, Malcolm, Myles Burnyeat, and Jonathan Barnes. *Doubt and Dogmatism: Studies in Hellenistic Epistemology.* Oxford: Clarendon Press, 1980.
Schulz, Fritz. *Classical Roman Law.* Oxford: Clarendon Press, 1951.
——. *History of Roman Legal Science.* Oxford: Clarendon Press, 1953.
——. *Principles of Roman Law.* Tr. Marguerite Wolff. Oxford: Clarendon Press, 1936.
Shiel, James. "Boethius and Andronicus of Rhodes." *Vigiliae Christianae,* 11 (1957), 179–185.
——. "Boethius and Eudemus." *Vivarium,* 12 (1974), 14–17.
——. "Boethius' Commentaries on Aristotle." *Mediaeval and Renaissance Studies,* 4 (1958), 217–244.
Sihler, E. G. *Cicero of Arpinum: A Political and Literary Biography.* New Haven: Yale University Press, 1914.
Slattery, Michael. "Genus and Difference." *Thomist,* 21 (1958), 343–364.
Smethurst, S. E. "Cicero's Rhetorical and Philosophical Works: A Bibliographical Survey." *Classical World,* 51 (1957–1958), 1–4, 24, 32–41.
Solmsen, Friedrich. "Boethius and the History of the *Organon.*" *American Journal of Philology,* 65 (1944), 69–74.
Sorabji, Richard. *Aristotle on Memory.* London: Duckworth, 1972.
——. *Necessity, Cause and Blame: Perspectives on Aristotle's Theory.* Ithaca: Cornell University Press, 1980.

Souter, Alexander. *A Glossary of Later Latin to 600 A.D.* Oxford: Clarendon Press, 1949.

Stangl, Thomas. *Boethiana vel Boethii commentariorum in Ciceronis Topica emendationes.* Gotha, 1882.

——. "Pseudoboethiana." *Jahrbücher für classische Philologie*, 29 (1883), 193–208, 285–301.

——. *Tulliana et Mario-Victoriniana.* Munich: Programm München, 1888.

Stark, Rudolf, ed. *Rhetorika: Schriften zur aristotelischen und hellenistischen Rhetorik.* Hildesheim: G. Olms, 1968.

Stewart, Hugh Fraser. *Boethius.* London: W. Blackwood, 1891.

Stump, Eleonore. *Boethius's De topicis differentiis.* Ithaca: Cornell University Press, 1978.

——. "Boethius's In Ciceronis Topica and Stoic Logic." In John Wippel, ed., *Studies in Medieval Philosophy.* Washington, D.C.: Catholic University of America Press, 1987.

——. "Boethius's Theory of Topics and Its Place in Early Scholastic Logic." In Luca Obertello, ed., *Atti congresso internazionale di studi Boeziani*, pp. 249–262. Rome: Editrice Herder, 1981.

——. "Boethius's Works on the Topics." *Vivarium*, 12 (1974), 77–93.

——. "Dialectic." In David Wagner, ed., *The Seven Liberal Arts in the Middle Ages*, pp. 125–146. Bloomington: Indiana University Press, 1983.

——. "Garlandus Compotista and Dialectic in the Eleventh and Twelfth Centuries." *History and Philosophy of Logic*, 1 (1980), 1–18.

——. "Topics: Their Development and Absorption into the Consequences." In Norman Kretzmann et al., eds., *The Cambridge History of Later Medieval Philosophy*, pp. 273–299. Cambridge: Cambridge University Press, 1982.

Tacitus. *Dialogus de oratoribus.* Ed. M. L. de Gubernatis. Corpus scriptorum latinorum Paravianum. Turin: G. B. Paravia, 1949.

Thielscher, P. "Ciceros Topik und Aristoteles." *Philologus*, 67 (1908), 52–67.

Thomas, Ivo. "Boethius' locus a repugnantibus." *Methodos*, 3 (1951), 303–307.

Viehweg, Theodor. *Topik und Jurisprudenz.* Munich: Verlag C. H. Beck, 1963.

Wallies, Maximilian. *De fontibus Topicorum Ciceronis.* Berlin: A. Haack, 1878.

——. *Die griechischen Ausleger der aristotelischen Topik.* Berlin: A Haack, 1891.

Watson, Alan. *Contract of Mandate in Roman Law.* Oxford: Clarendon Press, 1961.

——. *Law Making in the Later Roman Republic.* Oxford: Clarendon Press, 1974.

——. *The Law of Persons in the Later Roman Republic.* Oxford, Clarendon Press, 1967.

——. *The Law of Property in the Later Roman Republic.* Oxford: Clarendon Press, 1968.

——. *The Law of Succession in the Later Roman Republic.* Oxford: Clarendon Press, 1971.

——. *The Law of the Ancient Romans.* Dallas, Tex.: Southern Methodist University Press, 1970.

——. *Roman Private Law around 200 B.C.* Edinburgh: Edinburgh University Press, 1971.

——. *Rome of the XII Tables: Persons and Property.* Princeton: Princeton University Press, 1975.

William Ockham. *Summa logicae*. Ed. Philotheus Boehner, Gedeon Gál, and Stephen Brown. St. Bonaventure, N.Y.: Franciscan Institute, 1974.

Winnington-Ingram, R. P., ed. *Aristidis Quintiliani de musica libri tres*. Leipzig: Teubner, 1963.

Wolfson, Harry Austryn. "The Problem of the Souls of the Spheres from the Byzantine Commentaries on Aristotle through the Arabs and St. Thomas to Kepler." *Dumbarton Oaks Papers*, 16 (1962), 65–93.

Yates, Frances. *The Art of Memory*. London: Routledge and Kegan Paul, 1966.

——. "The Ciceronian Art of Memory." *Medioevo e Rinascimento*, 2 (1955), 871–903.

Zulueta, F. de. *The Roman Law of Sale*. Oxford: Clarendon Press, 1945.

INDEXES

A. Philosophers and orators referred to by Boethius in *In Ciceronis Topica*, exclusive of references to Cicero's *Topica*. Where I have given the name in a form other than that used by Boethius, I have bracketed the part of the name I have added.

Aelius Sentius, 46–48
Aquilius ([C.] Aquilius [Gallus]), 104, 122
Aristotle, 25, 26, 28, 85, 103, 108, 117–119, 154, 160, 162, 168
  Categories, 77, 171
  Physics, 162
  Posterior Analytics, 28, 32–33
  Prior Analytics, 28, 32–33
  Sophistical Refutations, 28
  Topics, 23, 28, 33, 34, 36, 93

Boethius
  translation of Aristotle's *Posterior Analytics*, 32
  translation of Aristotle's *Prior Analytics*, 32

Cato, 22
Cicero, 22, 86
  commentary on *Timaeus*, 87
  Pro Caelio, 116
  Rhetorics [De inventione], 135
  Tusculan Disputations, 162
Crassus ([L. Licinius] Crassus), 115–116

Gaius
  Institutes, 89–90

Gallus. *See* C. Aquilius Gallus, 122

Merobaudes ([Flavius] Merobaudes), 107, 156
Mucius. *See* Scaevola, (Quintus Mucius)

Patricius, 21, 49, 105, 132, 167
Paul ([Iulius] Paulus)
  Institutes, 64
Plato, 25, 28, 97, 103, 115

Scaevola ([Publius Mucius] Scaevola), 73
Scaevola ([Quintus Mucius] Scaevola), 101, 109, 110
Servius ([Servius Sulpicius Rufus]), 109

Terence, 22
Trebatius, 22–24, 73–74, 104, 122, 159, 169, 170, 176, 179, 180

Ulpian
  Institutes, 58

Victorinus, [Marius Victorinus], 22, 24, 37, 93–96, 168
  commentary on Cicero's *Topica*, 21
  On definition, 93, 96
Virgil, 22

B. Examples used by Boethius to illustrate Topics in *In Ciceronis Topica*.

accuse, 151–152
adoption, 62
agent, 114–115
animal, 44, 143–144
authority
  of a husband, 58–59, 62, 69–70, 80, 128

boundaries, 70–71, 80–81, 115

captivity, 109
cattle, 55
census, 43–44, 129
child(ren), 63, 64–65, 66, 79, 121, 146
Cicero, 143–144

citizen(s), 43, 110, 150
citizenship, 62
city, 70–71, 80–81
civil law, 42–43, 45, 115, 129
civil rights, 62–63, 79, 109–110, 121
    forfeiture of civil rights, 62
coin, 56–57, 78, 144–147
common pasturage, 55–56, 77–78
common pasturing, 55–56, 77–78
comparison, 172
    an artisan is better than his material,
        174
    animate things preferred to inanimate
        things, 174
    desirable things are better than those
        you can do without, 173
    fewer preferred to many, 172
    many preferred to fewer, 172
    natural things preferred to things that
        are not natural, 174
    necessary things preferred to
        nonnecessary things, 173
    nonnecessary things chosen over
        necessary things, 173
    preference based on number, 172
    things in our power preferred to
        things in the power of others, 174
    things produced by art preferred to
        things produced without art, 174
    things sought for their own sake are
        better, 172
    things that are approved by more
        people are better, 175
    things that are completely developed
        are superior to things not
        completely developed, 174
    things that are more pleasant for more
        people are better, 175
    things that are more renowned among
        many are better, 175
    things that are natural are better, 173
    things that are ours are better than
        things not native to us, 173
    things that are permanent are better
        than things that are not
        dependable, 174
    things that are rare are better than
        things that are common, 173
    things that are self-sufficient are better
        than those which need other
        things, 174
    things that are voluntary preferred to
        those that are necessary, 174
    things that use reason are better than
        those devoid of reason, 174
    those which last a longer time are
        more to be chosen, 172

what is easy preferred to what is
    difficult, 173
what is honorable preferred to what is
    advantageous, 173
what is in the interests of leading
    citizens is better than what is in
    the interests of private persons,
    175
what is pleasant is better, 173
what is unimpaired is better, 173
wholes are superior to parts, 174
condemn, 151–152
contract, 116, 169
covering
    of a common wall, 73
Curius, 115

day, 121
debts, 60–61, 78, 117
deportation, 62
divorce, 64–65, 66, 79, 146, 170
    initiated by the wife, 64–65
dowry, 64–65, 66, 69–70, 79, 80, 146,
    170

earth, 121
equity, 42–43, 72, 129

farm, 71–72, 81, 115
father, 121
fear(s), 150
field(s), 55–56, 77, 110, 115
foreigner, 66
foundation(s), 44–45, 113
fraud, 113
free, 43–45, 129

good faith, 169–170
grounds, 73
guarantee against future harm, 68, 80
guarantor, 46–48
guardian, 62–63, 114–115, 117

heir, 59, 78, 115
    substitute heir, 67, 115–116
honesty, 114–115
house, 44–45, 60, 71–72, 73, 78, 81, 113

inheritance, 63, 67, 79, 116

judge(s), 115, 170

know, 151–152
knowledge, 42–43, 45

land, 112
law, 63, 72
    associated with Aelius Sentius, 46–48

C. General index to introduction and translation (exclusive of items in Index A or Index B).
References to Cicero are exclusive of citations of his *Topica*, which occur on virtually every page.

custom, 89, 103, 170

day, 53, 96, 118–119, 121, 125–126, 132–
    142, 145, 148, 152–153, 176
dead, 84, 116, 127
death, 84, 98–100
decrees of the senate, 89
deduction, 25, 26–28
deed, 107, 113, 122–123, 165, 169, 180–
    181
    name of a deed, 107
    nature of a deed, 107
definition(s), 5, 25, 26–27, 29, 34, 38–40,
    42–43, 45–46, 54–55, 76, 81, 83–85,
    88–90, 92–105, 111, 122–123, 128–
    130, 161, 162–163, 177–178
    Aristotle's description of definition,
        85–86
    Cicero's description of definition, 93
    Cicero's division of definition, 178
    definition by metaphor, 95, 104
    definition of a clan, 100–101
    definition of an idea, 103
    definition of enumeration of parts, 91
    definition of genus, 102
    definition of inheritance, 98–100
    definition of species, 102
    definition of the genus figure, 108
    differentiae of definition, 86–89, 93–96
    division into species (kinds) of
        definition, 16, 84, 89, 91, 93, 101,
        103
    ennoematike, 95, 178
    genera of definition, 88
    how division differs from
        enumeration of parts, 16, 46
    hypographike, 95
    hypotyposis, 95, 178
    kata diaphoran, 95
    kata lexin (kat' antilexin), 94, 178
    methods for making definitions, 16,
        90, 96, 98
    partition of definition, 93
    poiotes, 95, 178
    substantial definition, 91
    the nature of definition, 16, 39, 88, 94,
        96
    typos (typoi), 94, 178
    Victorinus's division of definition, 16
demonstration, 7, 25, 33, 74, 114
De Pater, Walter, 4n
De Rijk, L. M., 2n, 3, 3n, 4n, 6n, 7n,
    10n
description, 92–94
designation, 16, 75, 108–110
De Vogel, C. J., 1n

dialectic, 13, 15, 21, 25, 26, 28, 31, 49,
    90, 126, 154, 162
dialectical reason, 175
    the tradition of, 4–8
dialectician(s), 126, 148, 176
Differentia(e), 5, 6, 8, 15, 31, 34, 55
differentia(e), 10, 15, 16, 25, 26, 28–29,
    34–36, 41, 51, 57, 60–61, 75–76, 78,
    83, 85, 88, 91, 94–95, 97, 101–103,
    108, 110, 112, 116–117, 126, 130,
    177–178
    differentiae constitutive of species, 117
    differentiae divisive of genera, 117
    differentiae of definitions, 86–89, 93–
        96
    differentiae of opposites, 118
    inseparable differentiae, 116–117, 178
    species of differentiae, 116
    substantial differentiae, 116
discourse, 25, 26–29, 49
discovery, 21, 25, 26–29, 32, 149, 171
    See also arguments, discovery of
disjunction, 133, 139–140, 142, 152–153
disjunctive, 139
    See also proposition, disjunctive
disputation, 4, 25
dissimulation, 52
division, 40–41, 45, 89–94, 96, 101, 103,
    106–109, 113, 118, 120, 155, 175,
    177–179, 181
    the difference between division and
        partition, 16, 107–108
    See also Topics, division of the
doctor, 72
double, 77, 119–121
Duns Scotus, 7n

earth, 64, 96, 158, 163
eclipse, 64, 161
edicts of the magistrates, 89
effect(s), 15, 17, 50, 53–54, 69–70, 80,
    83, 154–161, 171, 177, 179
element, 74
emperor, 95
enmity, 52
Ennius, 158
ennoia, 87, 103
enthymemes, 7, 15, 31, 149–152
enumeration of parts, 16, 45–46, 76, 81,
    90–94, 105–106, 108, 113, 129–130
    definition of enumeration of parts, 91
envious, 33–34
envy, 105
epagoge, 114
equal(s), 33, 50–51, 64, 71–72, 81, 97–98,
    105, 130, 136, 171–172, 175–177

D. Index of names for notes and appendix.
Because the notes and appendix are glosses on the text, which is indexed in detail in Index C, the index to this portion of the book is just an index of names.

Library of Congress Cataloging-in-Publication Data

Boethius, d. 524
   [In Ciceronis topica. English]
   Boethius's In Ciceronis topica : an annotated translation of a medieval dialectical
text / Eleonore Stump.
      p.   cm.
   Bibliography: p.
   Includes index.
   ISBN 0-8014-8934-2 (pbk.: alk. paper)
   1. Topic (Philosophy)—Early works to 1800. 2. Cicero, Marcus Tullius. I. Stump,
Eleonore, 1947–   . II. Title.
B659.I52E6 1988   160—dc 19   87-23161

LaVergne, TN USA
14 June 2010
186117LV00001B/139/P